COUNSELLING: INTERDISCIPLINARY PERSPECTIVES

Edited by
BRIAN THORNE
and
WINDY DRYDEN

Open University Press
Milton Keynes • Philadelphia

Open University Press
Celtic Court
22 Ballmoor
Buckingham
MK18 1XW

and

1900 Frost Road, Suite 101
Bristol, PA 19007, USA

First Published 1993

A catalogue record of this book is available from the British Library

ISBN 0 335 15678 9 (pb)

Library of Congress Cataloging-in-Publication Data
Counselling: interdisciplinary perspectives/edited by Brian Thorne and
    Windy Dryden
        p. cm.
    Includes bibliographical references and index.
    ISBN 0–335–15678–9 (pbk.)
    1. Counselling.   2. Psychology and the humanities.   I. Thorne,
    Brian, 1937–   . II. Dryden, Windy.
    BF637.C6C674   1993
    361.3'23 – dc20   93–18531
                                                              CIP

Typeset by Colset Private Limited, Singapore
Printed in Great Britain by Biddles Ltd, Guildford and Kings Lynn

COUNSELLING:

I‌N

P.

Counselling

£17.99

Please return/renew this item by the last date shown
Thank you for using your local library

This book is dedicated to current and future trainers and trainees at the Centre for Counselling Studies in the University of East Anglia, Norwich.

CONTENTS

THE EDITORS

Brian Thorne has been Director of Student Counselling at the University of East Anglia in Norwich since 1974 and has recently been appointed Director of the new Centre for Counselling Studies in the same University. He is also a founder member of the Norwich Centre for Personal and Professional Development and a Co-Director of Person Centred Therapy (Britain). He has contributed extensively to the professional literature and his recent publications include *Carl Rogers* (Sage Publications, 1992), *Behold the Man* (Darton, Longman and Todd, 1991) and *Person Centred Counselling: Therapeutic and Spiritual Dimensions* (Whurr Publishers, 1991).

Windy Dryden is Professor of Counselling at Goldsmith's College, University of London. He has authored or edited 58 books including *Rational-Emotive Counselling in Action* (Sage Publications, 1990) and *Daring to be Myself: A Case of Rational-Emotive Therapy*, written with Joseph Yankura (Open University Press, 1992). In addition, he edits eight book series in the area of counselling and psychotherapy including the *Whurr Psychotherapy Series* (Whurr Publishers) and *Improve Your Counselling* (Sage Publications). His major interests are in rational-emotive therapy, eclecticism and integration in psychotherapy and, increasingly, writing short, accessible self-help books for the general public. His latest book in this genre is entitled *The Incredible Sulk* (Sheldon Press, 1992).

THE CONTRIBUTORS

John Barkham is Senior Lecturer in Ecology in the School of Environmental Sciences at the University of East Anglia, a counsellor and member of the Norwich Centre for Personal and Professional Development and one of five partners of FDI Training, which offers courses for staff in higher education as well as the long-standing summer and winter workshops. As Chairman of the Norfolk Naturalists' Trust, with 13 500 members, he is active in the field of wildlife conservation.

Michael Carroll is Director of Studies in Psychology and Counselling at the Roehampton Institute, London. Besides being Head of Department, he directs and teaches on the MSc in Psychological Counselling. For the past five years he has worked with the Metropolitan Police Welfare Branch, training and supervising their counsellors. He has recently organized a new Diploma in Counselling at Work, and is researching the generic tasks of counselling supervision.

John Foskett is the Anglican Chaplain to the Bethlem Royal and Maudsley Special Health Authority in London and is Hon. Canon of Southwark Cathedral. He was chairperson and is now a council member of the Association for Pastoral Care and Counselling. He is the author of *Meaning in Madness, The Pastor and the Mentally Ill* and *Helping the Helpers, Supervision and Pastoral Care*, both published by SPCK.

Mhairi MacMillan is Senior Student Counsellor in the University of St. Andrews, Scotland. She also contributes to training and supervision in the person-centred approach to counselling and psychotherapy. She has facilitated small and large groups in Britain and Europe for twelve years and remains fascinated with large group process. In recent years, she has had a growing interest in the study of Kabbalah as a spiritual discipline and is author of 'Miriam, wilderness leader' (in A. Pirani, ed., *The Absent Mother*, Mandala, 1991).

Brenda Meldrum is a dramatherapist, psychologist, theatre director and performer. Until May 1992, she was teaching psychology at the London School of Economics; she has now joined with Jane Hanna, also a drama therapist, in 'Theatre Therapy Partnership', an organization dedicated to creative therapy on a theatre model, with groups and individuals. She also teaches at the Institute of Dramatherapy and is on the editorial board of the Journal *Dramatherapy*. Her recent publications include 'Drama and dramatherapy – how are they linked?' (*Theatre and Therapy*, 1991, Vol. 2, No. 1, pp. 11–20) and *On Being the Thing I Am: An Enquiry into the Therapeutic Aspects of Shakespeare's* As You Like It (Jessica Kingsley, in press). She is also contributing three chapters to a *Handbook of Dramatherapy* to be published in 1993 by Routledge.

Judy Moore is a counsellor in the Student Counselling Service at the University of East Anglia. She took her first degree in English Literature in 1974 and completed a PhD in 1983. She has taught in schools as well as in higher and further education and was for nine years a tutor with the Open University. She was trained in the person-centred tradition by Person Centred Therapy (Britain).

Richard Morgan-Jones works privately as an Analytical Psychotherapist in Eastbourne having worked part-time in the NHS at Sussex University. He was trained at, and is a full member of, the London Centre for Psychotherapy. He teaches and supervises in counselling training. He also works as an organizational consultant and is developing a course that explores a group-analytical approach to teamwork and organizations. He belongs to the Group-Analytical Society.

Eileen Pickard established the Roehampton Institute's Psychology and Counselling Department, the first in Britain to launch a Master's in Counselling Psychology. Currently, she is Manager of its Consultancy and Training and Consultant to TDA Consulting Group Ltd. Her research and publications are in creativity and training in counselling and education.

Campbell Purton works as a counsellor and supervisor in private practice and at the University of East Anglia. He teaches philosophy in adult education. He trained in client-centred therapy, though his work is modulated by Jungian and Buddhist themes. His previous publications include 'The person centred Jungian' (*Person Centred Review*, 1989, Vol. 4, pp. 403–19) and 'Selection and assessment in counsellor training courses' (in W. Dryden and B. Thorne, eds, *Training and Supervision for Counselling in Action*, Sage Publications, 1991).

INTRODUCTION

Brian Thorne and Windy Dryden

At present, we have little information about the characteristics of counsellors in Britain. Nevertheless, it seems to us that such practitioners are, as a group, heterogeneous in a number of respects. One of these concerns their original academic discipline. We know counsellors who are, by initial training, psychologists, social anthropologists, chemists, sociologists, ecologists, teachers and artists, to name but a few. At present, in Britain, there are few restrictions on people wishing to train as counsellors as far as their academic background is concerned. Indeed, there exist highly professional training courses which do not even specifically require graduate status in their applicants.

It is our strong conviction that this is a healthy and desirable state of affairs and we view with alarm certain European developments, for example, which seem to be moving in the direction of restricting the psychotherapy profession to those with backgrounds in psychiatry and clinical psychology. Leaving aside for the moment the contentious issue of whether counselling can be truly differentiated from psychotherapy, it would seem to us calamitous if such developments came to fruition, for the next step might well be to seek to impose similar restrictions on the practice of counselling. As it is, in Britain currently the theory and practice of counselling is informed and powerfully enriched by the knowledge and experience which counsellors bring to the profession from the wide range of their previous academic and vocational disciplines. Strangely, however, very little has been published on the influence of different disciplinary perspectives on counselling. Indeed, on counsellor training courses, trainees are more likely to be taught counselling theory from the four dominant traditions in the field – psychodynamic, humanistic-existential, cognitive-behavioural and transpersonal – than they are to be encouraged to explore how their respective previous disciplines can contribute to this theory. It is our view, then, that counselling does not fully utilize the potential of its practitioners in this respect. In order to remedy this deficiency, we decided to put together a book which clearly demonstrates the contribution which a variety of disciplines can make to the understanding and practice of counselling. It is our hope that future trainees will be encouraged to give due weight to the influence of their previous disciplines upon their personal and professional development and to explore the nature of their own inter-disciplinary 'mix' and its impact upon their counselling relationships.

We went about our task by inviting eight counsellors and a psychotherapist to contribute chapters showing how their own discipline informs their therapeutic work. The eight disciplines included in the book – psychology, social anthropology, education, drama, theology, ecology, philosophy and English literature – are not intended to be comprehensive, rather to be representative of all the many disciplines that can contribute to our under-standing of counselling.

The contributors to this volume were asked to write for a readership which, while knowledgeable about counselling in general, would know little about the contributors' own disciplines in particular. They were urged to avoid jargon and explain any concepts that the readership was unlikely to understand. To ensure that the contributors addressed themselves to the same task, they were asked to write to a common chapter structure. First, they were requested to provide a description of their discipline, outlining its essential characteristics, explaining why they were drawn towards it and exploring their personal engagement with it. We considered this personal dimension of the chapters to be important, since counselling, by its very nature, emphasizes the relationship between the personal experiences of the practitioner and the development of a professional identity. Secondly, they were asked to outline how their discipline informs their understanding of persons. While this understanding may have many aspects – especially when it concerns the nature of the human being – we invited our writers to explore, if relevant, what light their discipline sheds on personality development, social and family contexts, ideas about meaning and purpose and even transcendental dimensions of human experience.

Finally, we invited the contributors to consider how their discipline informs their understanding of counselling. We asked them to do this, first, in a general sense, detailing how the discipline influences the way they under-stand what goes on in the counselling process and the relationship between counsellor and client. In this respect, we enquired, for example, whether our contributors communicate their discipline-derived insights to their clients or whether this understanding exerts only a private influence. The second way in which we wanted our contributors to show the influence of their discipline on counselling was directly and practically, through explicit case studies. Their task was to demonstrate, through these illustrations, how their disci-pline influenced their case conceptualization, their choice of interventions, their view of the counselling process in each instance and other aspects they considered relevant in the moment-to-moment interaction with their clients.

We want to thank the contributors for their participation. We believe you will agree that they have tackled a difficult task with success. They have provided in the process a powerful antidote to possible moves to restrict entry to counselling to those previously trained in a narrow range of disciplines. Human beings are complex organisms who defy understanding, especially if they are viewed from limited perspectives. If counselling is to do justice to the complexity and mystery of human beings, its practitioners need to understand and respect the contributions of a broad range of disciplines. If this volume contributes even a little to this process, then we will consider our primary goal has been achieved.

ECOLOGY AND COUNSELLING

John Barkham

ECOLOGY AND MY ENGAGEMENT WITH IT

What is ecology?

'Ecology' is one of those words which everyone now feels they understand. An ecologist is thought of as vaguely green, cares about the environment, and probably has a leaning towards organically grown foods. An ecologist may acquire these characteristics but they by no means define him or her. Ecology is a long-established science and academic discipline and is concerned with the interrelationships between plants, animals and the environment (Odum 1989). The word is derived from the Greek *oikos*, meaning home. The Earth is home to all living things and we ecologists are interested in explaining their distribution and abundance.

Human beings are a legitimate part of ecological study for a number of reasons. First, they are themselves animals, limited in their activities in all sorts of ways by their environment – just like other animals. This is not a popular notion, as so many people like to think of themselves as fundamentally different from things that are slimy or furry or merely primitive. Secondly, they are an extremely significant factor in the environment of plants and other animals, and with an increasingly destructive effect. Thirdly, we humans through our numbers and all-pervasive technology have suddenly become custodians of this planet and we have the capacity to manage it and its rich assemblage of ecosystems sustainably – in a way that keeps all options open for future generations – or exploitatively and destructively, which means we continue to destroy the living capital upon which our societies depend. In other words, we are managers of the Earth, the home of all living things.

Becoming an ecologist

I found my undergraduate course in Geography rather tough going, often tedious, and certainly laborious. Looking back, I can see it was an exercise of the head to which my guts were not firmly attached, at least not until my final year. It was then that I became involved in a subject of which I had not heard before going to university, 'biogeography'. This was in fact ecology by another name, but more concerned with distribution than with abundance. I began a project on the development of the woodlands in my own home area of south-west Wiltshire and, suddenly, there was a full connection between my work and the places I had learned to cherish as I grew up.

Norridge Wood was twenty minutes walk away from home – a sunken path with elms either side leading out to the hedged side of a large field before entering the wood near its middle. Here we picked dense posies of primroses to decorate the church for Easter. In mid-summer I saw wood white butter-flies flitting weakly along the sinuous rides and later, as autumn approached, elusive purple hairstreaks would occasionally make themselves known coming down from the tops of oak trees for a brief visit to oozing sap. Here, too, the four woodmen worked all winter, cutting the coppice with handsaw and hook, each section of the wood in rotation, stacking most of it into charcoal burners. Returning as a student I learned to recognize this as an ancient woodland with a continuous history since prehistoric times, and one that had been managed in the traditional way probably continuously for 600–700 years. I find this deeply moving. A place of beauty, managed sustainably, and within which a great variety of plants and animals live, most of them with an ancestry stretching back to the *wildwood* before human beings arrived to cut and clear. And yet wildlife is able to live side by side with – indeed, depends upon – the management activities of tradi-tional woodmanship.

The reason, therefore, that I find myself a professional ecologist now is because of the powerful, positive experiences with wild living things close to home when I was young. My principal research area is also directly linked with that experience – the population dynamics of woodland plants. I am very interested in the output of computer models, statistical analyses of long runs of data, and graphs of changes and relationships. Yet if I am wholly honest, the reason I do it is because of the personal delight at being able to sit quietly in a sunlit woodland in early spring among the wild daffodils, wood anemones and bluebells, listening for the song of the latest summer migrant warbler arriving back from south of the Sahara, staying quiet and still as a roe deer passes diagonally across the slope behind the yews.

The meaning of ecology to me

Being in my wood is a deeply healing experience. But what is it that I have needed to heal? It has slowly dawned on me over the last few years that the crowd of memories I have stretching right back to early childhood were not simply those of a fortunate and happy child. They were in fact experiences which I think were essential to my psychic survival. I am amazed at the number of these memories and their importance to me. The deeper meaning I attach to this is as follows. I now see my childhood as a time of survival through some appalling emotional traumas. As with so many of us, even when we can see so clearly the awfulness in the histories of others, it often takes an inordinate amount of time to begin to accept that our own childhood was less than the idyll we fondly imagined or were led to believe it to be.

So it was with me. My grandfather who died when I was two; my father who chose not to return home after the War when I was four; the houseful of adult women . . . what was the significance of me walking out of the house, across the village street and down Shutewater Hill when I was two? Was it just the little adventurer and explorer, or was it the little boy who at times had to escape from what was unbearable back in there? What was the real significance of that robin's nest we found in the ivy-covered bank – just like the illustration in the bird book – inspirational excitement and wonder? Or the projection of feelings of hiddenness and freedom? Maybe all those things.

The single-sex prep boarding school 100 miles away to which I was sent by my mother when I was nine was a malign place in terms of all of its human relationships. If it had not been, maybe I would have survived less damaged from being sent away by my mother. What made things so much worse for me there though, was being deprived of my freedom to roam. In those intervening years from the age of four and the robin, I had amazing freedom of movement – the golden post-war years when children were not threatened by molesters and when parents could afford to let them out of their sight. I knew every flower and where every bird's nest was. Whatever the shortcomings of love and emotional support inside the house, outside it I could find connectedness and a special kind of nourishment. Then, two years of imprisonment in that truly dreadful school in Sussex. The crocodile walks following the same path every Sunday killed what was precious to me and probably life-saving. I have yet to recover from the totality of this appalling experience. I can now see that, at that time, deprived of the love of my parents and deprived of my connectedness with the living world, I became almost deprived of spirit.

So, very simply, I have come to the conclusion that the meaning of the living world to me is that it saved my life, psychically, from a very young age. No wonder it is so precious to me. No wonder, then, that my survival feels threatened by the way in which human beings abuse and destroy other living things and their environment.

The nature of my engagement with the subject of ecology

I do feel very different from how I perceive that many, perhaps most, of my ecological colleagues feel. The ecologists who are deeply involved in issues that matter to me are in a small minority. Most consider themselves first and foremost as scientists. Science with a big 'S' and Research with a big 'R' combine to produce an ethos where cool objectivity (there is no such thing), fence-sitting and being value-free are highly regarded.

My ecology is about three things. First, my contract demands that I have to do research. I do it in a place which is sacred to me, on plants with special meanings for me, and in a subject area which contributes in a small way to managing such places in perpetuity for their wildlife. Secondly, I teach ecology from the perspective of environmental problems of which any intelligent citizen will be aware, so that my students, in gaining an understanding of how plants, animals and the environment interact in a dynamic system, may later if they wish (and many of them do) make a significant contribution to raising societal awareness of environmental issues. Thirdly, I am deeply involved in the voluntary conservation movement, using such time and skills as I possess in promoting wildlife conservation in the UK. I suppose my biggest contribution here is through a person-centred form of chairmanship in which I attempt to encourage and support others in achieving organizational goals rather than using my ecological expertise directly, although the latter provides the essential foundation for my credibility in this work.

So, my personal engagement with my subject comes from my guts, out of lifelong experience of living things, because they matter so deeply to me, and not from any particular love of science.

ECOLOGY AND MY UNDERSTANDING OF PERSONS

Animal behaviour

Ecology has something to contribute to an understanding of people because people are animals. *Ethology* is the scientific study of the behaviour of animals in the natural environment and is part of ecology. Most of this work is, of course, carried out on the great variety of non-human animal life. However, Lorenz (1970) shows how human beings can also be viewed from this perspective. Although rivetingly interesting, this area is also quite threatening. On the whole, we do not like to think of ourselves or our behaviour as being like that of other animals, and certainly do not like having it pointed out to us. If this is so today, it may also have been largely so throughout the latter period of human development, thereby being a powerful force in driving underground certain key components of human biological nature.

Competition

Competitiveness is one of these characteristics. The genes of dominant individuals (both male and female) in the animal world are represented in greater proportion in subsequent generations than those of subdominants. On the other hand, the genes of some individuals will be represented to only a very small extent, either because they produce fewer offspring, or because they fail to breed altogether and are represented only through the genes shared with siblings that produce offspring. Competitive success and failure is therefore measured in perpetuating genes, the biological road to immortality. This is such a powerful script for all animals that we would be foolish to ignore it in the context of human behaviour.

Without being naively literal,[1] it is easy to see the obvious and, to many, unpalatable parallels with human society. For both men and women there is a deep-seated biological component influencing individual behaviour. The feminist movement has focused on some of the cultural results of male dominance, but unless the biological basis of this behaviour is made fully conscious it will, like all unconscious forces, continue to have an intractable influence on the way individuals, and therefore society as a whole operates.

Men are closely associated with the major ills of the world, with most destructive possibilities, and not least with abuse of the global environment. This is presumably because men occupy most positions of power and influence in most societies. The biological imperative determining, at least to some extent, why they should do so, is the premium on competitive behaviour. There is a premium for men in being successful in competition with other men. In the vertebrate world, the defence of territory and the acquisition of mate(s) and resources are achieved through gaining dominance over competitors. In the human world, much similar basic biological behaviour has become so culturally ritualized as to be almost unrecognizable. Such ritual, like behaviour in committees, or the way the hierarchical power structures of institutions are arranged, serves to make such behaviour socially acceptable. Further, the acquisition of material resources is given the utmost prominence in our society. Arguably, the pressure to acquire more and more has never been greater, the marketing to achieve this never more powerful. This forms an unholy alliance with both male and female unconscious drives, yet has little or nothing to do with the fulfilment of basic needs beyond a certain, relatively low level. The operation of 'market forces' and 'freedom of opportunity' are the euphemisms given to an otherwise undignified competitive scramble, with winners and losers as there have always been throughout history, and throughout the animal world.

Unsatisfied needs

These reflections have led me to explore how it is that competitive behaviour among human beings can be expressed across a wide spectrum; from what we would regard as consistent with a healthy zest for life, proper establishment and care of a family, creative expression and individuation, through to the acquisition and hoarding of excessive wealth, power over others and, in some cases, a determination to destroy people, property and the environment. Maslow's (1970) hierarchy of basic needs reminds us that the need to meet the requirements of the basic bodily functions comes first:

> Starting from the bottom, if a need is relatively well gratified, then a new set of needs emerges – the next one up the list:
>
> the need for self-fulfilment
> the esteem needs
> the belongingness and love needs
> the safety needs
> the physiological needs

At the same time, it is also worth reminding ourselves that of the five billion people in the world, more than ten per cent are chronically malnourished or hungry all of the time – they do not have even their most basic needs met. Not much use talking to them about self-actualization, nor even of love:

> Freedom, love, community feeling, respect, philosophy, may all be waved aside as fripperies that are useless, since they fail to fill the stomach. Such a man may fairly be said to live by bread alone.
>
> (Maslow 1970: 37)

When we also remind ourselves that we have the knowledge, resources and technology to feed adequately many more than five billion people, we are confronted with some uncomfortable questions about the nature of men and women and the extent to which the thin veneer of civilized caring for our fellow beings masks in us as individuals a predominantly animal competitive behaviour. If this is not so, why do we not help these people to meet their basic needs?

Further, there is a relationship between deprivation and aggression in human beings which may also have its roots in animal behaviour in general. Maslow again:

> The child who is insecure, basically thwarted, or threatened in his needs for safety, love, belongingness, and self-esteem is the child who will show more selfishness, hatred, aggression, and destructiveness.
>
> (Maslow 1970: 121–2)

Unmet infantile needs have consequences later in life for the adult: 'It is precisely those individuals in whom a certain need has always been satisfied

who are best equipped to tolerate deprivation of that need in the future'
(Maslow 1970: 38).

Red grouse (*Lagopus lagopus scoticus*), characteristic of heather moor-
lands in northern Britain, show some parallels. Surviving offspring produced
in years of poor quality food supply show greater aggression and establish
larger territories when they reach adulthood (Watson and Moss 1970). In
humans it seems obvious that those who are subject to appalling degrees of
deprivation in childhood, and the anxiety and fear that accompanies it,
yet survive to adulthood, are likely to carry within them destructive rage
which will emerge at times of perceived threat to basic needs being met in
adulthood. Moreover, long periods of deprivation of the most basic needs,
physiological, safety and love, lead to despair. This has dangers, not only at
the individual but also at the collective level:

> This does not mean that the enemy of humanity can emerge under
> any conditions, suddenly and without warning. The pre-condition for
> him finding followers who yearn for destruction is a long-standing
> despair of millions of people, a collective humiliation which has
> corroded their self-respect to the core.
>
> (Enzensberger 1991)

And:

> When a collective no longer sees any chance of finding compensations
> for the humiliations, real and imagined, heaped upon it, it will commit
> all its psychic energies to hate and envy, resentment and thirst for
> revenge . . . Perpetual losers can be found an all continents. Among
> them the feeling of humiliation and the desire for collective suicide
> is increasing by the year. A nuclear arsenal is already available on
> the Indian sub-continent and in the Soviet Union. Where Hitler and
> Saddam failed – in achieving "final victory" – the final solution, the
> one who inherits their mantle, may succeed.
>
> (Enzensberger 1991)

This seems to suggest that we have reached a stage in human cultural
evolution where a deep-seated biological and archetypal response to deprivation, which may have had survival value in the past, now poses a serious
threat to our collective survival because of the complex social institutions we
have created, the potential for acquisition of power, and the technology
of weaponry.

Negative feedback mechanisms and renewable resources

All plants and animals are limited in their numbers by the availability of the
resources they require for survival, growth and reproduction. Normally for
this reason the numbers of any species vary to a limited extent around a

stable mean. Permanent rises or falls may indicate a permanent favourable or unfavourable change in the environment of the organism.

The numbers of humans rose only very slowly, presumably due to colonizing new areas, up until about 1650. The beginnings and subsequent spread of the industrial revolution, improved food supplies and the control of disease, have meant that the world population has grown very rapidly over the last 350 years. With over five billion at the present time, it is due to double again by 2050. However, ecologists know, and have been stating for a long time, the simple truth that people cannot outstrip the resources they require any more than wild animals or plants can. Ingenuity in plant breeding, in the technical provision of irrigation and in the creation of more crop land have helped growth in food supplies keep pace with population growth. Nevertheless, it is now no longer possible to expand the cropped area significantly and many currently cropped areas which are marginal for arable agriculture are badly and probably permanently degraded. More than ten per cent of the world population is chronically malnourished or constantly hungry. We seem to be close to a time when factors beyond our capacity or inclination to control – a primitive ecological triangle of famine, disease and social strife – will result in a nightmarish Malthusian outcome, determining the lives and their quality of a number of people in the world too large for the rest of us to ignore.

What ecology shows us is that this scenario is bound to come about unless human beings use their unique capacity for conscious choice and restraint. We have recorded past trends; we can predict future ones with increasing precision; the picture is there before us. We can make the painful choice of a change in direction if we choose to do so. For that to succeed, we have somehow to *raise to consciousness* the fundamental behaviour – competitiveness – which in its various guises taken to extremes results in destructive behaviour at both an individual and a collective level. Let there be no doubt that a continuation of the current trend of global exploitation will leave the vast majority living in terrible conditions. A few will prosper, as long as the majority are contained by force. This is not a pretty scenario, but nevertheless is an increasingly common occurrence. It may seem a far cry from the comfort of the counselling room.

However, where is the consciousness going to be raised? And where will the damaged children vent their rage harmlessly and with a creative outcome? The likely contribution of counsellors to this task may seem so small as to be trivial, particularly in the Third World. This may not be so, because the actions we take in the First World, both individually and collectively, will count. Each of us can do our bit. Counsellors and therapists have an awesome task ahead.

ECOLOGY AND MY UNDERSTANDING OF THE
COUNSELLING PROCESS

General reflections

Uniqueness of individuals

Ecology has been defined by a wag from outside the discipline as the study
of the impossible by the incompetent. This stems from the enormous complexity of ecological relationships.

If you sit down on Morgan's Hill overlooking the Vale of Pewsey in
Wiltshire in July and then focus down on the ground immediately around
you, you will first of all notice the wealth of beautiful, small flowers which
make up the characteristic sward of 'unimproved' chalk downland. If you
look more closely you will quickly add to these the numbers of grasses,
sedges and mosses and you may wonder at the total number of plant species
present. There may in fact be up to fifty different kinds in a single square
metre – all of them we may suppose 'doing' something slightly different,
using the environment in a different way from other species. It is a constant
puzzle for ecologists to explain how such a situation comes about (Mahdi
et al. 1989). The environment to our eyes, and indeed in the face of our
most sophisticated measuring instruments, seems to be more or less uniform
over such a small area. Why is it that the best adapted species fails to take
over all the space?

At this level of enquiry we are not concerned at all about differences
between individuals of the same species. We are inclined to treat them as
being all the same. If we dare to add this level of complexity to our single
square metre we risk gazing at the 'impossible'. Yet we know that everything that is biologically relevant takes place at the level of the individual.
It is the individual that grows from seed, matures if it is fortunately placed,
reproduces if the resources it requires are available, and then eventually
dies, leaving no, a very few, or multitudes of decendants. An individual
orchid may produce over a million seeds – or none. The possible variation
of individuals in growth and performance is enormous. We ignore this
capacity at our peril.

The problem for ecologists seems parallel to that of counsellors. Ecologists
have somehow got to come up with principles, concepts and theories which
throw light on the way communities and populations of plants and animals
behave – valid generalizations and emergent properties – yet at the same
time hold in their awareness that the behaviour of individuals may, and
probably will, confound the comfortable structural explanation we have
proposed and into which we would like, even at a subliminal level, to
shoehorn our client. I have recently found two books (Freudian and Jungian
orientations, respectively) which provide an interesting contrast in the

search for general principles and the recognition of unique individuality (Olivier 1989; Corneau 1991).

Each plant on Morgan's Hill is unique; similarly, each person in the counselling room is different from every other. To be pedantically precise, there will in the chalk grassland be individuals genetically identical to others as a result of clonal growth. Here, the analogy breaks down. Nevertheless, each is growing in an environment different in its details and the individuals, although genetically identical, will grow differently. Thus although as a counsellor it is immensely helpful for me to have as wide a range of knowledge and experience as I have the time and enthusiasm to acquire, bringing me a wider repertoire of ideas to place at the service of my client, as an ecologist I know that the moment they constrain my openness to her uniqueness, I cease to be of value to her.

The individual, its community and its history

The distribution of bluebells, wild daffodils, wood anemones and wild garlic in my sacred wood is, I know, the product of two things – the environmental history of the precise place where an individual is growing, and the current set of conditions. The unrecorded history of the wood, to say nothing of the individual square metre, is one of the frustrations arising from plants' inability to speak. However, the plant as it is now, right here before my eyes, does give me the opportunity to understand it if only I would suspend my judgement and let it speak in its own inimitable, silent way. I have to respect it in its place for its story to unfold.

As an ecologist, I know that to acknowledge the unique history of each client is a prerequisite for coming genuinely alongside him in his present. It is fine for me to have theories in my head about the growth of trees, but they are of little value unless I am prepared for my experience of the individual's story to confound them. Each of us is the product of the way in which we have rubbed shoulders with our kind from the moment, and before, we were born. Each of us is dealt a hand – the totality of our genes and our environment – and then we play it through our lives. We grow up, like a wild plant, in a community of others, and our experience of that community shapes the way we are, the way we grow and the way we continue to play our hand. We have very little choice over the way we play it when we are small and very vulnerable; we have increasing choice about our strategy and tactics as we grow towards adulthood, thereby increasing by the same measure the onus on us to accept responsibility, not for the cards, but for the consequences of the way in which we play them. My ecological knowledge is important for me as a counsellor at this point in two distinct ways: in helping me, first, to acknowledge fully the importance of the past experience of my client and, secondly, to understand and respect his present context.

I have also been helped enormously from a quite different perspective to understand the importance of the environment as experienced by the client, in my role as a *teacher* of ecology. In that role, I am actually part of what many students experience as stressful, daunting and, perhaps, frightening. In that role, too, I see them struggling to come to terms not only with a new and unfamiliar environment, but with the personal history and circumstances they bring with them. I see them struggling with great courage and fortitude to find the strength to carry on, seeking support for *not* dropping out; neither wanting models of human personality and behaviour, nor arcane explanations of how they feel involving early childhood trauma – just wanting the milk of normal human kindness; the acceptance and affirmation as human beings that they have never had from well-meaning and, equally, disastrous parents, and that they might find here in their first experience of being part of an adult world. I ignore at my peril the part of my client that *wants to struggle to grow where she is*, that wants to play the hand she has, rather than pick up a new one elsewhere which may or may not be either more growthful or what she really wants. Ecology tells me that my frustration with the silent otherness of the bluebell before me may simply mean that I project my own plantiness upon her, ignoring her complex and unfathomable story and her plea for it really to be heard.

Consciousness and the unconscious

How unpredictable the weather is in the mountains of the English Lake District! A lowering grey-black and large cloud obscures the sun as we labour up the side of Scafell above Burnmoor Tarn. But, suddenly, the cloud is past and a hot early July sun illuminates the subtle colours of growing green. Immediately, a small, dark butterfly wings past. This is not the sort of place you might expect to see butterflies at all, a normally cold, wet mountainside at 1800 feet. It is in fact a mountain ringlet (*Erebia epiphron*) in its only English haunt, flying swiftly above the mat-grass upon which its caterpillars feed. As soon as the sun comes out, the adults emerge, sometimes in their hundreds apparently (Thomas and Lewington 1991), from deep in the grass tussocks where they shelter from inclement weather. One can predict this, at least in a general way – certainly in terms of probabilities. These individuals are programmed to behave in a certain way in response to ambient temperature and sunlight.

The sea is a well-known archetypal dream symbol of the unconscious. Not that that works for everybody, but it does for me. I also find walking at the edge of the sea a most precious and healing experience. It symbolizes for me now the boundary between the conscious and unconscious, a zone of flux, of healthy tension, of energy, of movement, construction and destruction. The community of life on the rocky shore is a product of this, its occupants rearranged by the interplay of inundation and exposure;

and by the force of this interplay – the unconscious and dark, the conscious and light.

The idea that our behaviour is controlled by unconscious forces, or even programmed like the mountain ringlet, is challenging. It offends the ego of most of us. As an ecologist, though, I find it important to acknowledge our biological drives, the archetypal elements of our psyches and the forgotten parts of our individual histories. All three influence our responses to day-to-day events. My consciousness-raising role as an ecologist to me means not only introducing cognitive material about ecological and environmental matters to those whom it has yet to touch, but also raising the unconscious material bubbling up from the deeper recesses of the mind to conscious awareness. I am often appalled at the patterns of my behaviour which have caused me (and others) so much distress in the past, and which I can now address and change only because the pattern and the cause have risen to my conscious awareness. Even if at times they are infuriating, I have found dreams immensely helpful, like the regular lapping of the tide at the edge of the sea, bringing new material for exploration with every day. As an ecologist, I cannot ignore the unconscious drives of my clients.

Space, time and equilibrium

It is sad to reflect that most people, I dare say, think that when they become an adult their growth is complete. Entering a long-established and unmanaged woodland, one might think something similar. The cathedral-like calm and sense of it having always been like this may be both a superficial impression and coincident with the unconscious wish of the observer. The individual tree grows, matures and dies. Early ecologists likened the process of community change to that of the life-histories of individuals. A woodland was supposed to develop following disturbance, mature and then reach a stable state – stable and predictable in its species composition. In reality, we find that no two patches of a woodland are the same. Moreover, if we take a photograph at the same time in the same place in successive years, we will observe that changes *have* taken place, some startling, some subtle. Equilibrium is never reached, even though an organism or part of a community may approach it, only for a sudden disturbance to bring about renewed growth. This seems a close analogy to the human condition. In principle, the work of personal growth and development closes only with the death of the individual. During the process, long spells of little apparent movement may be interspersed with short, perhaps violent episodes of change. Or, from an initial crisis, there may be a plateauing out, a long period of subtle inner change without obvious external manifestations.

Changes in time are intimately linked with availability and quality of space both in the natural and in the human world. There is one particular wild daffodil in a permanent plot of mine at Brigsteer Wood which has been there since I set the plot up in 1969. Every year for the first thirteen years, it appeared with just two leaves. There was no apparent net growth at all. Then, all of a sudden, in year fourteen, it had three leaves. Three years later it had four, and then in the following (year eighteen of my records) it flowered for the first time. This seemed to me scarcely credible. Then in the succeeding years it produced first one and then a second vegetative daughter. So now, after twenty-three years, there are three bits to the plant instead of one. There is no lack of space for this plant in a simple sense, for it is the only one in four square metres of ground; but the place it is in is just beneath a yew tree – a dry, dark place, where only the slowest rate of growth is possible.

As an ecologist, I know that the quality of space I create for my clients, together with the quality of space which provides the context for their lives outside, combine to produce the environment in which they can grow. Each informs the other and the interplay may be subtle or stormy. As with the daffodil, nothing may appear to change, yet suddenly there is a flowering. After a silent hour, much may change. In the sacred space, every nuance is significant.

In addition, there is the act of waiting. Ecologists are no more patient than the average human being and, indeed, are usually under pressure 'to produce results' during the tenure of the standard three-year research grant. Consequently, we know very little about the actual changes that take place in a woodland over many decades. I turn up in my wood every year at the same time to record my plants. It is an act of watching, waiting for and noting change. I notice how easy it is for me to have an investment in things changing in a direction that interests me, and how easy it is for me to fall into the same trap as a counsellor! As an ecologist and as a counsellor, I need to stay open to the changes that confront me, as they occur, be patient, and work with them as best I can.

Disturbance, damage and destruction

I am struck by how, in ecology, disturbance is both a violent and creative process. It may not seem very violent. A raindrop, for instance, may be sufficiently weighty to kill a newly emerged small seedling. Thereby it creates space for something else to grow. On the other hand, the same raindrop for a more substantial plant would be of no significance.

The effect on the child of what, for an adult, is an emotional experience having minimal effect, can be very destructive – so severe that the effect is felt repeatedly when a trauma in the present is sufficient to trigger a response from the hidden memory. For:

> The truth about our childhood is stored up in our body, and although
> we can repress it, we can never alter it. Our intellect can be deceived,

our feelings manipulated, our perceptions confused, and our body tricked with medication. But someday the body will present its bill, for it is as incorruptible as a child who, still whole in spirit, will accept no compromises or excuses, and it will not stop tormenting us until we stop evading the truth.

(Miller 1990)

It is important to acknowledge that damage to any organism can be so destructive that the effects are permanent and result in disablement of some kind. The uncovering of that damage, like the exposure, cleaning and sealing the heartwood of a rotten tree, is essential for further healthy development, as Alice Miller (1991) has so eloquently expressed.

The traditional practice of woodmanship appears at first sight to be most destructive, involving as it does a major disturbance – the cutting and clearing of most of the woody growth in a stand of coppice with standard trees. However, coppicing involves the cutting at about a foot above the ground of all the shrubby growth, producing straight, clean stems, used traditionally for a great variety of farming and gardening purposes (Rackham 1976). The cutting does not destroy the coppice 'stool'. Far from it. Instead, vigorous new growth arises from the cut stumps to continue the cycle. One of the challenges facing the client with her counsellor is to determine which of her present structures are dead, dying or unproductive. It is a difficult task.

I do not find easy the notion of there being creative outcomes arising from disturbance, damage and destruction. I am quite sure that sometimes, perhaps often, there are not. However, the ecologist part of me well recognizes this possibility and its importance in the counselling room.

Shelter, growth and nourishment

An oak and a hawthorn just down the lane near my home are symbolic of a relationship between counsellor and client. The oak is healthy, young and growing. Either side, along the bank, the vegetation is cut to prevent the development of scrub, more for tidiness sake than for any good functional reason. Only beneath the oak, where the flail cannot reach, is it possible for a small shrub to grow, and there the hawthorn has found a place – in the shelter of the oak. The oak symbolizes protection prior to establishment and independent growth. Of course, the analogy may be taken further. In this case, the protection and shelter afforded will eventually develop into shading and result in the growth of the hawthorn being stunted. Another possibility is that competition for nourishment will become too great for the smaller to survive in the shade of the large. The analogy breaks down when we incorporate the counsellor's and the client's freedom of movement.

This ecological analogy informs me of both the benefits and the dangers of the counsellor–client relationship. The creation of a safe place is of para-mount importance. That safety will be a different thing for each person: safe for one will be claustrophobic for another and excessively challenging for a third. The counsellor may be perceived to be very big and powerful; may be perceived as Mother or Father or some significant other. More disturbingly, 'ungrown bits' of the counsellor are sure to be exposed sooner or later through the relationship and my capacity to own and work with these is a measure of the extent to which I am still growing and open to the challenge of change. To me the twin occupational hazards of being a counsellor seem to be, first, a feeling of 'having arrived' and, secondly, of needing the client to fulfil my needs, not least a pecuniary one. When either of these two condi-tions pertain, I find it difficult to imagine the relationship from the client's point of view being other than at best trivial or, at worst, damaging.

Case studies

As an ecologist researching woodland plants, I am conscious of needing and continuing to develop the following qualities in my work:

1 *Careful observation*: I note what I see, involving the plants themselves and their environment. At the time, I do not necessarily know the extent to which much, little or no change is going to be significant.
2 *Minimal intervention*: I try to minimize my own impact, involving clumsy trampling and disturbance.

As a counsellor at work, I draw deeply on these same learned qualities. They provide my client with the essential still place in which she can explore. However, there are fundamental differences too. If I have no impact whatsoever on the woodland plants I am observing, I believe this to be desirable. If my presence as a counsellor was similarly lacking in effect on my client, I would need seriously to question my value to her. Nevertheless, the quality of watching and waiting for the appropriate moments of clarity that I cultivate are similar in both environments. In the woodland, this is essential for yielding the appropriate management advice; in counselling, it is essential in enabling my client to move in her chosen direction. In both, I am an active witness of growth. My experience with two clients illustrates these principles:

Andrew

Andrew had already been a client for six months when he first saw me, following soon after his first counsellor had left the district. I recognized this to be a difficult time of transition – an ending not of Andrew's choice, and the ending of an important, developing and very much valued relationship, combined with the difficulty of 'having to start all over again'.

We have shared seventeen sessions together so far. In the early ones, the process I experienced was one of Andrew gently and slowly filling me in with key facts about his life. It was only occasionally that he said, 'Of course, I've already told Peter [his previous counsellor] all this.' My own anxiety about him wasting his time was heightened at these moments, almost tempting me to try pushing the process. I did not, and I think this was because he never once showed irritation, only acceptance of the change; the need to carry on at his speed, while at the same time filling me in with essential facts when it was necessary.

The process often felt slow, a session often beginning with him saying something like, 'I don't know that I have much to say today . . .', but almost always such sessions ended with the exclamation, 'And I thought I didn't have much to say today!' Nevertheless, I often wondered whether anything significant was happening. One of my personal difficulties as a counsellor is the wish to give value for money – a wish to see rapid change – a 'wow' at the end of every session. Andrew has taught me more patience and to be less anxious to please. This week, after a three-week gap during which he revisited his birthplace and, for the first time, the grave of the father he lost in his early childhood, he was in deep emotion – joy and vulnerability – at beginning to find part of himself, the part associated with his vibrant, daring father. I can see now that over the last six months, the painstaking process of piecing together a complex jigsaw, at times involving apparently bland and maybe meaningless pieces, was in fact preparation for this, and it was for me to watch, wait, affirm and accept. And, of course, the process goes on, and I know not where.

Imogen

When I first met her, Imogen knew what had happened to her as a child and had already done a great deal of work on the trauma that had profoundly coloured all of her subsequent life. She knew she needed to re-enact that early drama and deal with it anew, but this time with all her adult strength. She needed an orchestrator, props and additional players in order to exorcise the devil who gripped her from within and manipulated her behaviour in her present world. She carried with her a vivid and startling dream, experienced 18 months earlier, which acted as a guide for the play of her experience that I had to manage and the small group of trusted people had to act with her.

Here was a person who needed much more active intervention. The ecologist as environmental manager cannot always just watch and wait for outcomes. Some endangered plant and animal species need direct intervention in order to create the conditions in which they can survive and, subsequently, flourish in a world increasingly abused by human beings. The appropriate intervention is what is required to allow a species to be self-sustaining. Imogen needed me and members of a small group to complete the already well-advanced work of healing a deep wound. In the violent and, finally, exultant drama which followed, the work was completed in a single session. It was her work, executed and completed in her way, but in a setting resulting from the interplay between the knowledge and understanding of an experienced observer and the context of significant figures in her life provided by Imogen herself.

In both these cases, I cannot deny my own presence and the importance of that. Nevertheless, in neither did I have a set plan beyond following, tracking, listening with the utmost intensity to every sign and signal, both verbal and non-verbal, and responding when something within me demanded it. This is the quality of the waiting needed by the patient field ecologist – not being overwhelmed by the pressure to find out, to complete, to act. I am also aware of constantly taking risks and being prepared to be quite wrong and to continue none the less, suspending judgement and flying by the seat of my pants. These are the ideas, speculations, informed guesses of the ecologist that need to be tested out with specific observations and experiments. Similarly, no books, no theories, no models provided the prescriptions for attitude or action at every crucial moment in Andrew and Imogen's therapy; just guts, senses, intuition and experience within the unique framework set by the client.

It would be wrong to suggest that I drew directly from my primary discipline of ecology – that I was 'thinking ecology' in my work with these clients. Nevertheless, the depth of that experience is a key part of me and of the personal resources I made available to them. There are some common threads, and they are all 'ecological' in the sense that they have to do with the individuals and their adaptedness to their environment. These can be summarized as a series of key points from my ecological knowledge and experience which inform my work as a counsellor:

1 The importance of the quality of the environment I create – space, time, security, trust.
2 The uniqueness of the individual. No one else is like her, nor will ever be.
3 The way in which each of us is shaped by our history.
4 The destructiveness in our adult lives of as yet uncovered, traumatic early experience, the feelings around which have still to be revisited.
5 The liberation arising from re-experiencing and living through the awfulness of repressed feelings which were unbearable earlier in life.

It has taken me more than twenty years watching my woodland daffodils in order to discover what I have so far. Beyond those natural questions of the enquiring scientist, the daffodils are enough in themselves and their unique beauty is enduring. This is what I care about most. Watching and waiting, letting them be, staying open to each bit of the story revealed to me, sometimes having it revealed in an oblique moment when I am least looking for it – these seem to be qualities as important in my sacred wood as they are in the sacred space of counselling.

The lesson of ecology for me is that every individual counts in his community. The reverberations of his being will be felt to a greater or lesser extent throughout society. One can see this writ large through those who choose to exercise their power for good and those for evil – Mother Teresa and Ghandi, Hitler and Saddam Hussein. We do not know where on the continuum in between those extremes of greatness our client who has just stepped into our space for the first time will place himself. The environment we create there will be significant in determining where. And the future well-being of our global environment, upon which we all depend, will be affected by the outcome.

ACKNOWLEDGEMENTS

I owe to Suzanne and Patrick Barkham many of the good ideas for this chapter, and great gratitude to Frances Hines for touching the key point and, thereby, finding me.

NOTE

1 Much of the remainder of this section was first presented as part of the Fifty-fourth Public Lecture of the Associates of the Student Counselling Service, University of East Anglia, Norwich, UK, 8 March 1991, and forms part of the 1992 article 'Personal drive and the environmental crisis'. *International Minds*, 3(1), 12–15.

REFERENCES

Corneau, G. (1991) *Absent Fathers, Lost Sons*. Boston, MA, Shambhala.
Enzensberger, H. M. (1991) The second coming of Adolf Hitler. *The Guardian*, 9 February, p. 23.
Lorenz, K. (1970) *Studies in Animal and Human Behaviour*. London, Methuen.
Mahdi, A., Law, R. and Willis, A. J. (1989) Large niche overlaps among co-existing plant species in a limestone grassland. *Journal of Ecology*, 77: 386–400. (This recent paper explores this puzzle and finds very little to distinguish between the environmental requirements of a group of species living together.)
Maslow, A. H. (1970) *Motivation and Personality*, 2nd edn. New York, Harper and Row.
Miller, A. (1990) *Thou Shalt Not Be Aware: Society's Betrayal of the Child*, 2nd edn. London, Pluto Press.

Miller, A. (1991) *Breaking Down the Wall of Silence to Join the Waiting Child.* London, Virago.

Odum, E. P. (1989) *Ecology and our Endangered Life-Support Systems.* Sunderland, MA, Sinauer. (This is a readable, introductory book about ecology.)

Olivier, C. (1989) *Jocasta's Children: The Imprint of the Mother.* London, Routledge.

Rackham, O. (1976) *Trees and Woodland in the British Landscape.* London, Dent.

Thomas, J. and Lewington, R. (1991) *The Butterflies of Britain and Ireland.* London, Dorling Kindersley.

Watson, A. and Moss, R. (1970) Dominance, spacing behaviour and aggression in relation to population limitation in vertebrates. In A. Watson (ed.), *Animal Populations in Relation to Their Food Resources*, pp. 167–220. Oxford, Blackwell.

3

ENGLISH LITERATURE AND COUNSELLING

Judy Moore

ENGLISH LITERATURE AND MY ENGAGEMENT WITH IT

Anyone who spends several years studying English Literature is likely to emerge from that study with a deeper understanding of human nature. This point was succinctly made by the actress Glenda Jackson, interviewed during her campaign as a prospective Labour candidate in the 1992 General Election: 'Working closely with Shakespeare gives you a valuable perspective on life' (*The Independent*, 17 March 1992). It is also likely that the student of English Literature will emerge with a heightened sensitivity to language and some awareness of the social context in which various works of literature have been produced. Beyond that I think it is impossible to generalize and I am aware that my approach to the question of how my study of English Literature has affected my work as a counsellor is very much dependent upon my own areas of interest and specialism and also upon my particular therapeutic orientation, which happens to be client-centred. What follows is therefore a very personal approach to the subject. In this section, I will explain some aspects of the study of English Literature. In the remainder of the chapter, I will look at how some of these might affect my work and also how my understanding of Romantic literature (roughly that of the period 1790–1820) underpins my client-centred perspective on individual experiencing within the social context of Britain in the late twentieth century.

Terry Eagleton points out that 'Literature, in the sense of a set of works of assured and unalterable value, distinguished by certain shared and inherent properties, does not exist' (Eagleton 1983: 11). If we accept a definition of 'literature' as being 'fine writing' then 'anything can be literature, and anything can cease to be literature' (Eagleton 1983: 10). Different texts are given different value in different ages and so the study of English Literature at degree level will involve the study of texts

recommended by a body of academics in whose current opinion those texts
constitute 'literature'. That choice of texts will reflect their own personal
tastes and assumptions as well as reflecting the preoccupations of the age.
The study of English Literature today, for example, is much more likely than
twenty years ago to involve the study of texts that invite engagement with
the discourses through which social and political values are transmitted.
Eagleton and other marxist critics argue that this level of engagement is
necessary to bring us to a more clear-sighted understanding of the society in
which we live. One of the ideas which I shall briefly consider later is the
possibility of engaging with the client as a text through which we may learn
more of contemporary social reality.

Literary theory is now a great deal more sophisticated than when I
embarked upon my first degree in 1971. Although a profoundly questioning
activity, literary analysis was then much less rigorous in its focus on
language. Works of literature were then examined for their construction in
terms of syntax, metaphor, rhyme and sound, and these devices were linked
to meaning. More recent criticism, however, takes the process much further:

> It is a shift from seeing the poem or novel as a closed entity, equipped
> with definite meaning which it is the critic's task to decipher, to seeing
> it as irreducibly plural, an endless play of signifiers which can never be
> finally nailed down to a single centre, essence or meaning.
>
> (Eagleton 1983: 138)

This fluidity I find immensely appealing and it is something that I strive
very consciously to bring to my counselling relationships. The client-centred
approach lends itself to a notion of meaning as process in which there are
no absolutes and no final truths.

Literary criticism, as well as submitting texts to an exhaustive analysis of
language that can finally destroy meaning, may also involve the reading
of texts in the light of quite specific theories. Psychoanalytic theory, for
example, has played an important part in the field of literary criticism and
has offered valuable insights. A Freudian reading of Lawrence's *Sons and
Lovers* can clearly shed light on some of the processes at play in the novel.
Yet in his evident sexism and other blind-spots, Freud is as much the product
of his age and society as any writer and his theories say as much about his
subjective reality as they do about human development. The study of English
Literature has taught me to approach all theories with caution. Interpretation of any kind can easily cut short the process of exploration and divert
one from deeper levels of truth. Alice Miller, in *Breaking Down the Wall
of Silence* (1991), validates such caution by rejecting psychoanalysis after
her recognition that psychoanalytic theory can be used to blind individuals
to the reality of their own experience of abuse as children.

The final aspect of the study of English Literature that I wish to mention
is the reading of texts in the light of political theory, such as marxism or

feminism. My own awareness of the relevance of the need to understand works of literature in their social context derives from working on my PhD thesis, which I began three years after completing my BA. At first sight, no subject could offer a less promising topic for political analysis: it is the construction of Mary Russell Mitford's *Our Village* (5 volumes, 1824–32), an apparently innocuous and immensely popular idealization of everyday life in the village of Three Mile Cross in Berkshire. As I became more deeply involved in the process of examining Mary Mitford's cultural influences and set these against what I was learning of the probable social reality of rural life in Berkshire in the early 1820s, it became clear that *Our Village* can be read as a very persuasive political text, an idealization and hence an affirmation of the *status quo* in the aftermath of the social disruptions and repressions that characterized English society from *c.* 1790–1820. At the same time, Mary Mitford was a very cultured writer, saturated in the literature and art of the period. Her work is a careful, probably largely unconscious, synthesis of influences, offering, among other things, a socially palatable version of the beliefs of the Romantic poets, the relevance of whose work to contemporary society I will consider in the following two sections.

For the past four years, I have no longer been professionally engaged in the study or the teaching of English Literature and work mainly as a student counsellor. The habits of my academic study are nevertheless deeply ingrained and I recognize that, however profound our level of human contact, I do not leave the insights of the last twenty years behind when I am working with clients. Sensitivity to language, an awareness of the relativity and ever-changing nature of meaning, a limited regard for psychological theories of any kind and an acute sense of the relevance of social context, are all aspects of my work that derive primarily from my study of English Literature

ENGLISH LITERATURE AND MY UNDERSTANDING OF PERSONS

If the doors of perception were cleansed, everything would appear,
to man as it is, infinite.
For man has closed himself up, till he sees all things thro' narrow
chinks of his cavern.
(William Blake, *The Marriage of Heaven and Hell*, 1790–93)

I could have discussed many authors in this section whose work would reflect different aspects of human experiencing as I encounter it in my work. For the sake of presenting a reasonably coherent view, I have chosen to focus on the poetry of the Romantic period (roughly 1790–1820). I have chosen this period partly because very specific ideas about human existence emerge in the poems themselves as well as in a number of essays that serve to justify the poetry and explain its underlying beliefs. The other reason is that the Romantic poets were, in their most fundamental beliefs, revolutionary and demonstrate how threatening to the established social order it may be to enable individuals, as one does in the counselling relationship, to contact the truth of their own experiencing.

Between the early 1790s and 1820, government fears of popular revolt in response to the French Revolution led to nearly three decades of war with France as well as to repressive legislation at home. Imprisonment without trial became common, public protest meetings were banned, libel laws were strictly enforced and many radical intellectuals were forced to flee the country. At the same time, the vast majority of the population lived in extreme poverty, with no voice in government and with little hope of reform.

Since that time, the introduction of universal suffrage and decades of social reform have raised the general standard of living, but our age resembles Britain at the beginning of the nineteenth century in so far as we are currently experiencing a time of extreme reaction after a period of reform. Paul Foot, writing in 1980, comments on this similarity and expresses also how complex are the social issues with which we are now faced:

> By clinging to the control of every area of power and influence except Parliament – the Judiciary, the police and armed forces, the civil service, newspapers and television, bigger and bigger corporations – the rich have managed to defend and extend their power and their privilege.
>
> (Foot 1980: 262)

Parliamentary reform has clearly not achieved what the radicals of the early nineteenth century had hoped it might achieve in terms of justice and equality. Welfare services are currently being eroded, the gap between rich and poor is increasing and we are now culturally oppressed by an omnipresent mass media whose promotion of images of desire and fear serves to imprison us in the pursuit of pleasure. As Terry Eagleton (1983: 13) points out: 'We live in a society which on the one hand pressurizes us into the pursuit of instant gratification, and on the other hand imposes on whole sectors of the population an endless deferment of fulfilment.' Eagleton argues that we need to apply the searching analyses currently confined to the study of 'literature' to the images and texts that feed society as a whole. Such scrutiny would undermine the power of these images and begin to liberate us from the myths by which we live, a more complex goal than the achievement of universal suffrage, but as necessary to the establishment of a more truly just and equal society. To see through the fog of twentieth-century propaganda requires a clarity of perception advocated by the Romantic poets as the necessary antidote to a very different kind of oppression.

Blake, Wordsworth and Shelley, from whose work I take most of my examples in this and the following section, were acutely conscious of the social context in which their works were produced. All three, at the time of their most radical writings, were supporters of the levelling impulse that had inspired the French Revolution and were violently opposed to the repressive, and increasingly corrupt, British government that thrived in reaction to it. Yet Blake's work, which so effectively captured the revolutionary zeal of the early 1790s, lost its popularity after the middle of the decade. Wordsworth, significantly radical in his early work, withdraws soon after 1800 into creeping apostasy to become eventually a revered figure of the establishment. Shelley, of a later generation than Blake and Wordsworth, is the most outspoken critic of what has been described as 'the most monstrous and corrupt government the country has ever seen' (Foot 1980: 44). He died shortly before his thirtieth birthday in 1822. The revolutionary output of each was therefore short-lived and reflective of different aspects of the age, but the common thread to their most radical work is a belief in the authority of individual experiencing and the need to give a voice to that authority in the face of social corruption and repression.

Shelley, perhaps more than any of the Romantic poets, had tremendous faith in poetry as an instrument of social revolution. In some of his later works (written from exile in Italy), he expresses very direct bitterness about the state of contemporary British society. In 'England, 1819', for example, he attacks the monarchy (in the person of George III) in his opening line, 'An old, mad, blind, despised and dying king'; the country is described as being governed by 'Rulers who neither see nor feel nor know'; religion is 'Christless, Godless', while the ordinary people are 'starved and stabbed on the untilled field', a direct allusion to the massacre of eleven unarmed ordinary people by the British army during an unauthorized reform meeting at St Peter's Field in Manchester on 18 August 1819. Yet in all his works, directed, as was all writing at that time, to the privileged literate minority, Shelley's motivation was predominantly social. As he writes in 'A Defence of Poetry' (1821): 'The cultivation of poetry is never more to be desired than at periods when, from an excess of the selfish and calculating principle, the accumulation of the materials of external life exceed the quantity of the power of assimilating them to the internal laws of human nature' (Owens 1984: 69). When Shelley was writing about the subtleties of individual experiencing, it was within the context of knowing that his society was corrupt and human nature struggling with the distortions imposed upon it by that corruption.

Blake, writing almost three decades before increasing repression and corruption prompted Shelley's bitter outpourings in such poems as 'England, 1819', was equally aware not only of the existence of gross social evils but also of the relationship between these evils and the inner state of individual human beings:

In every cry of every Man,
In every Infant's cry of fear,
In every voice, in every ban,
The mind-forg'd manacles I hear.
('London')

'Mind-forg'd manacles' are constructed by society; truth derives from a deeper level of knowledge. Blake, coming from a background of Dissent, believed in the presence of God within us as the ultimate authority, beyond the authority even of church or state. In an imagined conversation with the prophets Isaiah and Ezekiel in *The Marriage of Heaven and Hell* (1793), Blake gives expression to his belief in a ubiquitous divine presence: 'Isaiah answer'd: ". . . my senses discover'd the infinite in every thing, and as I was then perswaded & remain confirm'd, that the voice of honest indignation is the voice of God, I cared not for consequences, but wrote"' ('A Memorable Fancy', Plates 12–13).
     Through the voice of Ezekiel he also addresses the issue of gratification:

I then asked Ezekiel why he eat dung, and lay so long on his right and left side? He answer'd, 'The desire of raising other men into a perception of the infinite. This the North American tribes practise, and is he honest who resists his genius or conscience only for the sake of present ease or gratification?'

The pursuit of gratification is, in this context, seen as inimical to the perception of inner truth, a point that I think is of some relevance given the promotion of desire in contemporary Western culture. Yet the search for inner wisdom, Blake suggests here, as elsewhere in *The Marriage of Heaven and Hell*, involves not only self-denial, but also the expression of 'honest indignation': 'Jesus was all virtue, and acted from impulse, not from rules'. Impulse comes from within and is sacred; rules come from without and are infinitely questionable.
     Direct apprehension of the divine was central to the revolutionary beliefs of the Romantic poets. All authority beyond that was open to question and it is not surprising that they were regarded in their own time, and in quite separate ways, as a distinct social threat. I think it is of crucial significance to our reading of their work today that they were not merely rejecting a corrupt and authoritarian society, but that they were questioning all forms of knowledge, including scientific knowledge, that do not relate to the truth of inner experiencing. Keats (although less obviously radical than the poets I have chosen to focus on) summarizes this position in a letter dated 22 November 1817: 'I am certain of nothing but of the holiness of the Heart's affections and the truth of Imagination . . . I have never yet been able to perceive how any thing can be known for truth by consequitive [*sic*] reasoning' (Gittings 1970: 36–7).

The scepticism of the Romantic poets is not cynical, however. In his 'Hymn to Intellectual Beauty' (1816) Shelley makes a direct link between receptivity to 'The awful shadow of some unseen Power' ('the Spirit of Beauty') and the ability to 'love all human kind'. Direct apprehension of some kind of ultimate reality, the capacity to love and the ability to empathize with fellow-beings are inextricably interwoven in Shelley's thinking as they are in Blake and Wordsworth. Put very simply, they believed that if we are able to perceive everything 'as it is, infinite', then our capacity to love is increased. The task of the individual, therefore, is to seek access to perception of the infinite, which, they believed, could best be found in direct visionary experience (possibly precipitated by mind-altering drugs), the natural landscape, contact with spiritually advanced individuals and the reading of poetry that celebrates all or any of these. Hence the claims made, by Wordsworth and Shelley in particular, for the status of the poet who, they believed, was able to perceive truths invisible to mere 'reasoners and mechanists' (Owens 1984: 73). Poetry, Shelley believed, was capable of 'redeem[ing] from decay the visitations of the divinity in man'. Meanwhile, in a section of *The Prelude* (1805) that prefigures Shelley's 'Hymn to Intellectual Beauty', Wordsworth describes how apprehension of what he terms 'intellectual love' releases feelings of compassion:

> . . . he whose soul hath risen
> Up to the height of feeling intellect
> Shall want no humbler tenderness, his heart
> Be tender as a nursing Mother's heart;
> (*The Prelude* XIII: 197–200)

The importance of direct experience of the divine is the starting-point of Romantic beliefs about human life. The goal of life is to reach a point of simplicity where such experience can take place.

In *The Prelude*, Wordsworth's autobiographical poem whose stated theme is the growth of the imagination and 'intellectual love', the poet describes his own process as being a movement from love of nature to love of humanity. Elsewhere in Romantic poetry, love and compassion are celebrated in many forms and often the link between the human and the divine is made quite explicit, for example in Blake's 'The Divine Image' where he says 'Where Mercy, Love and Pity dwell/There God is dwelling too' (II, 19–20). Believing that the divine is within us, as in all living things, their conviction was that we must revere all manifestations of that divinity.

The social implications of this position are clear. Vagrants and beggars, such as are celebrated in Wordsworth's *Lyrical Ballads* (1798), are given as much value as representatives of any other stratum of society. It is not surprising that, in a contemporary review of the *Lyrical Ballads*, Wordsworth was accused of 'levelling' and linked with Tom Paine [author of the *Rights of Man* (1791–92)] as a subversive influence likely to 'bring

disaffection and infidelity within the comprehension of the common people'
(Butler 1981: 62). Reverence and compassion for 'the common people'
lie at the heart of revolutionary Romantic poetry and it is paradoxical,
though predictable, given the propertied interests that were at stake, that
such an attitude of profound respect for humanity should be perceived as
threatening. The issue at stake is one of authority: how can the rich tolerate
a society in which all the assumptions on which their position is based are
challenged by the perception of more valid truths?

Blake, Wordsworth and Shelley each held a view of the person as intrinsically good. They believed that the more natural an individual's state of
being, the greater is their potential for good. For the poets I have discussed
here, individual life and the finite world exist both socially and within the
context of eternity. Perception of the infinite, they believed, fosters the
ability to love. Both animate and inanimate nature are meanwhile seen as
direct manifestations of the divine. What the Romantic poets express for me
is a sense of human potential as the most fundamental of truths that can be
perceived in any social context. At the same time, their emphasis on how this
truth can only be reached through felt experience validates what I understand of the process of human growth from person-centred theory. It is this
stress on organismic experiencing that I will explore in the first part of the
following sub-section.

ENGLISH LITERATURE AND MY UNDERSTANDING
OF THE COUNSELLING PROCESS

Experience is, for me, the highest authority.
                                    (Carl Rogers, *On Becoming a Person*)

General

In the first part of this sub-section, I shall explain how Romantic thinking
relates to my understanding of the client's process in the light of client-
centred theory. Then I shall explore how other areas that relate to my study
of English Literature influence the way I work.

The counselling relationship, as I see it, is one in which the client is
gradually enabled to reach a clearer awareness of their organismic experiencing. The role of the counsellor is to facilitate this process by validating the
feelings of the client that gradually come to awareness. Balanced with
this is the counsellor's sense of her own experiencing which she will, where
appropriate, communicate to the client. Moving between the sensing and
validating of the client's inner world and giving expression to her own inner
responses, the counsellor is able to establish an acceptant reality which
facilitates growth.

The organic nature of his view of this process is made clear by Carl Rogers:

> If we were studying the process of growth in plants, we would assume certain constant conditions of temperature, moisture and sunlight, in forming our conceptualization of the process. Likewise in conceptualizing the process of personality change in psychotherapy, I shall assume a constant and optimal set of conditions for facilitating this change.
>
> (Rogers 1967: 130)

Rogers summarizes the conditions in terms of therapy as that of the client's being psychologically fully 'received' by the therapist. The process that follows is a predictable continuum from 'fixity to changingness, from rigid structure to flow, from stasis to process' (Rogers 1967: 131). Rogers identifies seven stages of this process, acknowledging that only a few clients would actually reach the seventh or final stage. The characteristics of this stage are that the client:

> . . . is aware of himself, but not as an object. Rather it is a reflexive awareness, a subjective living in himself in motion. He perceives himself as responsibly related to his problems. Indeed, he feels a fully responsible relationship to his life in all its fluid aspects. He lives fully in himself as a constantly changing flow of process.
>
> (Rogers 1967: 155).

This Rogers sees as a fundamentally simple way of being. The client has discarded all external structures to make subjective reality the centre of his or her world. Citing Maslow, he acknowledges that this state is one which is close to nature. Maslow describes self-actualizing people in the following terms:

> Their ease of penetration to reality, their closer approach to an animal-like or child-like acceptance and spontaneity imply a superior awareness of their own impulses, their own desires, opinions, and subjective reactions in general.
>
> (Rogers 1967: 174)

This is very close to Romantic thought and recalls Wordsworth's elevation of simple rustic characters to illustrate an ideal state of being in the *Lyrical Ballads*.

Carl Rogers' view of the person is predicated on an acceptance of the superiority of the natural and organic over the civilized and structure-bound. Apart from his disregard of the divine in relation to this natural simplicity, his views are very close to those of the Romantic poets, whose fear was that, with the expansion of industrialized society, we would increasingly lose touch with our natural roots. Romantic poetry abounds with metaphors of animal and plant life as illustrations of healthy growth. Wordsworth, for example, describes his childhood in the following terms that clearly illustrate the beneficence for him of his own early influences:

> Fair seed-time had my soul, and I grew up
> Foster'd alike by beauty and by fear;
> Much favor'd in my birthplace, and no less
> In that beloved Vale to which, ere long,
> I was transplanted.
>   (*The Prelude* XIII: 176–7).

It is when we are torn away from nature that we become damaged. Blake's *Songs of Experience* (1793) spell out how our natural goodness may be perverted by the corruption of cities, the punitive narrowness of conventional religion, the distortions of a repressive educational system and the diversion of our instinctive lovingness into fear, jealousy, hatred and sorrow. Essentially, in all these contexts, positive energy becomes negative energy. This is quite simply expressed in a poem entitled 'The School Boy', where the schoolboy speaks of the destructive effect of a classroom presided over by 'a cruel eye outworn'. Using metaphors from the natural world, the point is made that human beings also need space and freedom to grow:

> . . . if buds are nip'd
> And blossoms blown away,
> And if the tender plants are strip'd
> Of their joy in the springing day
> By sorrow and care's dismay,
>
> How shall the summer arise in joy,
> Or the summer fruits appear?
>   (II: 21–7)

A repressive education breeds 'sorrow and care's dismay' and is clearly far removed from the notion of freeing the individual to learn at his or her own pace and motivation as advocated by Rogers nearly two centuries later.

The straight-jacketing of the individual into any path that is against his or her intrinsic nature was anathema to the Romantics. Even the suppression of a natural feeling is seen as having the potential to bring dire consequences. In Blake's 'A Poison Tree', he explores the consequences of suppressing anger. The poem begins with a clear, self-explanatory antithesis:

> I was angry with my friend;
> I told my wrath, my wrath did end.
> I was angry with my foe:
> I told it not, my wrath did grow.

The poem goes on to explain how the speaker nourished his wrath, as one would nourish a tree, but with the 'water' of his tears and the 'sun' of his deceitful smiles. Eventually, the tree bears an apple which is coveted and then stolen by his foe. The poem concludes:

In the morning glad I see
My foe outstretch'd beneath the tree.

My interpretation of this is that not only is the foe damaged (apparently poisoned) by the suppressed anger of the speaker, but that the speaker is also damaged by following a self-destructive path through fear and sorrow and deceitfulness to take pleasure ('glad I see') in another's suffering. He has become effectively divorced from what Blake would see as his natural goodness.

Within a counselling relationship I see myself as helping the client to get more in touch with his or her own suppressed and repressed feelings by offering a reality that is deeply accepting of the real truth of the client's experiencing. The more the client is able to trust this truth, the more complete he or she becomes. Rogers summarizes the process in the following terms:

. . . the individual moves toward *being*, knowingly and acceptingly, the process which he inwardly and actually *is*. He moves away from being what he is not, from being a façade. He is not trying to be more than he is, with the attendant feelings of insecurity or bombastic defensiveness. He is not trying to be less than he is, with the attendant feelings of guilt or self-depreciation. He is increasingly listening to the deepest recesses of his physiological and emotional being, and finds himself increasingly willing to be, with greater accuracy and depth, that self which he most truly is.

(Rogers 1967: 175–6, original emphasis)

Elsewhere, Rogers gives expression to the conviction that 'both personal and social values emerge as natural . . . when the individual is close to his own organismic experiencing' (Kirschenbaum and Henderson 1990: 184). He also acknowledges that such a state fosters 'loving interpersonal relationships' (ibid.; p. 185). Taking this a stage further, the Romantics claim that in our natural, uncluttered, organismic state, we are profoundly loving and compassionate beings nourished by unmediated access to 'The feeling of life endless, the great thought/By which we live, Infinity and God' (*The Prelude* XIII: 176–7). Whether or not a client gets anywhere near this point within the course of the counselling process does not matter, but I find it personally very important to acknowledge this potential as the possible outcome of an individual's growth. Entering the counselling relationship from this perspective makes it, I believe, easier to be accepting and trusting of the process on a very fundamental level, whatever difficulties the client and I may encounter on the way.

It seems to me that the Romantics and Carl Rogers are viewing human life from different, but deeply complementary perspectives. The Romantics' reliance on intuitive knowledge brings them to an understanding of the person that is very similar to that arrived at by Carl Rogers through scientific method. Rogers is also very clear about the fundamental subjectivity of scientific investigation: '. . . there is no such thing as Scientific Knowledge; there are only individual perceptions of what appears to each person to be such knowledge' (Koch 1959: 192). Rogers' belief in the authority of the subjective is in essence no different from that held by Blake, Wordsworth, Keats, Shelley and their followers.

I find great coherence and internal logic in Romantic thinking that carries my understanding of person-centred theory into another dimension. It is, nevertheless, a very personal amalgamation that I would find quite difficult to communicate within a counselling relationship. At the same time, the reinforcement of the two perspectives actually simplifies the counselling process for me: my concern is simply to move with the client to deeper levels of truth. The client's experiencing dictates that movement: the truth that is revealed is their truth and part of the process, as I see it, involves the rejection of all external forms of authority. Wordsworth's *Prelude* is an exhaustive analysis of the development of the poet's beliefs through subjective experience. Carl Rogers, meanwhile, makes a very clear statement on inner authority:

> *Experience is, for me, the highest authority.* The touchstone of validity is my own experience. No other person's ideas, and none of my own ideas, are as authoritative as my experience. It is to experience that I must return again and again, to discover a closer approximation to truth as it is in the process of becoming in me.
>
> Neither the Bible nor the prophets – neither Freud nor research – neither the revelations of God nor man – can take precedence over my own direct experience.
>
> (Rogers 1967: 23–4, original emphasis)

This attitude is as revolutionary in its implications today as it was in the early nineteenth century. Client-centred therapy is capable of reaching beyond all structures and culturally held beliefs to establish a level of truth in individuals that, taken to its logical conclusion, could destroy the hold of popular myths in our lives and bring about radical social change. Subjective experiencing, as it exists today, is inextricable from 'the mass-mediated public sphere' (Brenkman 1979: 94) and needs to be more fully deconstructed. Even the family, the allegedly private arena in which most of our conflicts are contained, is, as Terry Eagleton (1984: 122) points out, 'ceaselessly penetrated by commodity culture'. Neither the individual nor the family exists in a social or cultural vacuum. I can see little point in bringing theories of human development to the client, although these may offer some insight, when what is really needed is the ability to stay with and deconstruct the myriad discourses that the client has internalized to prevent him or her from reaching their full potential as a human being. This could not be achieved without profound acceptance and empathy, but I believe these qualities need to be accompanied by a willingness to search and question layer beyond layer to uncover still deeper levels of subjective truth.

My starting point is to accept the client, as far as I am able, exactly where they are. This often involves acceptance of their internalization of beliefs or discourses that I find objectionable. I know, however, that if I can really stay with the relationship, the client is likely, through contacting deeper levels of inner experiencing, eventually to reach a point where he or she will come to question even the most deep-rooted assumptions. It is interesting to me to reflect on how the two recent clients I have struggled with most in terms of acceptance are a woman who came to me steeped in psychodynamic theories as to why she experiences herself as worthless and a young man steeped in popular myths about sexuality. In both instances, it was hard to reach the individual person through the rigid belief structures. My own early irritation in both cases made it difficult for me to respond empathically. Through exploring my response in supervision and holding on to my belief in the likelihood of therapeutic change, I managed to stay sufficiently in touch with the clients to begin to work effectively with them.

What then began to emerge with the woman client was how the neat psychodynamic theories she would reiterate every session served to defend her against the absolute terror that she hits whenever she begins to contact her own experiencing. We are now able to work with the terror much more directly and, as the rigidity of her thought-patterns is breaking down, life is becoming much more difficult for her. At the same time, she is beginning to emerge as a real person and I am optimistic that we will eventually contact something more positive once we have uncovered sufficient layers of conditioned beliefs and deep-rooted fear. I never attacked the theories, but kept holding her instead to what she might be feeling as she reiterated them. By articulating my own response to some of the experiences she has described and trying to get some idea of her own felt sense, we have moved closer to an organismic rather than an intellectual level of relating. It is on this level that therapeutic movement has begun to occur.

The social implications of this movement are something that I would not at present address in our sessions, but they are potentially quite profound. The terror that this client experiences is very much related to abuse by a sequence of male authority figures on whom she has been dependent at various points in her life. These relationships reflect a particularly abusive form of the patriarchal structure that underpins most of our institutions. I think it is unlikely, as she is beginning to contact the authority of her own experiencing, that she will continue in such collusion. To address this issue on a cognitive level would, however, detract from the level of experiencing which I know is the level at which change must take place.

A belief in the fundamental goodness of human beings and some sense of the social implications of self-awareness, both so powerfully reiterated in Romantic poetry, validate for me the efforts with acceptance that make possible movement towards the deeper organismic truths that are revealed through congruence and empathy. At every point in the counselling process, I could give an interpretation of my perception of the client's reality and the possible causes of the problem(s) that may have brought them into counselling. Each interpretation would be slightly different and none of them would be true, except in so far as they would be the truth of my subjective perception at that time. Therefore, I am extremely tentative about formulating and even more so about offering interpretations.

At the same time, it seems to be the case that openness to one's own experiencing can be facilitated by a breaking down of the rigidity of one's thinking patterns. That has certainly been so with many of my student clients whose counselling process has been precipitated or assisted by academic study, particularly in the humanities, where truth is more likely to be acknowledged to be relative and where social myths are likely to be challenged. My own background makes me particularly aware of this process in students of literature. At present, I have four clients who are studying English Literature and all have acknowledged that the study of literature has assisted their movement towards greater flexibility of understanding and self-awareness. While recognizing – and being fascinated by – this dimension, I am nevertheless clear that, within the counselling relationship, my terrain is the affective rather than the cognitive.

In searching for deeper truths of experiencing, language offers many clues. I am conscious of sessions moving between a primary and secondary mode of narrative, characterized respectively by first-hand, carefully discriminating language and a more defensive, second-hand retreat into platitudes or the conventional repetition of learnt responses. My object would always be to move into the first-hand, primary mode. As language is a tool of defence as well as a means of self-expression, attentiveness to clients' defensive, regressive or obfuscating words and phrases seems to me a valuable way in to the truth of their organismic experiencing, providing it is done within a relationship that is also characterized by acceptance and empathy.

The second client with whom I have recently experienced difficulties of acceptance was a young man whose language revealed complete contempt for the women ('fluff') with whom he was (not surprisingly) having difficulties in forming relationships. In fact, after a series of rejections, he had lost all sexual desire. It eventually emerged that he was angry and disappointed that women were in reality not available to him as the commodities promised by the pin-up culture on which his adolescent sexuality had been fed. After many months (and great struggles with acceptance on my part), he is beginning to contact the pain of rejection and emerging as a much more likeable person, capable of relating to people rather than images and with some return of sexual feelings. I am able to feel anger towards the culture that presented me with a client who regarded me with initial contempt rather than feeling anger (as I did at first) towards a victim of that culture. It is now also possible for me to address his language and the feelings that underlie, for example, the dismissive terms he, apparently unthinkingly, uses to describe women. As a result, he has begun to address the distortions of the culture in which his sexuality has been constructed. It is fascinating to me how his distance from his own organismic reality was fed by the pursuit of desire and how it was only the death of desire that enabled him to begin to contact his own inner truth. His experience confirms how destructive to the individual the peddling of desire in our society can be.

The relentless questioning that I undoubtedly bring to the counselling relationship as a result of years of academic study is, I think, humanized and made more radical by the beliefs about the nature of the person that I have absorbed from the Romantic poets and Carl Rogers. It enables me to balance compassion for the damaged individual with anger towards the source of that damage, whether it be the mass media or other individuals, themselves damaged by the distortions of a society dominated by values that are destructive to the human organism.

Case study

In this section, I will describe some aspects of how I worked with one particular client whom I will call Anna. The aspect of the work that is most relevant to this chapter is the quasi-literary search for ever-shifting levels of meaning that enabled Anna to deconstruct her own experiencing more fully. It is possible to analyse this aspect of the work, while it is not possible to analyse the quality of our relationship. I strongly believe, however, that it was the quality of the relationship that we established that was the most significant factor in bringing about therapeutic change. Our reflections or interpretations were absolutely secondary to what was happening at an organismic level, although I know that what was happening at an organismic level was influenced by these reflections and interpretations. What I describe in this section is very limited – a small part of that area of the process that can be related to literary analysis.

I saw Anna at the student counselling service where I work for approximately ninety sessions spread just over a year and a half. Eventually Anna moved away from the city where I work and so our ending was, in my view, premature. However, I have chosen to discuss her in this section because, as well as being very fond of her as a person and having enormous respect for her sensitivity and intelligence, I have been fascinated by the complexity of working with her. For several years before I saw her, she had had problems with eating and for a while had been in hospital with suspected anorexia. She had been treated very dismissively by her GP at home and, in a climate of general misunderstanding, had finally retreated into a state of complete withdrawal. She worked mechanically at her 'A' levels and arrived at university where she lost all control of her eating. By the time I saw her, she had become more sociable but was bingeing constantly and terrified that she would again descend into the 'nothingness' that had characterized the past few years.

My first impression of Anna, who is tall and attractive, was that she held herself as if she wanted to disappear, stooping slightly and with hair covering much of her face. She talked a little about the severity of her eating disorder, was quite desperate to find some way forward and evidently in tremendous emotional pain. Nevertheless, she completely contradicted all this by saying repeatedly that there was 'no real problem'. I felt quite out of my depth and, as I wrote in my notes after that first session, 'almost consumed by her pain'. I remember picking up a book on eating disorders shortly after the session and quickly abandoning it. I wanted to stay very clearly with what was coming from Anna herself, despite feeling quite lost amidst the pain and confusion and her denial that anything was seriously wrong. In effect, I wanted to stay with the text of this new and bewildering client and work as far as possible without preconceptions.

In retrospect, I can see that the contradictory themes with which we were to engage over the following months had already been established: Anna had told me physically by her presence, verbally by her communication of her problem and emotionally by the transmission of her intense level of pain that she needed help, while at the same time physically 'disappearing' and verbally denying that there was any problem. What Anna had effectively established was a primary discourse of intense suffering and a secondary, but quite powerful and insistent discourse of the denial or trivialization of suffering. What I found difficult during our first and subsequent early meetings was accepting that this individual could encompass such extremes. Here I can see the usefulness of the study of literature in enabling me to suspend disbelief, to accept the validity of both parts of the client's experiencing, to give serious attention to each, however much I may have wanted to give voice to my incredulity that Anna could so readily trivialize her own pain.

One of the problems I had in letting Anna know that both discourses were being heard was that I was so deeply affected by the intensity of Anna's pain that I was often fighting back my own tears. I was quite clear in these early stages that it would have been inappropriate to let Anna know the extent to which I was moved by her suffering in case she withdrew from the relationship to protect *me*. My notes for the early sessions are full of expressions like 'knot of pain', 'a descent into more pain', 'incredibly low and hopeless', 'such pain and distress', 'in despair'. It was only when we got to the twelfth session that I began to understand something of what was going on. Midway through the session I 'thought she would never stop crying' and became anxious that I had 'said tactless things to upset her'. When I questioned her it turned out that all I had done was to validate what a very real struggle every little thing was for her and the impact of knowing that she had been heard and taken seriously was quite overwhelming. Anna told me, to my absolute astonishment, that she never cried alone because she couldn't believe what she was feeling was 'real'. This helped me to understand the concentration of feeling in the sessions and also helped me to believe that, however inarticulate much of it might have been, some of my empathic responding had been received.

Much more problematic, especially given the level of pain that I had picked up from her, was the task of engaging with Anna's discourse of the denial of suffering. It was evident from the fact that she never cried alone that she was accustomed to putting on a reasonably effective façade and that it was the façade that was generally perceived in her social environment. Her language revealed that she did not have a vocabulary adequate to describe her suffering. She would talk about 'making a bit of a fuss', being 'a bit of a moaning Minnie' on the occasions when she actually referred to this aspect of her experiencing. I have no exact record of how I addressed these trivializations, but I recall how, in the early stages of the relationship, I tried very hard to focus on what was going on underneath what was being said. A 'moaning Minnie' suggests to me someone who moans repeatedly about nothing in particular and therefore needn't be taken seriously. 'A bit of a moaning Minnie' suggests a rather slight version of someone who moans all the time. By giving fairly precise consideration to such language, I fed back to Anna that it seemed as if at times she really did believe that she shouldn't take her own condition seriously. This was indeed the case and it soon became evident, as Anna began to elaborate on this discourse, that she held herself responsible for her own problems and, indeed, had evidently been encouraged to do so by well-intentioned family and friends who would exhort her to 'pull her socks up' or 'snap out of it'. Such platitudinous dismissals reflected all the vocabulary Anna had at her disposal to articulate deeply painful areas of her own experiencing. This experiencing could simply not be dealt with at a conscious level until she could find words to give voice to a closer approximation of the truth.

As if to compensate for her lack of a truly expressive vocabulary of feeling, her control of food had become for Anna an alternative form of self-expression. In session thirteen, she first introduced the notion of eating being to do with relating: in her early teens, she had starved herself to win popularity, feeling that she was disliked for being fat; at some point the dieting had become completely obsessive and social relationships became of less significance than her relationship with food. Dieting had meant being in control of eating and hence in apparent control of her experiencing; bingeing symbolized being out of control. By the time she came to me, bingeing was clearly related to her inability to handle feelings that were coming dangerously close to awareness. I was very willing to work with the notion

of eating as a symbol that held a multiplicity of meanings for Anna. From
session thirteen onwards, as if engaged in textual analysis, we looked
exhaustively at her past dieting and withdrawal and at her current bingeing
in relation to the range of feelings that were beginning to surface. If Anna
had binged that morning we would look at what had been going on the
previous evening or earlier the same day, and always eventually something
painful or difficult would emerge. By seeing eating/dieting/bingeing not as
problems but as part of discourse that could be 'read', we were able to look
at how her relationship with food was a necessary part of Anna's recent
experiencing and had distinct meaning. Bingeing was clearly something that
she needed until she could comprehend and give more adequate verbal
expression to what was really going on for her.

Looking at all this retrospectively, I can see the therapeutic process from
my perspective as being one in which I strove to engage with a multiplicity
of discourses in order to bring each of them to a level of articulation that
Anna could herself accept and adopt. In literary terms, it was as if I was
trying to help Anna see herself as a text that could be read and understood
rather than as the confusing conglomeration of contradictions and irrational
behaviours with which she first presented. The deconstruction of symbols
and behaviours turned Anna's experiencing into something more manageable and acceptable and a significant part of this process was enabling her
to discover a language to describe feelings (such as anger, pain and self-
loathing) that were, in her social experience, unacceptable. Clearly, much
empathic responding involves giving a label to describe hitherto unacceptable feelings, but in Anna's case, where feelings themselves were so heavily
disguised or denied, the process of uncovering and identifying the layer of
organismic experiencing was more complex and involved giving serious
attention to non-verbal as well as verbal symbols. Anna's abuse of food and
her own body were the most powerful symbols of all.

A continuing difficulty I had in relation to Anna was being restrained in
offering my own reading of her situation and responses. Although I was as
open as I could be in trying to hear and engage with everything that she
presented, my perception of any human being is inevitably coloured by the
Romantic/Rogerian view of the person I have outlined in this and the
preceding section. Thus, for example, while Anna saw herself as intrinsically
worthless, I saw her as intrinsically good; while Anna sought, initially at
least, to deny her inner experiencing, I held to the conviction that all
authority other than her own experiencing needed to be denied for her to
reach her full potential as a human being. Anna would clearly have rejected
these views outright if I had stated them in the early stages of our relationship, but eventually I was able to convey some sense that I saw her much
more favourably then she saw herself and that I believed there were certain
aspects of her home environment that had been destructive to her. It was
particularly difficult for Anna to see herself in a positive light, but she did

eventually contact great anger and bitterness about certain aspects of the social environment that had led to her complete withdrawal. It was always necessary to go at Anna's own pace so that each aspect of her experiencing could be explored. If, for example, I had given expression at too early a stage to any sense of quite how destructive certain aspects of her home environment sounded to me, then Anna, whose own security is very much bound up in that environment, would probably have felt judged and rejected.

Finally, I should like to return briefly to Terry Eagleton's argument that textual analysis needs to operate in the context of the society which has produced that text. It was impossible to work with Anna without being aware of some of the common social pressures that operate within a rather conventional and judgemental local community. One of these is the pressure exerted on us all, and particularly on young women, to believe that thinness is desirable: a glance through any magazine reinforces this message, with the effect of subtly undermining the confidence of any woman who does not approximate to an appearance that is culturally presented as attractive. It is no wonder, given the universality of this message, that Anna should have believed that she would be more liked if she were thin.

Predictably, she did win some approval for her ability to lose vast amounts of weight and I find it fascinating how her eventual suppression of her own hunger was accompanied by her losing contact with all feelings. It is as if the covert message of the peddling of images of the thin, desirable woman is a plea for the suppression of the organismic self. Authentic experiencing is clearly a social danger and Anna was beset on all sides by pressure, often probably quite unconscious, to be anything other than her real self. There are many aspects to this pressure, which there is not space to discuss here, but I am conscious of how useful I find it to consider how inimical to the human organism are most of the pressures that operate in our society.

Eventually, as she became more self-accepting, Anna reduced her bingeing very significantly, contacted a vast range of feelings about her past, began to make some good friendships and at times was able to enjoy life. At the same time, it became impossible for her to continue with her degree course. With a raw sensitivity to slights and put-downs, daily life in a city hundreds of miles from home became more rather than less difficult for Anna and my validation of her experiencing for an hour or two a week was simply not enough. I believed that Anna needed the more acceptant social environment of a therapeutic community to consolidate her trust in her own experiencing; her own decision was to return home.

Anna's case illustrates the paradox of growth in contemporary society. It is impossible to be authentic in a society built on consumerist propaganda where the expression of feelings is generally regarded as an embarrassment. The family, particularly if it is a loving one, may be safer than other arenas, but it is as much penetrated by cultural myths as the rest of society. What is authentic is what comes from the human organism and in order to contact that truth we need to listen beyond the myths. An eating disorder may manifest as an individual problem, but it is fundamentally a social disease. By deconstructing the experience of individuals such as Anna, we may come to a more realistic appraisal of the society in which we live.

CONCLUSION

It is undoubtedly the study of English Literature that makes me see the therapeutic process as a relentless search for truth. It reinforces the empathic listening which lies at the heart of the client-centred approach and validates the notion that all meaning is relative and no conclusion final. At the same time, I believe that the view of the person that will emerge from such listening is that held with such conviction by the Romantic poets at the onset of industrial capitalism and reiterated by Carl Rogers in our own century.

I began this chapter with a reference to the 1992 General Election, an election that, in my view, was won partly as a result of the exploitation of fear and greed by the mass media. It is such awareness that leads me to believe that we need to bring the scrutiny that characterizes the study of English Literature not only to the contemporary texts, such as newspapers, that manipulate our day-to-day lives, but also to the clients whose own experiencing in many ways reflects the repressions and distortions of our culture. We, as counsellors, are as much engaged as the contemporary marxist or feminist critic in 'the cultural politics of late capitalism' (Eagleton 1984: 25).

Meanwhile, there is a real danger of counselling being appropriated to serve the interests of the establishment. The recent increase in redundancy counselling is one example of how counselling may be used to hive-off distress and thus serve the interests of big corporations in the 'caring' 1990s. It seems at this point that the political significance of counselling needs to be carefully considered by its practitioners. I believe we can learn a great deal about social reality through deconstructing subjective experiencing. At the same time, the radical questioning of literary criticism may not simply be helpful in terms of our awareness of client processes but also in terms of analysing the discourses that sustain our own practice.

REFERENCES

Brenkman, J. (1979) Mass media: From collective experience to the culture of privatization. *Social Text*, 1: 94.

Butler, M. (1981) *Romantics, Rebels and Reactionaries*. Oxford, Oxford University Press.

Eagleton, T. (1983) *Literary Theory: An Introduction*. Oxford, Blackwell.

Eagleton, T. (1984) *The Function of Criticism*. London, Verso.

Foot, P. (1980) *Red Shelley*. London, Sidgwick and Jackson in association with Michael Dempsey.

Gittings, R. (1970) *Letters of John Keats*. Oxford, Oxford University Press.

Hutchinson, T. (ed.) (1950) *Wordsworth: Poetical Works*. Oxford, Oxford University Press.

Hutchinson, T. (ed.) (1970) *Shelley: Poetical Works*. Oxford, Oxford University Press.

Kirschenbaum, H. and Henderson, V. (eds) (1990) *The Carl Rogers Reader*. London, Constable.

Koch, S. (ed.) (1959) *Psychology: a Study of Science*, Vol. III. New York, McGraw Hill.

Miller, A. (1991) *Breaking Down the Wall of Silence*. London, Virago.

Mitford, M. (1824–32) *Our Village*, 5 volumes. London, Whittaker.

Owens, W. R. (1984) *Romantic Criticism*. A362 Prose Booklet. Milton Keynes, Open University Educational Enterprises.

Rogers, C. (1967) *On Becoming a Person*. London, Constable.

Stevenson, W. H. (ed.) (1971) *The Poems of William Blake*. London, Longman.

4

SOCIAL ANTHROPOLOGY AND COUNSELLING

Richard Morgan-Jones

INTRODUCTION

I welcomed the invitation to write this chapter as it has provided me with the opportunity to explore again the importance of a subject I had studied as part of a degree course at university. I work as a psychotherapist doing analytical work. That is my training and orientation as examples in this chapter will illustrate. I also work with organizations as an external consultant. Both involve me in doing training and group work.

I begin with some of my own story that drew me to the subject. For the personal reflections I make no apology. These ruminations are the stuff of personal insights in the counselling and psychotherapeutic professions. I hope mine will provide thoughts valuable to others for the way the study of Social Anthropology shaped my professional development, readers will find to be a quite idiosyncratic tale, peculiar to me. Others have taken different routes and made different conclusions based upon the same evidence.

For the intellectual elements in the chapter, I do not claim to be writing as one up-to-date with currents in the field of social anthropology. My brief in this chapter is to lay out the discipline to readers, to illustrate how it informs my understanding of persons and to explore how it shapes my understanding of the work I do.

SOCIAL ANTHROPOLOGY AND MY ENGAGEMENT WITH IT

The dilemma was: 'What was I to study at University?' Two life experiences shaped my decision. First, at the age of sixteen, I had been a member of a year long weekly experiential group run by one of my school teachers. This experience totally re-orientated my search for what I wanted to be doing in my life. The worlds of inner feeling, quality of relationships and group dynamics beckoned me. This was a microcosm of society. As members we were active participants while at the same time being observers and students of the group we helped to create. This was a rich invitation into the methodology of social anthropology.

During the year before university, I eventually secured a post as social therapist at the Henderson Hospital, a therapeutic community in the Health Service, specializing in patients with psychopathic personality disorders, using group and community therapy. There, patients who had been the despair of the prison, probation and mental health services were invited to participate actively in their own therapy. They were asked to speak their impulses and feelings in groups rather than acting them out in ways that were as dramatic as they were destructive and without feeling to both others and themselves. I learnt that in groups irrational impulses in those who appear least responsible, can be brought under self-control by being talked through.

At the age of nineteen, this was a baptism by fire into the world of therapeutic work. The daily dose of violence, passion, pain, confrontation and group dynamics opened me to experiences I still learn from. Professional work was achieved by staff focusing on the dynamics and therapeutic norms of the unit. These were clearly spelt out in a research study that Robert Rapoport had done under the title *Community as Doctor* (Rapoport 1960). It was this study and its title that had first attracted me to discover more about the hospital. It also highlighted the nature of the work of the social anthropologist, which was to participate in the events going on around him, while being also an observer of them. For me the stance of the professional therapist as involved observer commenting on individual, group and organizational dynamics was parallelled by that of the social anthropologist exploring the unknown in a foreign culture.

The second experience was a personal and painful one that came in the form of a bequest, by which I mean an experience that cannot be dealt with by one generation and is left to the next one to come to terms with. I have discovered that such 'bequests' are not uncommon in the way many in the helping professions have experienced the invitation to caring work. Stierlin (1981) calls them 'missions'.

At the age of nineteen, my father had what was to be the first of a series of psychological breakdowns that were to haunt him for the rest of his life. His diagnosis as someone with a manic-depressive personality, and his subsequent admission to hospital for a course in ECT and amnesia-inducing drugs constituted for me a more devastating experience than his appalling states of anxiety, irrational guilt and aimless rage that searched for exorcism. All this was in a man who until that time I had experienced as a loving, intelligent, successful, extroverted person who had been the cornerstone of what had seemed a secure, loving family. Amid my personal pain I was also aware of the question and protest in me: 'How could a supposedly sane and caring society stigmatize so thoroughly one of its members?'

The contradictions of this massive personal revolution have rippled through my life ever since. At that time, I oscillated wildly between two extremes. One was a fascination with the irrational, with a determination to do what I could to combat the evils in the way medicine responded with induced amnesia and shame-creating treatments by searching out alternatives. The other was a terror of madness, mad thoughts, mad feelings, mad behaviour, mad treatments, in others, in me, everywhere. The study of social anthropology offered me the chance of studying the way societies shaped individuals and dealt with what was experienced as beyond the norm.

Readers in the counselling and psychotherapy professions, at home with hearing stories of this kind, will recognize the painful ambivalences that are at the heart of our work. There is also the painful dilemma to resolve; namely, 'Am I therapist or patient, or always what Jung would have described as a wounded healer?' (Fordham 1978: 15).

A quarter of a century later, after a psychotherapy training, fifteen years of clinical work with patients, and two personal analyses – one Jungian, the other Freudian – I no longer think this to have been the most traumatic of many life experiences, merely an echo of the worst. Interestingly, it is not what motivates me in the work the way it did in the early years, and the fascination with and terror of madness that once drove me no longer have the same hold over me, nor is it such a central conflict. None the less, you will hear cooler echoes of it through my examples later in the chapter.

That I was able to think at all during this period of my life was in some measure due to an effective defence structure, with intellect and humour high on the list of techniques for banishing feeling. It was also in large measure due to the teacher who had run the experiential group that I had been a part of, who, in addition to developing his group skills, was beginning to discover his considerable ability as a counsellor to people as confused, searching and distressed as I was. This in fact was Brian Thorne, one of the editors of this book, who invited my contribution. As a generous and vital reference point in my chaotic seeming life, for me he opened doors to find ways of turning my step into higher education into a positive experience, instead of one where I was unable either physically or psychologically to leave home.

Let me return to the dilemma. What to study at university? With hindsight, studying social anthropology was a creative compromise between order and rationality on the one hand and strangeness and seeming irrationality on the other. On the one hand, it allowed me access to unfamiliar behaviour in cultures distant in time and geography; on the other, it introduced me gently to the possibilities of deeper reflection and meaning on how to be an observer who also participates and makes sense of what goes on around them.

SOCIAL ANTHROPOLOGY AND MY UNDERSTANDING OF PERSONS

Definition

Social anthropology is the study of man. This definition is so broad that it suggests that almost any aspect of mankind could be studied. In 1926, the young anthropologist in Melanesia was expected by his professor to study 'religion, secret societies, and kinship in the local culture. In addition he was expected to collect artifacts for the local museum, research the local language and spend half his day carrying out statistical analysis of the shape of people's skulls' (Leach 1982: 21).

My own course in social anthropology also included elements of physical anthropology and archaeology. The vision that had inspired this combination was the idealized hope that one day there would be a Science of Society, capable of linking ancient developments in mankind to those of primitive peoples today. This imperialistic 'museum of curiosities' approach to the so-called primitive in man became outdated in favour of the search for academic theories about the nature of society. Happily, a less patronizing, white, colonial and Western European set of values prevailed. As the enlightened French humanitarian writer Montaigne had put it in 1526, in his essay on Cannibals: 'We are justified in calling these people barbarians by reference to laws of reason, but not in comparison with ourselves, who surpass them in every kind of barbarity' (Montaigne 1958).

What you will see from the exploration of three key themes that follow, is that the study of social anthropology stemmed from learning from societies with less developed technology and very different kinds of rationality to Western European cultures. In essence, it is a kind of micro-sociology, interested in finding meaning in the detailed analysis of interaction between persons in defined role relationships, and particularly interested in searching out possible creative analyses for the relationship between these and the functioning of the whole society. This seems to have much in common with the work of the sociologist George Herbert Mead (1934) and his 'Symbolic Interactionism'. Indeed, the overlaps with sociology are considerable, particularly in the sociology of organizations that deals with the micro-analysis of organizational interactions. Organizations, like the societies studied by anthropologists, have clearer boundaries drawn around them to contain and give meaning to their members.

Key theme 1: The methodology of participant observation

The social anthropologist joins a society, observes people's behaviour and asks them for their explanation of it. He or she then makes up theories about the behaviour and the explanations. It is in joining a society with the intention of studying it that the social anthropologist defines his or her role. Like the members and staff of the experiential and therapeutic groups described above as well as later in this chapter, he or she is a participant who observes. For those who want an introduction to the texture of the work of a social anthropologist, I recommend Nigel Barley's (1983) bitter-sweet, but humorous account of the trials and tribulations of gaining access to the Dowayo people in West Africa. Particularly significant is his agonizing with the values and virtues of doing fieldwork at all.

But who is studying who in this process? The story was going the rounds when I was a student, of the earnest graduate anthropologist, replete with first-class degree, Columbia grant and supervision through a doctorate pro-gramme interviewing the recommended informant about an ancestor cult in Burma. The researcher was surprised by the conditions laid down in return for the valuable information, not just a percentage of the grant, but also the promise of a copy of the final doctoral dissertation. A return visit some years later revealed the reason for this sophisticated sounding request. The pro-mised gift of the dissertation was followed by an introduction to the inner sanctuary where the informant revealed the shelf of bound doctoral disserta-tions he had received from each of '*his* students'. He grinned and accom-panied his revelation with the triumphant claim that he was interested in following the different theoretical conclusions each had reached based upon the slightly modified version of his cult that he had delivered to each researcher!

Perhaps this story illustrates that every member of a society is potentially an anthropologist, quite capable of examining his or her own social milieu aided simply by reflection. This, however, raises the dictum of Gregory Bateson: 'How can you hear the music if you are one of the notes' (Bateson 1972). This was from a man renowned for doing research both into the cultural interactions of primitive societies as an anthropologist as well as the interactions of families where one member is diagnosed as psychotic. In each area of work, the search for a theoretical vertex from which to stand and perceive human interactions is crucial, complete with a value analysis of the chosen point of view. In the end, it was Bateson's creative solution to this problem that enabled him to extend his theory of 'Schizmogenesis' from the Naven ceremony among the Iatmul people of New Guinea, to inventing the valuable clinical theory of the 'double-bind'.

Bateson studied gender role differentiation. Each gender role was discrete, the women being given the childcare, food-gathering and cooking tasks, with men claiming the right to preside over how they performed them. Women were excluded from the ceremonial meeting houses, as well as hunting, fishing and canoe-making. What Bateson observed was the way detailed interactions between individuals, indeed even the meanings of words, reinforced these cultural differentiations. He defined schizmogenesis as 'a process of differentiation in the norms of individual behaviour resulting from cumulative interaction between individuals' (Bateson 1958: 175).

This kind of social anthropology is also familiar in the work of Margaret Mead, whose investigation into sex-role stereotyping was entitled *Male and Female* (1950). But we should notice also how much of this kind of social analysis is familiar in the Women's Movement.

> Struggles which have focussed on women's equal rights outside the home seem doomed to be ineffectual unless they also take account of women's domestic and familial responsibilities; but this is very difficult when women still have negligible power in the trade union movement, national government, the Labour party or any other political party.
>
> (Segal 1987: 43)

Many doing counselling and psychotherapeutic work have had to confront their own prejudices induced by overconformity to stereotyped role models.

When it came to exploring psychological and social pressures on the person diagnosed schizophrenic, Bateson coined the term 'double-bind' for the particular way in which an identified patient's feelings and behaviour were discounted as real or of value. He produced the well-known example of the 'schizophrenogenic' mother who advances towards her child with a demonstration of affection, then, when the child responds in kind, both withdraws and says something like, 'Well, aren't you going to kiss your mother then?' (Bateson 1972).

This approach to studying the pressures that produce madness is also familiar in psychoanalytic investigations, found in Harold Searles' (1965) paper 'The effort to drive the other person crazy'. This pre-dated Laing's popular work in which he explores the personal and social stereotyping that earns individuals the psychotic diagnosis (Laing 1967, 1969), as well as his theory of 'disconfirmation', where the person feels 'guilt or shame at being honest about his "real" feelings' (Laing 1961: 91).

Jules Henry combined both the disciplines of social anthropology and psychoanalysis. In the early 1960s, he pursued the naturalistic study of families of disturbed children by living with them. His compassionate study, *Pathways to Madness* (Henry 1973), records the ways in which daily routine and family interactions are mismanaged to undermine the confidence and self-identity of the children of these families, as well as the adults. In one example, the father in a family, having proposed an outing, fails to take the normal precautions in relation to timing. Stimulating excitement to get in the car for a trip to the local seaside precedes preparation of food or equipment. Meanwhile, others are blamed for the family frustration as all are kept waiting while these crucial tasks take place. Fixed and flexible time in our society, says Henry, is governed by social rules. Fixed time dominates flexible time. An important meeting with the boss dominates family priorities.

However, when the father of the family uses this prerogative to assume his family will submit to his failure to plan his home life, failing to think how long the food, the baby and the beach gear take to prepare, individuals' sense of their own needs and identities is systematically undermined. It is mad driving (Henry 1973: 11–24). This detailed micro-analysis of a family as a social system illustrates well the carry over from the methodology of participant observation in social anthropology to that of the psychotherapist doing clinical work.

In training analytical psychotherapists, it is common to offer seminars based on the naturalistic observation of the development of relationship between a mother and a baby, weekly for an hour, over a period of a year. The task of observing without intervening is of the essence in analytic work, where the role demands noticing what is being said without being thrown either by the weight of emotion or by the pressure to intervene. Readers will find excellent examples of this work in Bick (1968), Piontelli (1986) and Perez-Sanchez (1990).

A similar stance to research is found in the work of James and Joyce Robertson on the effect of separation on babies and young children taken into nursery and hospital. It was their ability to observe and film without intervening in painful scenes that enabled them to present findings that have changed a whole generation's attitudes to parents having access to their children in hospital (Robertson and Robertson 1989). Their work, along with Bowlby's, has also influenced a whole generation's attitudes to attachment and loss in child care and the importance of continued quality of care in the face of inevitable experiences of separation in daily life (Bowlby 1979).

Key theme 2: Religion and mythology

Accounts of primitive religious beliefs and mythologies abound in social anthropology. The gods of a society may be anthropomorphic and a dramatized reflection of the attributes esteemed by man as in many ancestor cults. They may be reflections of aspects of nature such as the sun, the sea or the wind, as in the Nordic or Greek pantheon (Thor, Neptune), or they may be more sophisticated versions of the same thing where it is aspects of life experience that are venerated, gods of destruction, creation or death. Whatever is found, social anthropologists seem to take one of two approaches. They see religion either as a way of upholding accepted social and moral values or else as a cultural way of legitimating real and powerful personal experience.

Functionalism and its limits

What makes a social anthropologist a functionalist is the commitment to showing how social institutions, norms and beliefs fit together to produce a coherence that is shaped by the members of a society. Radcliffe-Brown focused his attention on the rites and ceremonies that make up a religion. He claimed that rites 'can . . . be shown to have a specific social function when, and to the extent that, they have for their effect to regulate, maintain and transmit, from one generation to another sentiments on which the constitution of the society depends'. He suggests that religion is the expression of 'a sense of dependence on a power outside ourselves, a power which we may speak of as a spiritual or moral power' (Radcliffe-Brown 1965: 157). In support of his views, he quotes Confucius: 'It is through the sacrifices that the unity of the people is strengthened' (p. 158). He also quotes his own work among the Andaman Islanders, the totemism of the North American Indians and the Aborigines, as well as the way clergy on both sides during the Second World War prayed for victory for their nation.

The risk of this view is that it provides but a 'suitcase theory' in which the conclusions 'discovered' are already 'packed away' in the presuppositions embodied within the theory. The functional anthropologist looking for examples of ritual and ceremonies attaches importance to them in the way they uphold the values of the assembled members of a society.

As sociologists will know, functionalism does not adequately describe how social change comes about. Perhaps for the anthropologist in his remote society, change was rare. Neither does functionalism take account of the revolutionary aspects of religion as an agent for social change. This is well illustrated by the 'Confessing Church' in Germany that plotted and only just failed to assassinate Hitler, by the left-wing criticism of dictatorial regimes by the Latin American Catholic bishops and by the self-immolation by Buddhists in South East Asia making political protests. The point is illustrated poignantly by MacKinnon when describing the way Christianity was accepted as the state religion in the year AD 312 after Emperor Constantine won the battle of the Milvian Bridge: 'It was from that moment that the Church could begin to speak with the voice of Caiaphas and it was once more expedient that in the name of religion one man should die for the people' (MacKinnon 1965).

Mythology as cultural legitimation of personal experience

Rosemary Gordon is not untypical of a different approach. She writes as a social anthropologist who is also a Jungian analyst. In her book *Dying and Creating – A Search for Meaning* (Gordon 1978), she attempts to connect the difficulties people have in being creative with their difficulty in facing the reality of death and in some way coming to terms with it. Among her illustrations are stories where man chooses death, in a way dignifying the process of owning the time of death, a feature described by a number of workers in the Hospice movement. A Polynesian myth describes the Island of the Dead, where the Navigator celebrates his past life, officiates at his funeral party, then withdraws to the place of the dead with his apprentice to instruct him before putting himself to sleep and death. This myth is movingly brought to life in Morris West's (1976) novel *The Navigator*. Gordon concludes that different stories about the origin and meaning of death reflect man's attempt to face the powerful feelings engendered by the experience of death and dying. Each story provides a sense of value for creative activity during life.

I have described this work by another social anthropologist, partly to illustrate another approach, partly to add colour and detail to anthropological work, but partly also to make the connection to the work of the psychotherapist. Gordon makes the point that in order to be creative, people have to be able to sustain their own particular moods involved in states of ego loss. These include any experience where despair, depression or narcissistic rage can obliterate a creative attempt to face living. The creative act means experiencing the risk of not knowing quite where ideas have come from nor where they are leading. It means trusting what is not conscious nor predictable. All this suggests the vital importance of practitioners in the therapeutic field having also spent a substantial time as patients themselves exploring the difficulties they have with their own creativity and ability to face dying.

Nowhere is this more important than in the work of bereavement counselling. However, it is also at the heart of all intensive psychotherapy as the attachment between patient and psychotherapist becomes increasingly experienced as the vehicle for understanding truths about self-identity, and the weekly, termly and final ending of the sessions becomes the model for surviving the process of letting oneself know that one has been born or weaned into a world that once felt inhospitable.

Throughout this chapter, we explore the interface between society and the person's experience of it. As we have already seen, the social anthropologist explores the nature of society without judgement. The psychotherapist explores the way particular individuals have had their emotions and relationships patterned to find their culture and society more or less welcoming.

The above example illustrates how there is perhaps a secular shift in Western societies away from religion or medicine, towards searching for psychological meanings for personal and social phenomena. Most people in Britain are now aware of the importance of grieving after loss. Places of work are now acknowledging this in their conditions of service and agreements on compassionate leave. However, we are not yet in the position of the USA, where those with private health insurance are covered for 12 sessions of grief counselling!

Key theme 3: The meaning of belonging – culture and kinship

Early anthropologists tried to distinguish between culture as that which was created by man and nature which was not. So Tylor defined 'Culture or civilization . . . [as] that complex whole which includes knowledge, belief, art, morals, law, custom, and any other capabilities and habits acquired by man as a member of society' (Tylor 1871, in Leach 1982).

Structuralism

If functionalist social anthropologists tended to focus upon what was observable in behaviour and people's explanation of it, the structuralist social anthropologists were concerned with cultural forms that exposed ideas revealed through symbolism and linguistic use. One problem here was to distinguish between what was held in the mind as part of socialization and what was observable in behaviour. Many followed Levi-Strauss, whose 'structuralist' perspective was more concerned with 'the patterning of ideas in the mind rather than with facts on the ground' (Leach 1982: 47).

If we ask people, 'Who do you feel you belong with?', we might find that their *affinity* is with a range of biological relations spread all over the country, and for many of them all over the world. If, however, we observe their behaviour, we should notice that they belong to a range of possibly localized social contexts organized by institutions and groupings in our society, including the workplace, school, social contexts, including pubs, clubs, sport and friendship networks.

Here we can see the diversity facing anthropologists in what weight they glve to different evidence. Levi-Strauss thought that it was the structures in people's minds that provided the key evidence. For him, legitimate membership of a society is epitomized by having two parents and a name that belongs to them. He concludes that there is an underlying structure to the patterns of cultural identity.

Cultural anthropology and life stages

Analysis of culture, then, can begin from a whole variety of perspectives. What may be important is the collection of evidence in order to tell a simple story. An early example of this is Ruth Benedict's early work entitled *Patterns of Culture* (Benedict 1954). She explored not just the kinship patterns, but the specific institutions, legal and religious, in a number of societies, and also their norms for behaviour and socialization. Margaret Mead also provides a valuable approach for cultural analysis in her study of female socialization entitled *Coming of Age in Samoa* (Mead 1928). It was this 'cultural' perspective on anthropology that provided the psychoanalyst Erik Erikson with an approach in which to integrate two elements:

1 A close description of eight stages in life development, beginning with Erikson's version of the three coined by Freud – oral-sensory, muscular-anal and locomotor-genital. Each stage was characterized by a particular

emotional conflict. He suggested that where earlier developmental stages were not well resolved, then their patterning of emotions could be found repeated in later stages – hence psychological conflicts (Jacobs 1986, 1990). This is a kind of legitimating psychological approach to 'rites of passage'.

2 The exploration of different cultures in order to examine how in different social contexts people found a benign or hostile environment for coming to terms with their central emotional dilemmas.

We have seen that one of the major preoccupations of social anthropologists is to explore the question, 'What holds people together collectively through personal and social changes?' This question is at the heart of the functionalist pursuit, the search for the upholding of common values and beliefs in social institutions and norms, as well as of Structuralism, with its search for common underlying collective themes, reminiscent of Jung's 'collective unconscious'.

As we saw earlier, collective behaviour in groups and organizations is studied by social anthropologists and those doing therapeutic work alike. A rich vein for exploring in detail – 'What holds people together collectively during personal and social change?' – is the study of group dynamics and organizational behaviour. It was in this aspect of therapeutic work that I came to see the principles of social anthropology applied in the service of psychotherapy.

Group dynamics and belonging: Bion

Bion's study of groups was a functionalist pursuit. He wanted to know what held groups together in behaviour that was at times creative, at times destructive. He studied small group behaviour in the army, in leadership selection and in small therapeutic groups (Bion 1961). He distinguished between the work group (W-activity) that was able to apply itself to a specified task, and people's basic assumption activity that used survival mechanisms to defend themselves from unbearable anxieties (S-activity). Basic assumption activities seemed to be formed unconsciously as members of the group clustered around a certain way of behaving. The three types of group dynamics Bion described as people behaving as if the only way they might survive was:

1 To find a replacement leader, object or cause upon whom or which to depend.
2 To find a pair who would in their intimacy or quarrel serve to resolve the group's difficulties by simulating family life.
3 By searching for the adrenalin escape from depressive feelings into fighting or fleeing.

Group dynamics and belonging: The Tavistock approach to organization

Bion also suggested that particular institutions in society require group phenomena that depend upon the expression of these basic assumptions. Combining these phenomena in order to maximize the flexibility as well as the emotional maturity to find collective feeling and motivation for specific tasks, could be the aim of sophisticated teamwork or organizational work. Bion's followers at the Tavistock Institute for Human Relations developed his approach to groups and applied them to organizations and wider social phenomena. A large number of them were trained as social anthropologists (Trist and Murray 1990: 613–14).

An early Tavistock contribution to organizational dynamics came from Isabel Menzies Lyth, whose report on why the nursing profession lost so many staff soon after or during training was entitled, *The Functioning of a Social System as a Defence Against Anxiety* (Menzies Lyth 1970). Her analysis focused upon how the nursing profession functioned within the general hospital in a way that required crisis procedures at certain times. Because of this, and because of the powerful emotions that had to be suppressed in order to function in life and death situations, equally powerful nursing procedures were not just available for crises, they dominated the routines of the hospital. This made it impossible for nurses to innovate individual approaches to solving challenges in patient care. Thus their creativity and motivation that had lead them into the profession were sapped, while it also made for inefficient solutions to problems that seemed to require a crisis to produce results.

Robert and Rhona Rapoport, also at the Tavistock Institute, provided a social anthropology research of the therapeutic community at the Henderson Hospital, where I worked briefly (see p. 45). They analysed the unit's ideology of democratization, where patients and staff are engaged with equal responsibility for: (1) therapy; (2) permissiveness, so that behaviour normally not tolerated could be experienced in order to be understood; (3) communalism, where all activities were shared in a tight-knit inter-communicative web of activities, so that 'everything that the patients say and do . . . should be used for treatment'; and (4) reality-confrontation, where 'patients should be confronted continually with how their behaviour is perceived by others' (Rapoport 1960: 54–64). They also analysed the specific roles and organization of the daily programme in order to explore how these values were transmitted and held in place against powerful testing by staff and patients alike.

Group dynamics and belonging: Foulkes and group analysis

A quite different approach to understanding the micro-culture of small groups was pursued by Foulkes and his followers at the Institute of Group

Analysis. His approach to the theory of the functioning of small therapeutic groups allowed for groups to work at widening and deepening communication not just at one of Bion's two levels, but at four:

1 The level of current adult relating, or working alliance.
2 The level at which individual emotions or patterns of relating from the past may be transferred onto the conductor or members of the group, the transference level.
3 The level of projected and shared feelings and fantasies, often from early pre-verbal stages of development, prior to separation and individuation from symbiotic merging.
4 A primordial level of archetypal universal images.

(Brown 1985: 211)

Brown compares two approaches: 'Bion's relative neglect of the group's ego functions and its work task, and his failure to discuss where and how it is achieved, are made good by Foulkes' central concept of the *matrix* as the place in which group communications are made, distortions are corrected and group culture develops' (Brown 1985: 211). This approach pays more attention to the ebb and flow of trust through the stages of a group's life. At a theoretical level, it includes approaches that are functionalist in searching for the sense of the group as a whole, as did Bion. It also includes structuralist elements in searching for common themes expressed by individuals, that reveal fundamental patterns in the mind.

Conclusions

We can see from this debate that some of the central concerns of the social anthropologist about how to approach and analyse data in a society, are echoed in the technical dilemmas of the group psychotherapist and organizational consultant. I would also suggest that these theories illuminate some of the central dilemmas within the discipline of social anthropology, particularly in the debate between functionalists and structuralists.

So far, I have explored three key issues in social anthropology, begun to make some connections to social anthropological work in a mental health context and introduced issues around psychotherapeutic group work and the task of understanding and consulting to organizations. I now want to present my own understanding of the key elements in doing psychotherapeutic work, many of which have already been heralded by an exploration of the themes above.

SOCIAL ANTHROPOLOGY AND MY UNDERSTANDING OF THE COUNSELLING PROCESS

General reflections

First, I want to gather together eight aspects of psychotherapeutic work already indicated in this chapter and deriving from the discipline of social anthropology.

1   The privacy of the self and shame

Most people who seek the services of a psychotherapist or counsellor rely enormously on the confidential aspect of the relationship. They come with secrets they do not want to expose to others. In many ways, they feel their identity has been spoiled and they experience a degree of shame. This was clearly the case in the personal story I told at the beginning of the chapter. Paradoxically, it suggests that the role of the therapist is to be asked to socialize what cannot be socialized, to hear the story that cannot be told.

2   Participant observation

My initial theme in exploring social anthropology was about the discipline and value base of being one whose task is to participate and make a relationship that is about openness and understanding, while being detached enough to be able to think clearly and to analyse in detail. With a patient this has to be a joint task, but one which the nature of the material being discussed will hide from view. There is an alliance in the work. There is also the potential for conflict, as what surfaces are thoughts and feelings that are unwanted because they are painful.

3   Double-bind

Bateson's theory of the double-bind takes us straight from the anthropologist's fieldwork into the consulting room. Perhaps the important thing to bear in mind is that excessive focus on feeling reactions can give the impression that these are unreasonable in a patient, whether in a work or personal context. Reality needs interpreting as well as inner response, lest self-knowledge be over-socialized by the idealized norms of others.

4   Search for meaning and truth: Religion and myth

Psychotherapy sessions offer the chance for someone to tell their own story as it happened to them, not as others over-socialized them to produce a false truth. It is a chance to review how religious experience, by which I mean 'the gods that have gripped people', has been coloured by life experience and inner objects. Jung rather dramatized the idea by suggesting that people were in search of their own myth. His view was that people needed to individuate out of the collective unconscious into something of their own. Yet, seemingly, many of his followers have tried to over-teach their patients with mythological analogies in a way that has prevented this process. It may be that there is a similar problem with the paradigm of human development as schools of psychotherapy and counselling teach their students to interpret 'known and familiar' arenas of development and ignore a person's own theory of his or her development. Gordon and her colleagues at the Society for Analytical Psychology in London seem less bound by Jungian orthodoxy by making rich use of developmental theory (Samuels 1985).

5 Belonging and attachment

The social need to belong catches the individual's drives to find an object for one's desires, a pathway courageously pioneered by Freud. He considered that civilization demanded too high a price from the individual. What is at the heart of analytical psychotherapy is that the shape and patterning of each individual's style of emotional attachment is brought to the moment by moment feeling and attitude to the psychotherapist. This opens the gateway for the professional and creative use of bodily, emotional and thoughtful responses to a person as their way of relating is revealed. This is what is meant by transference of feeling, sensation and relationship on to the psychotherapist and his or her reciprocal counter-transference response.

6 Developmental stages

It may be true that Erikson's and others' attempts to delineate life developmental stages is a modern version of secular society's rites of passage. Hopefully, it provides a more understanding socialization process that is less bound by tradition and less thoughtlessly applied than those used by all societies to give meaning to life stages. The point for psychotherapy is that an interpretation about the past is not to provide a new rationality as each life stage is encountered; it is to open up yet new doors for the expression of self in personal exploration in depth, feeling and meaning.

7 Group phenomena

The application of the method of participant observation to groups and organizations illustrates that we are all caught up in group experience that can be as destructive by its unchangeability as by its apparent innovativeness. All the time it suggests that psychotherapists and counsellors need to carry a mental map of the social and interpersonal context of their patients and clients in order not to re-socialize them in a restricted way.

8   Work

Despite the fact that Freud identified work and love as the key arenas for growth, most therapeutic work focuses on the latter. Anthropologists and those who have applied their approaches at the Tavistock Institute provide a rich arena for how individuals limit their creativity and satisfaction in their workplace by refusing to know the anxieties and pleasures that are evoked deep inside them. Perhaps with the increased alienation caused by trust in staff being undermined by new forms of work contract that are based in increasing bureaucracy and computerized accountability, more people are seeking meaning for their own experience in the world of work.

I now want to outline four more issues where it is not so much that the study of social anthropology indicates aspects of psychotherapy. It is rather that there is an overlap or common cause, as analysis of the individual and of the social context are almost inseparable in providing important insights that can belong to either discipline.

1   Free association

Freud's fundamental principle of encouraging patients to express thoughts without inhibiting what seems meaningless, embarrassing, shaming or full of strong feeling or none, flies in the face of the social norm which conditions what is said to the current context, and therefore screens out or represses appropritate thoughts that approach the surface of consciousness. These thoughts may be strangely familiar when revealed and can thereby earn the title given by Bollas of the 'Unthought Known' (Bollas 1989). Herein lies the revolutionary aspect of psychotherapeutic work. It also echoes the task of the social anthropologist whose search is for the theories individuals hold of their own patterning of behaviour.

2   Sexuality and forbidden love

The universality of the incest taboo is well established by anthropologists. Its existence in all cultures reveals the existence of incestuous feelings that are unacceptable at a conscious level. The Freudian social revolution has now enabled generations to know publicly about the sexuality of infants and its reflections in the 'polymorphous perversity' of adults' fantasy lives. It is not less revolutionary today, particularly when we see how little those involved in the scandal of child sexual abuse are able to take on board the reality that children are sexually tempting. Psychotherapy and counselling are designed to help people to acknowledge unwanted feelings, including the hostile or aggressive 'delightful, damage doing' element in normal as well as perverse sexuality. The social anthropologist might also reflect upon our civilized society's failure to acknowledge such feelings that become expressed in abusing pornography and advertising, that present men as exploiters and women as idealized sexual objects.

3   Gender certainties and gender confusions

Andrew Samuels (1985) has explored the inevitable confusions that face the person looking at such a bewildering array of role models in society today. While he used to feel that the anima or female principle in men was the 'jewel in the Jungian crown', he now feels that it might inhibit a quite reasoned and reasonable gender uncertainty. It is not just a matter for inner discovery. He also points to the social refusal to admit to gender certainties like the need to value the male role of the father in both social commentary as well as in psychotherapy. Balance is needed between certainties and confusions, between inner and outer realities and between maternal and paternal psychologies. Clearly, this is a matter for exploration by social anthropologist and psychotherapist alike.

4   Alienation, schizoid, psychotic and autistic aspects of the personality

Psychotherapists and counsellors have been responding for four decades to the increasing need to work with more disturbed patients, or with those aspects of overly adjusted people that are alienated, split off or schizoid (Meltzer 1975; Tustin 1986; McDougall 1989). This could be said to indicate a change in society as its structure becomes more automated and dislocated. An echo for this theme can be found in social anthropology in Phillip Slater's (1970) evocative book, *The Pursuit of Loneliness*.

Case studies

An early session

A man in his fifties fumbles while untying his shoelaces before lying down rather stiffly on my couch. He smiles ironically and points to how clumsy he feels in being reluctant to expose himself by talking. He senses a mood of apprehension, as he approaches something that is fearful. I find myself experiencing the bodily sensations of unwanted sexual intrusiveness. This I decide is a clue to wait with. It determines in me that I shall not say anything, but let him begin the session as he will.

I sense the pressure to say some of the things I have in mind that may be empathic, useful, insightful, encouraging, yet I feel he is someone who may have been encouraged too much in how to be, with his well-educated voice, scrupulous conformity and self-doubt about whether he is pleasing me. My counter-transference fantasy about intrusiveness which may or may not contain some unthought truth confirms this.

Eighteen months later, he confirms my initial impression by telling me of his sexual abuse as a child. He had feared I would home in on this issue like an investigating social worker and not let him find his own way of telling his story.

Discussion

In this patient, the wish to conform and belong is strong. Yet the cost of it has been high. He has lost not only his sexual innocence but parts of himself including openness and trust. As anthropologist, I sense the high cost of feelings of social acceptance and legitimacy and the need to claim permission for waiting time until he can trust me. These ritual hesitations in the 'therapeutic dance' play out cultural themes about the risks of exposure to 'intrusive investigation' of an abused person who confesses.

Dealing with anger

A psychiatric nurse is newly qualified and distressed by feelings of being out of control, generated partly from never having left, psychologically, an over-protective home. Why does she feel so angry about some of the ways patients are treated? Her anger frightens her. She wants help to understand it so that it will not get in the way of her work. She feels it is irrational and that I, as a psychotherapist, will be able to interpret it away. She searches desperately for reasons. She has read enough about psychotherapy that she knows to search for moments and persons that have produced similar feelings in her. Throughout, anger has a negative connotation for her.

I ask her what makes her angry at the hospital. She stops in her tracks and looks at me in surprise and shock. She looks for a moment as if she might lash out at me or as if I might have hit her or be about to. The momentary mood passes. She reflects: 'the ECT of course'. 'What about that particularly?' Suddenly she erupts with rage that turns rapidly to tears. She just cannot stand the way the patients are treated and the effect it has on them. She has never dared to say so to anyone at the hospital. Gradually she calms.

Her next thought is the pleasure at seeing a child, her niece, walking for the first time, gaining real independence. Eventually, we are able to discuss what happened in the session and I am able to show her some of my perceptions, including her very mixed reactions to me. I tell her also that she is trying perhaps to find the independence to walk with her own feelings and be strong enough to learn how to stand on her own two feet. This seems to be what has brought her to psychotherapy. Once more a premature intervention by me might have prevented the recovery of powerfully repressed feelings. She goes on to talk about her difficulties in her family and in the hospital of expressing independence let alone anger which seems to make her cry and evokes images of her father being drunk, and frighteningly withdrawn. I make a mental note that if I am too unobtrusive she may also experience me as withdrawn.

Discussion

This story illustrates the search for what anthropologists would call a 'rite of passage' for leaving home. The only provision in a developed culture seems to be the step into professional training. Yet this, too, echoes the same dilemma. At first, she sees me as someone who will maintain her role as conforming and dependent. Eventually, she sees the possibilities in her angry reaction to finding a voice and feelings of her own that are autonomous. This opens the door to further experiences that inform her need to find order in conformity.

Issues of race, gender identity and regression

A 45-year-old highly educated Kenyan Asian manager of a personnel department in the retail trade has been married twice and is now contemplating leaving her third husband. She is confused. She has always seen herself as an assertive, westernized feminist. Her first two husbands were frightened by her assertiveness, she claims, and by the fact that she never wanted to have children. She now finds herself in the grip of a longing to have children, and quite unable to initiate sex with her present husband, whom she chose because during their courtship she was drawn by his ability to deal with her wish to take the initiative. She has since found that he is bisexual and is totally fascinated in going out with him to 'oggle' at the beautiful men in the gay bars he likes to frequent. She has a companion but not a lover.

In the first three months of our twice-weekly sessions, she found that she could not seduce me with the considerable charm, insight and intelligence that she brought to the sessions, together with a fascinating articulation of the Asian woman identity she had left behind in Africa in order to fulfil her true personality as a twentieth-century woman of the world, liberated and successful, sexually and professionally.

As the therapy moved on, she became more ashamed, then upset during sessions, both tearful and angry with herself and with me that her marriage had gone wrong and that she had discovered her longing for a different kind of man so late in her life. Yet everything with her husband seemed to be wrong. She also started to come early to the sessions and to use my waiting room. She always used the toilet after leaving. Occasionally, she came with notes written between sessions. She also began to feel something new, a kind of homesickness, but where was her home? This I saw as

the beginning of regression to an earlier stage of development. She wanted
to belong.

She had had a dream in which a woman who had the same coloured hair
and eyes as me nestled her on her lap. It was a peaceful dream – a peace she
yearned for. Her associations to the dream included the long-planned
journey to the village where she was born. Three weeks later, having
followed the mood of the dream in her relationship to me, she eventually
recalled a memory of running across a dusty street in her home village and
throwing herself into the arms and lap of her grandmother who had been the
one tender and comforting person in her life. There were tears of loss, then
peace. From this moment on, she began to come to sessions in saris,
something her Western feminist side would never have countenanced. She
became less brittle and angry, and began to realize that the child she grieved
was also a part of her, not just a longing for a child of her own.

The work that remained in the psychotherapy was how to integrate these
two diverse sides of her. What sort of a woman did she want to be?
Gradually, she found that in addition to her 'black feminist woman's consciousness', she also had 'a tender brown skinned caring part' (her words) to
her personality. She wanted to use the rest of the psychotherapy to explore
both with me.

Discussion

This work illustrated for me the possibilities of needs and figures from the
past being transferred on to me – at first unconsciously as an Asian grandmother. It also illustrates the interrelationship between racial identity, body
image and the ability to regress in order to understand something. She had
begun to re-evaluate the startling cultural and social transition that leaving
Africa meant.

From the viewpoint of the social anthropologist, this story demonstrates
the identity problems of belonging to two cultures. This interweaves with the
cultural issue of gender uncertainty and the range of alternative solutions
open to women in modern society.

Case studies in organizational settings

Work with a staff group in a therapeutic community

The community was part of a specialized provision used by social service
departments for disturbed young people. I was asked to run a weekly con-
sultation group for the whole staff, including managers. The main focus at
the beginning of each session is on who is there. People account for absences.
There is an important ritual element to this task. As they put it: 'we need to
know who we are with'. We focus on who has arrived and who is leaving
the unit and when. This focus on the membrane, boundary or skin that

surrounds the group seems to have enabled the staff to have time of their own to explore how they often feel invaded by the powerful emotions of the young people, many of whom are physically or sexually abused.

An issue that appears frequently as a division between sub-groups is whether it is more important to focus on the depth of feelings in the staff group – whether depression, loss, violation, anger – or whether there are crucial management issues that need to be addressed in order to try to reduce the scale of the impact of the young people. The fear is that if we do not address the feelings in the group, the young people will act them out in a way that cannot be contained. If the management issues are not dealt with, individuals will leave because they cannot stand the emotional pressure. This will cause more grief. I see my job as ensuring that both issues get addressed and become legitimated, as well as exploring in detail what the group is preoccupied with each week. I also refer regularly to the reality aspects of the work: the pressure from diminishing referrals of even more disturbed young people from under-resourced social services departments, and the genuine difficulty in sustaining the work.

Discussion

In this work, inner experience and social reality encounter one another. It is like a meeting point for the two worlds of psychotherapy and social anthropology. The staff group want the meetings with me in the hope of providing meaning and legitimation for their own responses to abused young people. In the group, the task is to create a mini-society that can cope with and ameliorate violent and disturbing experiences. As a social anthropologist, I observe and comment on the short-cuts that seem to create answers but that do not address the pain and conflict being expressed. Often the staff long to be as one, yet they are individuals in their responses and care and badly need sub-groups to belong to.

Teamwork across cultures

I was invited by a colleague to run a two-day management training course in Italy for a group of European managers from an international electronics company. The focus of the course was to be on teamwork. One aspect of the work was to help a group develop skills in checking cross-cultural assumptions. Just because Germans are always seen as over-bureaucratic and Italians quite the reverse, it does not mean that individual managers are necessarily out of the same mould just because they come from these countries. The work focused not just on team dynamics and the analysis of the typical group roles that individual managers occupy, but also involved careful learning and unlearning of the stereotypes each member brought to the training event. It also meant realizing that individuals are ambassadors and representatives of others' stereotypes about them.

Discussion

Social stereotyping is at the centre of social anthropology's study of 'tribal conflict'. This theme is clearly echoed in inter-group as well as inter-national dynamics. What was significant in this work was the role of the marginal person from a nation who can be at home abroad in another language and culture, manage the conflicts and ambiguous role, and still do business. Social anthropology has a rich vein in studying outsiders and marginal people in society and the way they serve as leaders.

Supervision of a group in a rest home

A couple run a rest home. Each of them also has training in group work using a group-analytic model. One of them is training to be a psychotherapist. I meet both of them every six weeks to discuss the group they run for residents. There are personality issues as one or other member becomes confused, ill, difficult. The work is courageous for the specific reason that all know in some way that a fundamental issue underlying the group is that the house is not their home; often it has been chosen for them, however much they are made to feel it is theirs. There is much loss. There is also a sense that an unspeakable element in the group is the fact that most of them have come to the house to die sooner or later. The issue is how they spend their last months and years.

My role is in supporting the couple to do this work by focusing closely on the boundary issues, the difficulty in getting people to remember the group and in sharing the task of getting it started. That way the leaders can focus more clearly on issues of trust and suspicion in the group. I also pay attention to what is introduced about individual group members' attempts to come to terms with their own ageing processes, including loss of hearing, of memory and of their sense of themselves. Together we discuss possible group interventions that respect the dignity of group members while confronting them with realities.

Discussion

A functionalist approach to supervising this group suggests how much belonging there is and how much members have in common. A structuralist approach suggests the individual means by which members and the group structure the experience to avoid the painful transitions into old age and dying. Either way, the social anthropologist can make common cause with the group worker in attending to boundaries, rituals in the group and the search for dignified ways of dealing with the marginal role to which these individuals seem consigned.

CONCLUSION

In this chapter, I have described what drew me to social anthropology and introduced the reader to some of the elements in the study of it. I have provided definition, chosen three key themes and connected each of them to aspects of counselling and psychotherapy. I have also provided examples of social anthropologists working with issues of mental health and with organizations. I have included cultural perspectives on psychotherapeutic work. Finally, I have provided examples from my own work to illustrate these points.

On a final note, I do recall that one of the clear choices open to me at university was studying psychology. I was put off as the psychology was very behaviourist. I am grateful that I chose social anthropology, as it opened me to a more flexible way of thinking about people than I have encountered in colleagues or patients with a psychology training.

REFERENCES

Barley, N. (1983) *The Innocent Anthropologist*. Harmondsworth, Penguin.
Bateson, C. (1958) *Naven*. London, Wildwood House.
Bateson, G. (1972) *Steps to an Ecology of Mind*. New York, Ballantine Books.
Benedict, R. (1954) *Patterns of Culture*. Oxford, Oxford University Press.
Bick, E. (1968) The experience of the skin in early object relations. *International Journal of Psychoanalysis*, 49: 484–6.
Bion, W. R. (1961) *Experiences in Groups*. London, Tavistock.
Bollas, C. (1989) *Forces of Destiny: Psychoanalysis and Human Idiom*. London, Free Association Books.
Bowlby, J. (1979) *The Making and Breaking of Affectional Bonds*. London, Tavistock/Routledge.
Brown, D. G. (1985) Bion and Foulkes: basic assumptions and beyond. In M. Pines (ed.), *Bion and Group Psychotherapy*. London, Routledge and Kegan Paul.
Fordham, M. (1978) *Jungian Psychotherapy*. Chichester, John Wiley.
Gordon, R. (1978) *Dying and Creating: A Search for Meaning*. London, Society for Analytical Psychology.
Henry, J. (1973) *Pathways to Madness*. New York, Vintage Books.
Jacobs, M. (1986) *The Presenting Past*. Milton Keynes, Open University Press.
Jacobs, M. (1990) *Insight and Experience*. Milton Keynes, Open University Press.
Laing, R. D. (1961) *The Self and Others*. London, Tavistock.
Laing, R. D. (1965) *The Divided Self*. Harmondsworth, Penguin.
Laing, R. D. (1967) *The Politics of Experience and The Bird of Paradise*. Harmondsworth, Penguin.
Leach, E. (1982) *Social Anthropology*. London, Fontana.
MacKinnon, D. M. (1965) *The Stripping of The Altars*. London, Fontana.
McDougall, L. J. (1989) *Theatres of the Body*. London, Free Association Books.

Mead, G. H. (1934) *Mind, Self and Society*. Chicago, IL, University of Chicago Press.

Mead, M. (1928) *Coming of Age in Samoa*. London, Pelican.

Mead, M. (1950) *Male and Female*. Harmondsworth, Penguin.

Meltzer, D. (1975) *Studies in Autism*. Perthshire, Clunie Press.

Menzies Lyth, I. (1970) *The Functioning of a Social System as a Defence Against Anxiety*. London, Tavistock Institute of Human Relations, Tavistock Pamphlet, No. 5.

Montaigne (1958) *Essays*. Harmondsworth, Penguin.

Perez-Sanchez, M. (1990) *Baby Observation*. Perthshire, Clunie Press.

Piontelli, A. (1986) *Backwards in Time*. Perthshire, Clunie Press.

Radcliffe-Brown, A. R. (1965) *Structure and Function in Primitive Society*. London, Cohen and West.

Rapoport, R. N. (1960) *Community as Doctor*. London, Tavistock/Thomas.

Robertson, J. and Robertson, J. (1989) *Separation and the Very Young*. London, Free Association Books.

Samuels, A. (1985) *Jung and the Post-Jungians*. London, Routledge and Kegan Paul.

Searles, H. F. (1965) *Collected Papers on Schizophrenia and Related Subjects*. London, Maresfield Library.

Segal, L. (1987) *Is the Future Female? Troubled Thoughts on Contemporary Feminism*. London, Virago.

Slater, P. (1970) *The Pursuit of Loneliness*. Harmondsworth, Penguin.

Stierlin, H. (1981) *Separating Parents and Adolescents*. New York, Jason Aronson.

Trist, E. and Murray, H. (eds) (1990) *The Social Engagement of Social Science. Vol. 1: The Socio-Psychological Perspective*. London, Free Association Books.

Tustin, F. (1986) *Autistic States in Neurotic Patients*. London, Karnac.

West, M. (1976) *The Navigator*. London, Fontana.

5

THEOLOGY AND COUNSELLING

John Foskett

THEOLOGY AND MY ENGAGEMENT WITH IT

I was not brought up to believe in God in any explicit way. On the rare occasions I entered a church my eyes turned heavenward not to glimpse the light of the world, but to negotiate the doorway with the cub scout standard. At school, religion was something to be studied rather than believed in. We were given copies of William Temple's *Readings in St. John's Gospel* (1955). It was the first theological book I read, and I cherished it more for its being mine than for anything in it. Nevertheless, our discussions showed me that there was more to my book, and the book it was about, than a mere possession. What appeared to be simple stories, dramatic as they often were – water made into wine, the sick healed and the dead raised – were, according to Temple, the signs of much more. He took us behind the words to their author, his purpose in writing and our reaction in reading. The gospel was a proclamation of good news – *gospel* means good news. The author's testimony was of a man called Jesus, whose birth, life, death and resurrection revealed most fully God's nature and intentions. This was disclosed to the characters in the story, as to actors on a stage and to us, the readers, as the audience. Unlike a real play, the cast knew as little of the plot as we did. We had the benefit of their spontaneous reactions to stir and challenge our own.

I learnt that other gospel writers with other preoccupations had alternative versions of the play. And others still had written about the same revelation, and its effect on an ever widening circle of people and communities in prayers, poems and letters. There came a time when these writings were collected together to form the sacred scriptures of the followers of Jesus. In their turn, the followers wrote of their reactions, and of the meaning to be derived from all the writings. Christian theology embraces the stories passed down, and the countless responses and interpretations evoked by them. In our own humble way we, in 4E, were making our contribution to theology. Like generations before us, we were trying to relate our experience to the story of Jesus and the theologies born of that story, in the expectation that they would help us make sense of ourselves and our world.

Theology's task has always been to try and make sense of the universe we inhabit and our place within it. Despite the scepticism and disinterest of many in our post-modern age, the thirst for understanding has remained unquenchable, particularly among those whose lives are troubled and precarious. In the gospel stories themselves, the good news was for the poor, the sick and the oppressed, those most likely to have an interest in it. In the west, Jewish and Christian theologies have dominated the questioning of believers and critics alike.

Jewish theology

For Jewish theology, the answers to humanity's questions lie in the nature and activity of God. Jewish theology is monotheistic and attests to a God who is active in history and especially in the history of the Jews. From their formation out of a disparate collection of tribes into a single covenanted community, their story is the basis for their explanation of life's meaning and purpose. Here is no simple chronological history, but *salvation history*: the record of a succession of significant events, some real and others mythological, which revealed that the destiny of humanity was dependent upon God's purpose for it. Humanity had a special place in the created order, being made in the image of God, and having authority to help bring creation to its completion. The problems encountered in this work extended people's capacities and abilities. Men and women were overwhelmed and unequal to the task, demoralized they turned from God and his purpose, and began to strike out on their own. This, their *sin*, compounded their problems, and reinforced their alienation not only from God, but from one another and from the whole of creation. God chose the Jews to overcome this fault, to expose sin and its consequences, and to bring about reconciliation. The Old Testament is the record of how succeeding generations strove to follow God's lead in the process of reconciliation, and of the theologies born of their efforts:

> One of the things which modern Old Testament scholarship has made abundantly clear is that in the Old Testament we are in touch, not with one monolithic theology, but with a series of traditions which often coexist side by side and interact upon one another, and which are capable of being adapted, expanded and reshaped. These traditions gave the community of Israel its identity and enabled it to respond creatively – or negatively – to situations of crisis.
>
> (Davidson 1983: 1)

It is the inclusiveness of this response and Judaism's readiness to embrace the good and the bad within its theology, which has attracted me most to the Old Testament and to the prophets in particular.

Christian theology

Christian theology has its roots in the saving history of Israel. It, too, unearths meaning through its exploration and interpretation of significant events. As Jewish theology revolves around the events of Exodus and Exile, God's choosing and leading of his people, so Christian theology does around the birth, death and resurrection of Jesus. In these events, Christians believe, God brings to fruition what he began among the Jews. The transcendent word of God which guided people is made incarnate in a human being. God is a person reconciling humanity from within as well as from without. Christians look to the Bible, and its many interpretations, for answers to their questions, guidance for their behaviour and wisdom in times of crisis. For much of their history, they have depended upon a literal understanding of its meaning. It was, and still is sometimes, read as though it were written specifically for the readers of any and every generation. But it has also been the occasion of dispute and disagreement, as one person's interpretation differed from another's, and as the texts themselves revealed conflicting views.

Theology has been fashioned out of the raw material of those differences. For Jews and Christians, God is still active in reconciling human beings within themselves, with one another and with the universe. Humanity's waywardness and disobedience – its *sin* – is the opportunity for its *salvation*. The history of this process, complete with its tragedies and triumphs, is a resource for each generation's own salvation. In time, their experience will come to make its theological mark upon salvation's story as well.

Pastoral theology

This interaction between received tradition and present experience has always been implicit, but not always recognized. Historically, theology's task has been to propagate the unchanging truths of religion. Religious authorities have depended upon it for their leadership and control of the faithful. Change and development have only come about by the sustained pressure of contemporary experience and need. In the West, the Reformation was the most far-reaching challenge to, and reformulation of, the received faith among Christians. It established the principle of a dialogue between scripture and tradition. It exposed the way in which the original biblical stories were continually modified by the traditions built upon them. The illiteracy of the faithful left them dependent upon the custodians of the traditions for their meaning and significance. As the dialogue between scripture and tradition has evolved, so has the realization that scripture itself is not something handed down from God complete and consistent, but a collection of the earliest and most influential traditions.

Increasingly, theology has come to focus on two areas of exploration.

First, to allow its treasures to be more than mere possessions, stories and traditions have to be unravelled both within scripture and in the faith's historical development. Theologians have to do what we, in 4E, were trying to do. They have to look behind the words of the text to their author, his (the authors were men) purpose in writing, the circumstances for which he wrote, and the reactions he might have expected among his readers. Theology attempts to distinguish between these things and our, or any, generation's reactions to them:

> Gone are the days when we can read the Gospels as if they were the work of people of our own time with our criteria of truth, our (in effect 'my') way of regarding the world, alive to our distinctions and standards of evidence. The fact that we may be fellow participants with them in the Christian tradition does nothing to render their world less alien to us and only serves to domesticate them, usually naively and thoughtlessly, to our time.
>
> (Houlden 1991: 35)

The second focus has been upon the contemporary side of the dialogue in theology's development – the application of the belief that God continues to be active in the lives of people and nations. Here theologians look to those disciplines which analyse contemporary experience. The social, behavioural and human sciences have figured most in what is now known as practical or pastoral theology, and more recently, liberation, black and feminist theologies. Most significant for counselling has been the pastoral care and counselling movement, in which the dialogue has been between theology and contemporary experience understood from the perspectives of psychology and sociology. The high point of the theological analysis of scripture coincided with the growth of psychoanalysis. As the methods of literary and historical criticism, and the disciplines of archaeology and anthropology, were harnessed by theologians in their efforts to untangle biblical documents, so pastoral theologians drew upon pyschology to help them sift the mysteries of the soul. Anton Boisen (1920), the founder of the American pastoral care and counselling movement, coined the phrase *living human documents* as the subject of his study of his own and other people's experience. It was his belief, confirmed by generations of pastors and theologians since, that unravelling the mystery of humn beings would tell us as much about God as it did about people (Boisen 1945).

As a newly ordained Anglican curate, pastoral theology and counselling offered me a way to reconcile my bewildering experience of ministry with my preparation for it. That preparation had included both a liberal theological education and a catholic ordination training. I was already confused about my role before I had set foot in the suburban parish to which I was sent. Soon the demands of the faithful, and the not so faithful, were to confuse me even more. My theology, myself and now my job had precious little in common. In desperation, I signed up for a course in human relations with the Richmond Fellowship College. I dimly sensed that a combination of practical experience, personal awareness and pastoral theology could help me get myself and my job together. The course did introduce me to many of the fruits of pastoral theology and the care and counselling movements, but it was living in a therapeutic community which had the greatest impact upon me. The residents were more interested in my problems with myself and my ministry, than they were in helping me overcome them. They wanted me to explore these things for their sake as well as my own, and they were thorough in their oversight of my education. They convinced me of the validity of Boisen's belief that our humanity is not so much a problem to be solved, as it is a vocation to be revealed.

THEOLOGY AND MY UNDERSTANDING OF PERSONS

People, and indeed life itself, are not problems to be solved, they are mysteries to be loved.

(Pattison 1988: 139)

There is much in the current culture which construes people, situations and events as problems to be analysed, understood and in the end solved. The pursuit of excellence in every kind of speciality, and the attainment of higher qualifications in problem solving, reinforce the notion that life and the universe are a vast examination paper. Indeed, counselling is often defined as a way of helping people overcome problems. In societies strongly influenced by rational thinking and technological expertise, it is hardly surprising that skills relating to these activities are the most highly prized, for people as well as things. Our health and welfare services are beginning to share in these values. They, too, have framed their work in terms of goals and measurable objectives. As a consequence, priority is given to those activities and services which are the most responsive to being audited and assessed. The services which are less easily measured are increasingly devalued. 'Our attention to problem-solving can also mean that situations which do not actually have solutions are liable to be neglected. Chronically ill and mentally handicapped people, for example, are not going to get "better"' (Pattison 1988: 139).

Valuable as the problem-solving perspective can be in analysing situations and difficulties, and in bringing the appropriate resources to bear upon them, like other equally valuable things their usefulness can be inflated, and is always driven by the predominant culture. 'Psychotherapy typically takes the shape of helping selves to fit more comfortably, productively, and adaptively into roles of acquisition and consumption, which culture promises, will bring us meaning and fulfilment' (Hinkle and Hinkle 1992).

This is particularly the case when the same people set the goals and evaluate progress towards them. Even with Citizens' and Patients' charters, 'It is often professionals and experts who define objectives and goals which are carefully selected to fit in with their own knowledge, expertise and abilities' (Pattison 1988: 140). In counselling, despite our concern for the rights and autonomy of clients, we regard the counsellors as professionally and ethically responsible for their own knowledge and expertise, and in this they are judged by their peers rather than their clients. Pattison goes on to point out how regularly professional and expert solutions to problems turn out to be worse than the problems themselves. Therapy, medication and solutions to economic and social ills can and do make matters worse. The Rabbi and family therapist Edwin Friedman adopting the strategy of an Old Testament prophet, has been trenchant in his condemnation of experts manufacturing knowledge, and then inflicting it upon others in books like this. Publishers and editors have become the pushers of the literary substances to which practitioners are addicted. For him it is just like the idolatry that the prophets railed against (Friedman 1992: 57–9).

The making and breaking of idols

Theology has a particular interest in the way in which people are attracted to and bewitched by solutions. The book of Genesis begins with God's creation of the world including the first human beings: 'And God saw everything he had made, and behold, it was very good' (Genesis 1:31). God is satisfied, but Adam and Eve, the first man and woman, are not. They are tempted to overcome their anxieties by the promise of a foolproof problem-solving technique. All they have to do is bite on the apple from the tree of the knowledge of good and evil (Genesis 3). This kind of temptation is as irresistible now as it was mythically then, and theology has been vigilant in watching out for it.

There is something in human nature which lends itself to what theology knows as idolatry, the making of idols. We take a good idea, method, person even, and convince ourselves that their significance has an application beyond our experience of their usefulness. Rather than put this belief to the test, we turn our assumption into a certainty and organize our lives around it. Christian doctrines, practices and traditions including the Bible, have been used and abused in this way. There is a certain logic to this. If we can find ideas or people or beliefs upon which to depend, then our fears are more manageable. The more we depend, however, the more vulnerable we become. Theology provides many examples of truths which have been exhausted by the demands placed upon them, and of many reformations constructed out of the crises of their demise.

Davidson (1983) demonstrates how ideas about suffering evolved in the life and traditions of the Jews. Generations struggle their way to a theology which makes sense of their history, suffering is punishment, the prelude to blessing, the cost of redemption, the travail of a new creation, the mystery to be borne not understood. Each theology has its value in making the distress of suffering more manageable and living more possible. Its validity for the generation who have laboured long in its creation is unquestioned. It is a treasure to be preserved and passed on intact. Out of humble origins it grows from sign to symbol, icon to idol. But tomorrow's pains may not be soothed by the balm of today's doctrines. Tomorrow's sufferers will prise the idol from the hands of its guardians, break it open and use the pieces to build something of their own. In the book of Job, one man's theology of suffering comes from the disputes he has with his comforters, the custodians of a theology whose time is up.

Sin

Theology, through the concepts of sin and salvation, offers us an alternative to the problem and solution way of understanding persons. Because of their narrow and prejudicial use, neither term is easily accommodated in contemporary discussions about people. Sin is mostly associated with individual behaviour; the sinner is a breaker of moral (often sexual) codes as the criminal is of legal ones. Salvation, too, is an individual business involving the heart more than the head. They are ideas which have little currency outside religious gatherings. This is as unfortunate as it is understandable given the way in which religious people often propagate their beliefs. Set free of such prejudicial restraints, the theology of sin and salvation provides a view of persons which is both realistic and hopeful. It helps me engage with the ambiguity of my humanity and the ambivalence I have about my destiny. For me the story of Adam and Eve's temptation and fall from grace is symbolic rather than historical in its account of what it is like to be a person. Here are representative human beings inherently good, responsible and capable, and yet in their uncertainty about themselves open to temptation, self-deception and in the end their own self-destruction. '"Eat this", said the serpent, "and you will be like God." Eve was like God, her breath was God's breath, but she couldn't believe that of her self' (Gaden 1987: 71). Sin is as normal as it is lethal, and penitence, the acknowledgement of this, is a prerequisite for human survival and fulfilment. Although sin is identified with humanity in the story, there is more to it than human self-doubt and disobedience. The serpent, as representative of creation, provides the occasion for humanity's disgrace. The opportunity for sin, that which is evil, is already there. Some but not all of the responsibility rests with people. Sorting out what we are and are not responsible for is a major task for human beings, especially when we are in trouble.

In the New Testament, evil is cosmic, present in demons and supernatural powers, which invade creation and possess human beings. St. Paul (Romans 5) traces sin back to Adam – through his disobedience all of humanity has been infected, and from it the whole of creation. Suffering and death are the evidence of this contagion. But sin, too, has a positive part to play in this mysterious drama, for without it there would be no salvation. St. Augustine's doctrine of Original Sin was the culmination of the early church's attempts to make theological sense of our human condition. Augustine tried to steer a course between Pelagian optimism and Manichean pessimism about people (Williams 1983: 172–7). The current disputes between the theories of nature and nurture, and between the positive assertions of humanistic psychology and Freud's bleaker view of our neurotic condition, illustrate that it is as difficult for us as it was for Augustine to maintain a middle way in the understanding of persons.

As the mystery of what is wrong and right with people continues, it becomes clearer that the responsibility for it is not simple but multiple. Individuals and groups have a part in it, as did Adam and Eve and the serpent, but so, too, do forces, principalities and powers, present among people but shadowy, unrecognized and unpredictable. Our short-cuts and solutions are susceptible to becoming problems themselves, but equally our faults are fertile soil for the growth of our well-being. The unknown author of one of the Bible's most serious examinations of the human condition explains it in this way:

> I perceived it that God has so ordered it that man should not be able to discover what is happening under the sun. However hard a man may try, he will not find out; the wise man may think he knows, but he will be unable to find the truth of it.
>
> (Wisdom 8: 17)

Theology helps me approach people with this mystery in mind. Part of what any person faces or endures will be his or her responsibility. We need to recognize what belongs to us, what is our *disobedience*, our *temptation*. Then with sorrow and regret we can be *penitent*, and find forgiveness. But there will be much that affects us for which we have no responsibility, and about which we can do little or nothing. It is as important to our well-being that we recognize this, and resist the urge to assume responsibilty for what is not ours. The theology of salvation goes some way to help me sort out what belongs where.

Salvation

The doctrines of the atonement attempt to explain how salvation works. Jesus, as the representative human being, gets things right, just as Adam got them wrong. He is the example of how people can be, and the antidote to Adam's infection of the human race. He overcomes alienation, suffering and ultimately death, and is both the model and the medium of our salvation. Scripture and Christian tradition describe this atonement with images unfamiliar to our culture and ill-fitted to our reasoning. Redemption and sacrifice, like sin and evil, take some digesting. And yet the object at the heart of these theories holds people's attention in a way few other symbols ever have. The *Cross* adorns buildings and hangs around people's necks as a remarkable sign of its significance to human beings. People may never be able to explain satisfactorily what it does for them, but they are safer in its presence.

Wesley Carr (1989: 111–36) argues that the Cross more than any other symbol represents the ambivalence and ambiguity common to all human experience. All that people try to ignore or deny about themselves and their condition is held before them in the Cross. Try as we will to separate the good and the bad, the positive and negative in our lives, like weeds and flowers they will surely grow together. The psychological mechanisms of splitting and projection cannot in the end untangle them. The Cross makes no attempt to separate good from bad. For Christians it is the sign of God's action on behalf of creation, which is good, and at the same time it is the means of a good man's execution, which is bad. Evil is affirmed for what it is. There is no ignoring it, nor any magical conversion of it into good, but in all its horror and starkness it is incorporated into God's action for humanity's well-being.

In the characters of Judas, the follower of Jesus who betrayed him, and Peter, the one who denied knowing him, we have, according to Carr, 'the whole drama of salvation from the human perspective' (1989: 131). Despite all the negative projections he has received, Judas appears in the story as 'neither completely evil nor determinedly responsible, but rather confused, misled and ultimately tragically mistaken' (ibid.). What could be more human than that? Jesus, in his death, purposefully accepts the consequences and cost of that confusion and mistakenness. Judas, in his subsequent suicide, shows that he cannot tolerate what he had done nor what had happened to him. In taking more of the responsibilty than is his, he is broken by it. If Judas took too much responsibility, then Peter took too little. Peter's denial of Jesus shows a human being's capacity to belittle himself. In denying his knowledge of Jesus, Peter disowns what is most important to him – he lets go of his authority as a person. 'The disciples are classic instances of all who wrestle with guilt and splits that result from our failure to live competently with the authority which is ours as human beings' (ibid., p. 132).

In the conversation recorded in St. John's Gospel (21), Jesus helps Peter recognize both his failure and his worth, his denial and his love. Salvation, reconciliation and forgiveness work not by forgetting but by remembering, but remembrance has to be complete and not selective. Theology plumbs the depths of this understanding of persons in its recognition that, 'In the cross God aligns himself with the fundamental experience of life which is common to us all – the evil and guilt inevitably linked with the exercise of our authority as human beings' (Carr 1989: 133).

THEOLOGY AND MY UNDERSTANDING OF THE COUNSELLING PROCESS

Whenever people exercise their authority as human beings, they step forward from the crowd, and risk separating themselves from others. In so doing, they fulfil things for themselves, and for the crowd. Some will identify with and invest in them; others will react negatively, and project upon them feelings of anger, envy and fear. In the exercise of our authority as human beings, we carry the expectations and projections laid upon us, and others will expect a dividend from their investment. This understanding of persons clarifies for me the essence of the counselling process. Counselling is an exploration of the exercise of a person's authority as a human being, and the consequences of that for him or her and for others.

The biblical parallels

The stories of Jesus and his followers are a resource for this exploration, and biblical theology offers us some vivid parallels to the counselling process. New Testament theologians like counsellors enter a world which is both alien and familiar, and try to make sense of the confusion. The historical and geographical distances between the theologian and the New Testament help accentuate the differences, the common Christian tradition the familiar. Houlden (1991: 108) describes the task of the theologian in terms astonishingly reminiscent of counselling.

> I believe in trying to sharpen the historical awareness as we interpret Paul or John, and I resist treating them as if they were my contemporaries, seeing the world as I see it. Yet how can I avoid intruding myself into the picture as I interpret them?.

How, indeed, and especially when mine is not some disinterested study of ancient and foreign peoples, but the humanity of which I am a part, and in whose survival and fruition I have a very personal interest.

Religious people come upon the writings of Paul and John eager to find answers to their questions and relief from their anxieties, so much so that they are bound to draw their own conclusions. Christianity has a long history of believers interpreting the scriptures according to their own needs and aspirations. Human beings who try to help one another have a similar history of confusing the familiar and the alien, and of working out their own salvation through the lives of those they try to help. Theologian and counsellor have each to learn a method whereby they can harness what they have in common with the object of their work, while respecting what will always be unique and different. Houlden (1991: 35) says of the theologian, what I aspire to as counsellor: 'What can I do to intrude diffidently and provisionally, refraining from final judgements? I can only converse with them as sensitively as I can, making sure that I try to hear their voices through their lips and not through mine.' In their article, 'Surrendering the self: Pastoral counselling at the limits of culture and psychotherapy', Hinkle and Hinkle (1992) demonstrate the way in which pastoral counselling, fed as much by theology as psychology, can enable counsellors to transcend the dominant cultural pressures, and question their own subjugation to them.

Conversation and intercourse

The practice of conversing sensitively touches upon another aspect of contemporary theology which has parallels in counselling. Narrative theology is that branch of the discipline that focuses upon dialogue. It conceives of revelation as the fruit of the interaction between different stories:

> A narrative theology . . . recognises that the identities of persons
> and communities cannot be separated from an interpretation of their
> respective histories, and that in most cases it is the narrative identity
> of the community (articulated in its scripture and traditions) which
> provides the context for the interpretation of personal identity.
>
> (Stroup 1983: 110)

For some theologians, the process is more mutual than Stroup suggests. In their work of care and counsel, pastors are being encouraged to think in terms of a conversation between three stories. The story of the one to whom they listen, their own story, parts of which are often evoked by what they hear, and the Christian story or stories that come to mind as they listen to the others. Revelation works when 'it becomes an experienced reality at that juncture where the narrative identity of an individual collides with the narrative quality of a pastoral situation' (Stroup 1981: 170). It is the situations where experience and belief collide that are most often brought to the pastoral counsellor.

In trying to describe this interaction or collision of stories, a colleague and I were tempted to use another metaphor:

> Perhaps the imagery of sexual intercourse captures more accurately
> the reality of what happens. For intercourse implies a sensitivity in
> meeting with both parties giving and receiving, so that something new
> is brought to birth in a relationship which is mutually satisfying.
>
> (Foskett and Lyall 1988: 50–51)

Not all intercourse is as good as that implies, especially in the early stages of a relationship. So, too, in the counselling process, stories and identities will miss, as well as collide with, one another. But patience and practice in counselling, as in sex, will foster confidence and make for better and better intercourse. The stories of Jesus and his followers have about them the flavour of patient discovery. His parables are a model of illumination, and his readiness to leave stories to do their own work, unencumbered with explanations, a salutary lesson to me as a counsellor.

The stages of faith

How people believe is as significant as what they believe in, particularly for counselling. Jung (1961) in analytic psychology and Tillich (1957) in theology have contributed most to the understanding of this aspect of faith in the lives of people and communities. More recently, James Fowler (1981), Michael Jacobs (1988) and Paul Fleischman (1990) have examined the significance in a culture often antipathetic to religion. Fowler embraces the psychological theories of Piaget and Erikson with those of the moralist Kohlberg in his analysis. He specifies six faith stages from primal to universalizing faith, which apply not only to religious faith, but to *faith* of any kind. He shows that people move backwards and forwards between the stages depending upon their experiences. Just as we are likely to regress psychologically in the face of trauma, so we do in our beliefs. A colleague remarked on his amazement that he, a confirmed atheist, began to pray at his father's graveside, and was comforted that he did. Most people, in post-rationalist Western society, find themselves somewhere in the mid-point of Fowler's stages. They may be literalists, who treat the dogmas of their faith, be they religious, scientific or commonsensical, as quasi-literal facts. The King James version of the Bible is literally the word of God. Dreams are the voice of the unconscious. Liverpool is the best football team in the country. Others function at a stage where truth is more symbolic than literal. There is inspiration in the Bible without every word coming from God. Dreams reveal our unconscious wishes. On their day, Liverpool can play better football than any other team. The simpler the faith stage, the easier to explain and believe, but the more vulnerable to anything which conflicts with it. The more symbolic the faith, the more open to uncertainty and doubt, but the more flexible and compatible with other points of view.

Transitional objects

This clarifies for me the part that faith and religion, as one major expression of faith, plays in people's lives. It is like a foundation upon which world views are built, and out of which behaviour develops. Like a parent with an infant, at first it is impossible to separate us from our world view. We are unconscious literalists who cannot separate subject from object. As we grow, like toddlers, we begin to draw apart from the object of our faith, and to manage the attendant anxieties, faith provides us with transitional objects. Not the object itself, but things which remind us of it, and its presence with us in this unfamiliar territory. McGlashan (1989: 507) describes this intermediate state in the life of a new born child as one of intense imaginative play:

> The infant may light upon, or may create, a transitional object. This object, be it a soft toy, an old piece of cloth, or whatever lies to hand, may come to assume vital importance for the infant, such that the infant may have an absolute need for it at going to sleep time, and during the day may often refuse adamantly to go anywhere without it . . . For the parent to question the significance of the object or to demean its importance is tantamount to blasphemy. The child itself may attack its transitional object in play, and eventually discard it, but no one else is permitted to do that for the child.

Our faiths, of whatever kind, give us transitional objects, things and ideas, which we keep by us as we move from the objects of our faith literally and metaphorically. The Jews carried their ark, Christians have bibles, crucifixes and icons, analysts the transference and Liverpool fans their red and white scarves. Everyone has theories and philosophies, hidden *transitional objects,* the fruits of our imaginative play, which inspire and comfort us, and protect us from the blasphemies of other people's opinions. These are things which come to our aid as we celebrate the joys and negotiate the traumas of our lives. World views are made up of many transitional objects, which we alone can treasure or renounce.

All objects of faith are transitional in the sense that they are never the object itself. Faith is defined as 'the substance of things hoped for, the evidence of things not seen' (Hebrews 11:1). Of course, they are often treated as the object and cannot be separated from it, any more than small children can from their comforters. But children know the difference between the scraps of cloth and their parents. It is in the knowing of the difference that inspiration arises. From these small beginnings, the artist and scientist first contemplate the matter which will captivate them, and become the objects of their life's work. In so far as we can celebrate and separate ourselves from the object of our faith, with the aid of whatever transitional things come our way, we will resist the urge to deify things, people and ideas. In so far as we fail, our transitional comforters will imprison and suffocate us.

Theological and psychological traditions (Erikson 1965; Winicott 1974; Reed 1978) document the way in which individuals and groups move between a regressed and a mature use of their transitional objects. They lead us to respect the inevitability of this and to anticipate the conditions which impede the necessary and healthy oscillation between the two. External trauma and internal conflict provoke regression. The child within each of us is inconsolable without its comforter. Significantly, it is in times of crisis and confusion that both religion and counselling are called upon, as if they have a particular part to play when we need to regress. They are the security blankets in which people wrap themselves, and of which a great deal is asked.

How can they best manage the demands we place upon them? The disciplines of theology and psychology remind us that religion and counselling are not ends in themselves, even if for a while they are experienced as such. Once comforted we need to separate ourselves from the things which kept us afloat and see them for what they are, the spiritual and psychological life belts which saved us in the storm. Religion and counselling divorced from theology and psychology are likely to hand out straitjackets rather than life lines.

In practice, I aim to clarify the *faith stage* at which a client is, and how that varies from the stage I am at, in order that I can be aware of how each of us is likely to construe our experience. I try also to identify a client's *transitional objects* – the significance that they have, and how they differ from my own. Baldridge and Gleason (1978) suggest that people at different faith stages have problems with one another, and will want different things from their relationship. The literalist client, whose faith and experience must not be allowed to conflict, will not be helped by a counsellor bent upon the exploration of faith as myth. Such a client will be helped in a relationship which allows the conflict of faith and experience to find its own means of expression, and a counsellor who uses a facility with symbols to help make sense of the client's transitional objects. The following example illustrates my own attempt to think theologically in my work with James.

James (a case study)

As I walked on to the ward, he greeted me.

'I've been waiting for you. God has told me not to eat, and everyone here wants me to disobey God's word.'

I suggested we go somewhere quiet to talk about this impasse. He agreed and led me to his room.

'You do believe me? God does not want me to eat.'

'I believe what you are telling me, but I would like to know more about what God actually says to you.'

Less anxiously now, James described the voices he hears. Some are to do with his illness, but God's voice is different. When first he heard it, he had a vision of Christ. He told me he is fasting because that is what God wants him to do. I asked if he was doing it as some kind of penance, and he looked at me incredulously. Our stages of faith were by no means compatible.

'I do it to suffer.'

'Why do you have to suffer?'

'Jesus suffered and so do I.'

He told me triumphantly that his longest fast was six weeks, about the same as Jesus' fast of forty days. Apparently, the voices say dreadful things about his parents, and he cannot eat until they stop. I asked him if he was worried about his parents, and he told me they were due to visit him but that their train might crash. Although this had never happened to them before, there was news of a derailment on the radio. I concluded our conversation by telling James that I understood his belief about God, although I did not agree with it, admitting that I, like others, had often misunderstood what God expected of me. I suggested that he keep a record of what God said to him, and of what other things happen at the same time. If he wished, he could tell me about them when next I came. He agreed enthusiastically, and said he would eat now. I did this to help me and I hope him find some connection between external reality and the reality as viewed from his internal world of faith. Twenty-four hours later, he refused food again, and told the staff that the chaplain did not understand him either. So much for my attempt to make connections.

James is in a new enviroment because the last one could not help him overcome his fasts. So it is reasonable for him to be disorientated and alarmed. The ward staff and the patients are disturbed by him and the strength of his convictions. His psychiatrist contacted me, a relatively rare event, and another patient directed me to James the moment I came on the ward. The nursing staff were divided between those who wanted to call James' bluff, aud those who were doing their best to persuade him to eat. I found that once I listened to him, and his beliefs about himself, he became calmer and more able to manage the anxiety of his new environment and the wait for his parents. I and the role I exercised offered some security to both internal and external worlds.

He appeared to be at a very literal stage of faith, no doubt driven there by the torment of his voices, which he hears almost continuously, and the changes brought about by his move. Internal and external worlds are equally unpredictable, and his response is to obey the one direction which comes with unambiguous authority. God says he must not eat until the critical voices stop. The voices including God's and the fasting are his transitional objects. Taken literally, in this crisis, they provide a tenuous link with his parents. His actions also ensure the maximum care and attention from busy and distracted hospital staff. Initially, my presence and authority provided an alternative comforter, which allowed him to begin to address the real anxieties he had about himself and his parents.

More of what he has said makes sense to me when viewed from a theological perspective. James connects his fasting to Jesus' suffering. When Jesus fasted he was suffering in order to overcome temptation and to prepare himself for his ministry. Perhaps there are parallels here with James' experience. On my second visit, he tells me of the crudely sexual things the voices say. In contrast, he never thinks or feels anything about sex. So the voices, as well as being split off aspects of himself, begin to sound like the tempter who must be resisted, and overcome by the suffering James has to endure. By asking him to keep a record of what the voices say and what happens to him at the same time, I hope to encourage a conversation between him and the parts of himself that he splits off, the object being to see where his *experience* threatens his *theology*, and how to create the conditions that will reduce the threat and aid the integration of the two.

In subsequent visits I hear more of James' story, and of a family for whom trauma is all too familiar. His parents had tragic early deaths in their families. His mother's father died when she was a baby, and the family fragmented with his grandmother leaving to go abroad and not seeing her daughter again. According to James, his mother has always suffered, and he became like her in this respect. She lives and suffers for him, he says, and now he suffers for Christ. A picture emerges of a family clinging to their illness as to a vocation. Treatment in hospital may confirm the family's solution of always having a patient, that is, a person become a sickness, a transitional object become a reality. Family therapy introduced carefully and gradually could help to address the external splits, which may reflect the internal ones emerging from my conversations with James. In so far as it is effective, this combination of approaches will begin to unravel the vicarious nature of this family's sufferings. It will help them recognize and mourn their losses and contain their anxieties in ways less costly to each of them and to James in particular.

Theology, particularly the theology of the Cross, provides me with a way to acknowledge the intricate elements in this family's story. Here loss and death and destruction are borne more and more vicariously in each succeeding generation. James' mother and now James become the bearers or scapegoats. There may be little I or anyone can do to bring these scapegoats back, or to lift their burdens from them, but at least I am better equipped to follow them into their wilderness, and to respect the significance of their actions in trying to save their family from more suffering and distress.

Failure

> Wherever people have longings, goals, purposes and aspirations, failure, or at least relative failure, enters the picture.
>
> (Pattison 1988: 153)

Counselling is bound up with longings and aspirations, and with failure, and so is religion. The good and the bad, the destructive and the creative aspects of people, which theology holds together in the ambivalence and ambiguity of the Cross, is the stuff of counselling. People often enter into counselling because of a sense of failure; failure to achieve what they wanted in their relationships, their work and their faith. Despite its importance in a success-orientated society, failure has not figured prominently in either theological or counselling studies. They, too, have their eyes on this world's treasure. There are, however, some important exceptions. Henri Nouwen (1979) and Alastair Campbell (1981) explore failure theologically through the figure of the Wounded Healer; Casement (1985), Jordan (1979) and Brandon (1976) in social work and therapy.

> From the start I realised that social work, even with the best of intentions, could as readily be unhelpful as helpful. It was clear to me that every attempt to influence a person in trouble entailed a risk of making things worse for him, and that social work often did just this. Far more painful for me was the gradual recognition that often it was when I minded most about my clients, tried hardest or liked them best that I did them the most harm. The risks of damage were highest where the investment was greatest.
>
> (Jordan 1979: 13–14)

In his book the *Critique of Pastoral Care*, Pattison (1988) devotes a chapter to the subject of failure, and the problems it poses for carers and cared for alike. He notes how little the subject is addressed in the Christian tradition despite the fact that Jesus' death and, by implication, his failure are so central to it. 'The word was made failure and died among us', is Maria Boulding's (1985 :71) rerendering of St. John's (1.14) 'the word was made flesh and dwelt among us'. The initial responses of Jesus' followers to his death were brimful of their failings, their doubts, their despair and their terror. There are as many failures as achievements in Christianity's chequered history.

Christians are as prone as anyone to splitting good and evil. And yet the Cross, the occasion of Jesus' failure, was also the opportunity for his success. Theology encourages me to look for this combination in counselling. So I expect to find in a client's failure, and more so in my own failure with clients, something that cannot be reached in any other way. Neither I nor the client will like it or want it; probably we will do everything in our power to avoid or ignore it. Like the disciples we will run away and hide behind closed doors. If we stop running, emerge from our hiding place and face our failure, there will be a revelation, the news of which may be good. By providing an environment conducive to the optimistic exploration of failure, supervision provides an essential contribution to counselling. In so far as it helps me look for treasure there, I will be fortified in helping my clients look too. My recent conversations with one client, who was facing failure on every side, were illuminating in this respect. The more so because I found myself to be a very reluctant counsellor to Catharine. I had met her husband first and by identifying with him I had begun to see their relationship from his point of view. At first I tried to avoid involvement with Catharine. I think I was unconciously sensing reverberations with my own life story. Now I am grateful to her for the faith she showed in me, and for what I learnt from her about the facing of failure.

Catharine (a case study)

She has a long history of depression for which she has felt responsible but powerless to alleviate. She has been very dependent upon her husband for understanding and support. When this was denied her by his own breakdown and subsequent decision to leave her, she became acutely depressed. In our conversations, she expressed how desperate and hopeless she felt. Her family grown up and now her husband gone from her, there was nothing to live for, a life with only mental illness was untenable. I encouraged her to explore these feelings further in order to try and distinguish the shapes in the fog of her depression. As she told me about her life, she revealed a fuller picture of her relationship with her husband. He did look after her, but also he depended upon her for support in his work, her determination had helped him fight for his rights: 'It made me mad when people took advantage of him. I wish I could stand up for myself as I did for him.' It emerged that standing up for herself had always been difficult. She recognized the roots of this in her own childhood, but she also felt a personal responsibility for it. She painfully regretted the way she had been towards herself, confessing the *sin* she recognized as her own. At this point, the counsellor within me wanted to encourage her to be less critical towards herself. But theology reminded me of the significance of repentance, and so I bided my time, and had her explore her own responsibility for what had happened to her.

It was at this point that she began to fight for her rights. She pushed her husband to be clearer about his plans for the future so that she could be about hers. The organization for which he worked had responsibilities both to him and to her, and they were reluctant to admit them. Patiently and persistently she pursued them too, until they began to admit to their failure, and to show some willingness to help in reparation. At each stage she was anxious about the disasters likely to accrue from her newly discovered assertiveness. At times she withdrew again into the relative safety of her illness. But there, too, she would find the roots of her power and authority. What was significant to me was the multiple nature of responsibility in her story, and how the unravelling of that contributed most to her beginning to believe in herself. As she recognized the parts played by her own family and upbringing, her husband and his needs, his work and those who employed him, she could begin to see herself in more proportion. She had said things for which she was sorry. They and she were important, not only as parts of the whole, but as the raw material of her new found personal authority. In one joint meeting, I witnessed how her penitence and sense of forgiveness, fuelled by her passion, induced something of a conversion in her husband's former employer. When others could express their doubts and responsibilities, and they are still reluctant to do that, her confidence in herself is confirmed. Failure reaches the places other things can never find.

REFERENCES

Baldrige, W. E. and Gleason, J. J. (1978) A theological framework for pastoral care. *Journal of Pastoral Care*, xxxii: 4.

Boisen, A. (1920) Theological education via the clinic. *Religious Education*, 25:235.

Boisen, A. (1945) *Religion in Crisis and Custom*. New York, Harper.

Boulding, M. (1985) *Gateway to Hope*. London, Fount.

Brandon, D. (1976) *Zen in the Art of Helping*. London, Routledge and Kegan Paul.

Campbell, A. V. (1981) *Rediscovering Pastoral Care*. London, Darton, Longman and Todd.

Carr, W. (1989) *The Pastor as Theologian*. London, SPCK.

Casement, P. (1985) *On Learning from the Patient*. London, Tavistock.

Davidson, R. (1983) *The Courage to Doubt*. London, SCM Press.

Erikson, E. (1965) *Childhood and Society*. Harmondsworth, Penguin.

Fleischman, P. R. (1990) *The Healing Spirit*. London, SPCK.

Foskett, J. and Lyall, D. (1988) *Helping the Helpers*. London, SPCK.

Fowler, J. V. (1981) *Stages of Faith*. San Francisco, Harper and Row.

Friedman, E. (1992) The Relevance of the Biblical prophets. In O. Stange (ed.), *Pastoral Care and Context*. Amsterdam, VU University Press.

Gaden, J. (1987) Pastoral response to the movement towards sexual equality. In *Pastoral Ministry in a Fractured World*. Proceedings of the 3rd International Congress on Pastoral Care and Counselling, Melbourne.

Hinkle, J. E. and Hinkle, G. A. (1992) Surrendering the self: Pastoral counselling at the limits of culture and psychotherapy. *Journal of Pastoral Care*, 46(2): 103–16.

Houlden, J. L. (1991) *Bible and Belief*. London, SPCK.

Jacobs, M. (1988) *Towards the Fullness of Christ*. London, Darton, Longman and Todd.

Jordan, B. (1979) *Helping in Social Work*. London, Routledge and Kegan Paul.

Jung, C. (1961) *Modern Man in Search of a Soul*. London, Routledge and Kegan Paul.

McGlashan, A. R. (1989) Symbolisation and human development: The use of symbols in religion from the perspective of analytic psychology. *Religious Studies*, 25: 501–20.

Nouwen, H. (1979) *The Wounded Healer*. New York, Doubleday.

Pattison, S. (1988) *A Critique of Pastoral Care*. London, SCM Press.

Reed, B. (1978) *The Dynamics of Religion*. London, Darton, Longman and Todd.

Stroup, G. W. (1981) *The Promise of Narrative Theology*. London, SCM Press.

Stroup, G. W. (1983) Revelation In P. Hodgson and R. King (eds), *Christian Theology*. London, SPCK.

Temple, W. (1955) *Readings in St. John's Gospel*. London, MacMillan.

Tillich, P. (1957) *Dynamics of Faith*. New York, Harper.

Williams, R. R. (1983) Sin and evil. In P. Hodgson and R. King (eds), *Christian Theology*. London, SPCK.

Winicott, D. W. (1974) *Playing and Reality*. Harmondsworth: Penguin.

6

DRAMA AND COUNSELLING

Brenda Meldrum

DRAMA AND MY ENGAGEMENT WITH IT

I have been engaged in drama all my life. I have performed, directed, taught and watched theatre and drama ever since I was taken by my mother to see the first production of A *Midsummer Night's Dream* in the Open Air Theatre at Regent's Park, just after the war.

I was born in 1938; my mother was Irish and a nurse, and my father an officer in the Royal Air Force Medical Corps. If I ask students nowadays the question, 'What are your earliest memories?', they often find it hard to answer, but people of my generation have memories etched in clear colour on their minds, like the photographic slides we took of our own children in the 1960s and 1970s. When I hear the tales of childhood stoicism and grief from friends who were evacuated, then I am glad my mother kept me by her side in the family house in South London. It was a family house, because my uncle and aunt lived on the top floor, my grandmother and grandfather on the middle floor and we, my mother and eventually my sister and I, had two bedrooms and a sitting room on the ground floor. Everyone shared the kitchen and the beautiful garden. But in the war we lived on our own; gran and grandad went to the seaside with my aunt and my uncle, who was a Quaker and drove ambulances, and my father was posted to West Africa. The house in West Norwood had no glass in the windows, just board because of the blast when the house next to us was bombed and we slept in a most exciting way for some of the time under a huge iron table in the kitchen, surrounded by sandbags.

Some of my earliest memories, when I was between three and four, were of fear – not so much my own fear (as I recall it), but my mother's fear. Light behind the slide switches on to show me, looking at my mother, sitting crying with a baby on her lap and saying, 'Don't cry, Mummy, we'll be all right'; the next slide shows me and my mother again, this time without my sister, running along the road silent and breathless while overhead, as though it were following our path, a doodlebug sputtered, before the terrible silence and the inevitable explosion. It was a life without men and, specifically, a life without a father, except for very short periods when he came home from leave. Of course, we were not alone; almost every family around us had the same experience. And I suppose, because it was such a common pattern of existence, it was rarely talked about; in our family it was never talked about. When fathers returned to their families, it must always have been difficult for them to accept their children and for the children to understand that mother had to be shared. Maybe too, the five years of almost continual separation of husband and wife and totally different life experiences, often led to problems in marriages; then as now, children cope in the best way they can. For some children, in those days of compulsory 'games', physical activity gave them a way of expressing frustration and energy, for me the great coping strategy was drama. Not, indeed, that I was encouraged to improvise or express my anger, or act stories which were thinly veiled representations of my own experience as I allow the young people in my drama groups today; but I could try on all sorts of different roles and costumes and lose myself in pretending to be someone else. I was on the rung of the ladder to drama school when my mother died and life changed.

For several years, I studied and worked as a psychologist. But I found that working as a research developmental psychologist was not satisfying my need to work creatively, so I began teaching at the London School of Economics on a part-time basis while I worked in drama – directing, performing, teaching – with many different groups from young children to professionals.

Through working on courses run by Cicely Berry, the Director of Voice at the Royal Shakespeare Company, I became interested in the director Peter Brook's methods of 'preparation' or rehearsal. Through improvisation workshops with the British Theatre Association, I became involved in working with groups using Keith Johnstone's methods; these influenced my performing and directing. At the same time, I was reading Dorothy Heathcote and Cicely O'Neill, whose radical approaches to drama in education were influencing drama work in the then Inner London Education Authority schools. Meanwhile, I started up weekend drama classes for children based in a theatre in South East London, not far from the house I lived in as a child, eventually setting up a theatre for young people called 'The Prompt Corner Youth Theatre'. One of the plays we devised and wrote together was called 'Blitz: The Children's War', an anti-war piece on the tragic effects of war on the children of South London.

In the late 1980s, because I was very concerned about the 'real life' difficulties some of the teenagers in my group were experiencing, I enrolled with the Institute of Dramatherapy to train as a dramatherapist, thus integrating my training as a psychologist with my drama work, in order to be able to work with young people in a therapeutic way, using drama. Dramatherapy has its roots in theatre art, not in clinical psychotherapy, and I am thus able to use all my theatre and drama training and expertise in my group work and counselling as a dramatherapist. I now use drama structures in my dramatherapy practices and dramatherapy techniques when I direct and with my drama groups and there is a very fruitful interchange.

What is drama?

The *Shorter Oxford English Dictionary* defines 'drama' as: 'A composition in prose or verse, adapted to be acted on the stage, in which a story is related by means of dialogue and action and is represented with accompanying gesture, costume, and scenery as in real life.' Thus, drama is a story, whose content and meaning is communicated physically and symbolically, as if it were real life. 'Drama' in Ancient Greece meant something that is acted out, or lived through: communication through action (Taplin 1978). Although the OED definition does not make it explicit, drama, as O'Neill and Lambert (1982) say, is: '. . . essentially social and involves contact, communication and the negotiation of meaning. The group nature of the work imposes certain pressures on the participant, but also brings considerable rewards.'

Dorothy Heathcote, a great drama teacher and pioneer of drama in education, describes dramatic activity as 'the direct result of the abiliity to role-play – to want to know how it feels to be in someone else's shoes' (Johnson and O'Neill 1984: 49). When the infant can distinguish herself as separate from her mother or care-giver, then she can begin deliberate social communication with the people around her. We see the very young child playing games of pretence, where she takes the role of her mother or father or her siblings and even the very young infant will imitate facial expressions and sound. We are able to be social because we have the ability to take the role of the other person. We can recognize the emotional responses of others, because we feel what the other person feels and we can recognize similar responses in ourselves.

In drama, we use our experience of the real world and our knowledge and understanding of roles and relationships in order to create a make-believe world. In drama, we enter dramatic reality which is different from everyday reality. Since we are suspending disbelief and working in the 'as if' mode, we can use this dramatic reality in any way we like. In drama, a person may express a creativity she has not experienced since she was a child. She is allowed to be spontaneous and to use her body, to relax and to engage in activity with full energy; to shout and to keep completely silent; to practise emotional expression and to learn how to control it and to use language in ways that are sometimes quite different from everyday experience. Above all, drama allows us to enter what Brecht calls 'visiting another room', where we can experiment without dreading future repercussions and where we can control what happens to us, in a way that is often impossible in 'real' life. In drama, we may express emotions and ideas that we are unable to express in any other way, through the use of aesthetic distance. Dramatic or aesthetic distance allows us, both as actors and spectators, a continuous passage between two planes: objective and subjective. As audience, we stand in with the actor as the character, but we still maintain our own artistic separation or distance as members of the audience. By standing in with the actors, we are creatively stretched and released and, as Bruce Wilshire (1982: 10) says, 'We accept our kinship with monsters; we enlarge the domain of our being'. The actor, on the other hand, does not become the character she is playing, but brings herself to the character as she interprets it from the text. So the actor is also experiencing objective and subjective reality through aesthetic distance.

Jonothan Neelands (1990), writing about drama and theatre, says, 'Theatre is a direct experience that is shared when people imagine and behave as if they were other than themselves in some other place at another time' (p. 4). So drama and theatre are social encounters in special places at agreed times, where some people will be behaving as if they were someone other than themselves; they will be taking different characters and different roles, while the spectators suspend their disbelief and accept that in that space and in that time, the actors are the characters they are playing.

My experience of drama, particularly in my role as director, has deeply informed my therapeutic practice. As director, my role is to help the actors interpret the text, find their characters, and meld with each other and with me in a joint enterprise, very similar to groups in psychotherapy and, of course, intimately akin to dramatherapy. Working with an individual actor on a one-person show, however, is very similar to individual counselling. However, while keeping to a similar structure as that used in group work, there is, when counselling an individual, generally more talk and less overt role-playing. The drama with the individual client will usually concern aspects of her own story perceived through myth, or stories generated by the client herself. Many different techniques other than role-play may be used in the drama of the session, including art and music – movement being an integral part of drama anyway. I often use masks, particularly in individual counselling, as they have an uncanny ability to free the person and the voice.

When I am working with an actor or a group of actors on a text which we are rehearsing for performance, I will use insights and techniques which are the same as those I use in counselling and in dramatherapy. First of all, there is the audition. Here, I am not looking for the actor with the beautiful voice and the charismatic stage presence – although these qualities are important – but I am seeking the person who is willing to try different techniques and who is motivated to work with a group and with me and who is able to accept a challenge. I explain that the way I work will involve improvisation and self-exploration, which can sometimes be upsetting.

Clearly, assessment for a counselling group will be different from audition-
ing actors for a play, but just as at auditions there are actors who are not
attuned to working with a particular director, so there may be some clients
who would be better suited to a different counsellor or form of counselling.
My assessment procedure is designed to see if the person wishes to work
in a physical as well as an intellectual way, for my model of counselling
is based on engaging the whole person.

When the cast is assembled for the first rehearsal, we will play games
designed to bring the different personalities of the group together. This is
a difficult stage in the development of the group; for it is important both
to recognize each person's individuality and to encourage group activity.
This stage is similar in a counselling group. The director's role here is
crucial, for if she loses the confidence of the group members by insisting
that they try to get to know each other intimately too quickly, she may lose
them for ever. At this rehearsal, or at the first group meeting, ground rules
are laid concerning attendance, time keeping and confidentiality. It might
be thought that confidentiality would not be an issue with a group of actors;
however, like Peter Brook, I believe that actors, just like our clients, need
to feel secure and safe in the knowledge that they may explore personal or
inner issues without fear of disclosure.

With actors, we have the text to interpret; with clients, we have their
own stories which they can explore through the medium of the drama.
The script will give the actor a time and a place and a character in the
dramatic reality of the play; the client projects her own script on the stories
we use in the sessions. She may take different roles and characters and
give herself the opportunity to play them out in the dramatic reality of
the session, which also takes place in a special place within a given time
period.

During the rehearsal period, the audience for the actor is the director and
the other actors; in the counselling session, the audience consists of the
facilitator and the other group members who witness and affirm the work
of the client.

Drama uses metaphor, where the characteristics of one thing, object,
concept or feeling is transferred to another. Jacques in As You Like It says,
'All the World's a stage, and all the men and women merely players' – the
stage is frequently used as a metaphor for life. Drama offers a metaphorical
way in which the client may explore feelings and relationships and 'working
through metaphor is a way of developing communication between people
free of the rules and restrictions of rationality' (Campbell 1990). A metaphor
may take many forms and unlock many doors in the edifices we build around
ourselves to avoid the pain of living. That is why I use drama in counselling
and that is why I translate my theatre and drama knowledge and skills
to my counselling practice.

DRAMA AND MY UNDERSTANDING OF PERSONS

A developmental perspective

When we are infants, we are unable to distinguish ourselves from others and in order to become a person, i.e. a member of a complex social world:

> . . . children must develop powers of recognising and sharing emotional states, of interpreting and anticipating others' reactions, of understanding the relationships between others, of comprehending the sanctions, prohibitions and accepted practices of their world.
>
> (Dunn 1988: 5)

Were we to substitute the word 'actors' for 'children', in the first line of this quotation, we might think we were reading a passage from a book on drama instead of from a volume on developmental psychology, from which it comes.

In the social group of drama, the person observes the sounds, gestures, body language of others and their effects on her. She also becomes more aware of the effects of her body language on others. In drama, the person learns to interpret and anticipate the reactions of others in all sorts of different imaginary contexts.

Children learn social knowledge within the family group. They learn about role relations and social rules from the world in which they grow up. The member of the drama group has the opportunity to play all sorts of different roles and relationships and through drama is able to experiment and 'try on' different personae and explore and express emotions which she may be too inhibited or actually forbidden to indulge in. Thus in drama the person, by exploring herself in different roles and characters, is able better to understand the rules, prohibitions and acceptable behaviour in her social world and in the cultures of others.

Theoretical perspectives

The three major influences from the field of drama on my work in theatre and also in counselling are first, Cicely Berry, who seeks to give sound to the inner voice of the actor; secondly, Peter Brook, who gives the actor the opportunity to find the real person in herself through the character; and, thirdly, Augusto Boal, who helps actor and spectator to have the courage to change. These three directors give me models of practice which have influenced me greatly in my perception of persons.

Cicely Berry's influence

Cicely Berry's work allows the actor to find her own voice in both physical and psychological terms:

I think the person has so little self-esteem when it comes to expressing their inner self, that they then resort to accepted cliché responses and the thought crosses one's mind as to what extent we then define ourselves through clichés. Perhaps our greatest fear is the fear of appearing ignorant.

(Berry 1992: 192)

Actors and clients need to find their inner voices to be able to express themselves and their emotions in a true and straightforward way, not censoring their true feelings by blocking them with the opinions of others through fear of being mocked or appearing ignorant. Thoughts may be expressed in language and language is communicated through speech. Actual voice production, however, is a physical activity. We don't know what animals are 'thinking' although when we know our pet well, we can give meaning to its body language and behaviour. Humans express their thoughts and their feelings both through their bodies and through their speech. We can often tell that a person is depressed by the way she walks and sits and by the tone of her voice. So there are physical connections between the voice and our emotions. Words, says Berry, 'both define and release feelings and are never separate from them'. How we use language expresses the self; we are trapped in the sounds and patterns of sounds that we make and we make a statement about ourselves when we speak. That is to say, my voice, my sound is bound up with my self-image and the way in which I want the world to see me. If, for example, a person has been criticized as a child for talking too much, for expressing opinions the adults didn't like, for being stupid or bad, then she may be inhibited from speaking at all. People with power have language. Berry (1992: 192) says: 'So in fact, language rules: that is, it is the people who have a facility with language who can manipulate and invade and inhabit our secret voice'. Many of the clients we see are literally at a loss for words. They cannot find words to express how they feel. Berry trains actors literally to use their voices in different ways, for it is her belief that the more dynamic and muscular the movement of the words, the more the speaker becomes attuned to her inner self.

I use voice work, adapted from Berry, in drama, in dramatherapy and in counselling to help people find the inner voice. To quote Berry again: 'There are many ways of opening up the hidden agenda in the language, so that we realise the extent to which feelings are ambivalent and complex' (Berry 1992: 198). This last point of Cicely Berry's is very important to us and to our clients. It is often very hard to tolerate ambiguity: it is easier to see the complex in terms of the extremes of polarities, and to judge ourselves and others as good or bad, loveable or hateful. In finding the inner voice, we can discover our complexities.

The influence of Peter Brook

Peter Brook is a great and innovative theatre director still – he began work
on the English stage in 1946! For years, he has been an inspiration to actors
and directors and also to all of us who find in drama and theatre a *modus
vivendi*. Brook says that theatre has 'the strange possibility' of inhabiting
several different levels at one and the same time. Theatre breathes life
into a story or a myth, which has its roots in the unconscious, while at the
same time it deals with the reality of the play as a story and the spectator's
life in the here and now (Brook 1992).

I have taken from Brook (1987) his model of 'existence' and adapted
it because it helps me to understand my self and my work. Brook says that
our existence may be represented by two circles: the inner circle contains
our impulses, emotions and fantasies which we keep to ourselves – the
core self; the outer circle represents our social lives and our relationships
with others in work and in play and in the life roles we assume or have
forced upon us. But there is an intermediary circle, which drama and
counselling can stimulate; it works like an echo chamber because it tries
to relate different aspects of the inner circle and to connect inner with
outer. If the outer circle is rigid and inflexible and the person is caught
in a destructive social role and does not allow insights from the inner circle
to impinge on the outer, then the director or dramatherapist or counsellor
helps the actor or client to bridge the inner and the outer through the
intermediary circle.

If, for example, I have a client who finds herself in difficulties relating
to her child because she is over-possessive and controlling, I will give her
the opportunity to play this role in a drama that she improvises herself,
or we may use a mother and child myth – the story of Oedipus is great
for this – or take a text from a play. Playing in role with me or with other
members of the group, she can see from their reactions the effects of her
behaviour. We can then change characters; she may play the child to see
what it feels like to be trapped by her overbearing parent. We may then
alter the mother role into a different sort of person, one who is less anxious
and domineering, one who gives the child a secure base from which she
can explore. Thus the client is given insight into more positive aspects of
herself, which she can bring to bear on her interaction with her child.
She has been helped to connect different aspects of her inner self with her
role of mother.

The influence of Augusto Boal

Augusto Boal has been a great influence on my practice ever since I attended
a course he ran at the London Bubble Theatre. Boal made theatre a weapon
of liberation in countries where political change was an imperative. Because

people who work with words are more powerful than people without words, Boal starts by working with images. With images, you can project your own feelings on to the image – a picture paints a thousand words. Images can bring us closer to our own true feelings because words allow us to censor ourselves. Images allow us to recognize what Boal calls 'the cops in our heads' placed there by our own experiences as children, which prevent us from doing what we want to do and realizing our potential as individuals. Making an image, the client uses her body to express what she feels.

Using Boal's (1992) 'Image Theatre' techniques in counselling is particularly apt. Working with groups, I start with pairs and end with a whole group exercise. With individuals, I might ask the person to make an image of the way in which she is feeling at the moment. I ask the person to freeze the image and then, perhaps, give her three wishes to move her body out of that (possibly oppressed) position and into some other way of being. The person finds real liberation in progressing from, say, crouching in unhappiness to standing upright and facing the world. Not a very significant thing, the reader may think, but surprisingly effective. It is ludicrously simplistic, of course, just to ask a depressed person 'to smile' and then expect her to 'feel better' – but there is certainly some good in moving the body – and taking responsibility for oneself – from an abject to an empowered physical position. The counsellor/director does not ask the person to describe or define her image, but the person, by seeing herself in her reality, is encouraged to change herself, which, of course, is the aim of all counselling.

So, through Cicely Berry's voice exercises, which give power and flexibility to the physical production of the voice itself and by helping the client to use words in a dynamic and muscular way, the counsellor may help the client find ways of expressing vocally her inner voice. Peter Brook's model of existence can be helpful in counselling; allowing the client the opportunity to inhabit disparate characters may paradoxically help her get in touch with her core self. Augusto Boal's image theatre gives the client a way of expressing herself without the need verbally to explain. All three directors have had an immeasurable effect on my life and work.

DRAMA AND MY UNDERSTANDING OF THE COUNSELLING PROCESS

The counsellor as empathic director

As Stephen Murgatroyd (1985) emphasizes, the role of the counsellor or helper is to enable the person or client to live the life she wishes to lead, without being more dependent than she wishes on other people and helping her to act in a way which makes her content, without oppressing others.

Drama helps me view the counsellor as a director – not the authoritarian director of the old actor/manager school, but the empathic director whose task is to facilitate and encourage the actor to get in touch with her body, develop an ability to express the full range of her emotions and to empathize and appreciate the emotions of others and to develop her knowledge and appreciation of herself and others. The empathic director is non-interpretive, that is to say, she allows the actor to make her own interpretations, to use drama and characterization and role to discover things about herself. This director/counsellor is but another person who has artistic and therapeutic skills and a professional training. The director and the actor, the counsellor and the client are embarking on a joint journey.

Action in counselling

In drama, there is by definition action. Drama is holistic; it uses the body and the mind in equal proportions; drama does not recognize the mind/ body split but says that all emotions are expressed in physical terms. As director and counsellor, my aim is to help each person seek out resistances and blocks that militate against her ability to express herself. I begin each session with warm-up exercises designed to help the client get into her body and also to stimulate cohesion within a group. I may use the theatre games of Augusto Boal (1992), who believes that through games and play, we get in touch with ourselves and our bodies and our environment. Through these games we are encouraged to see what we look at, to listen to what we hear, to feel what we touch, to remember what we have learned and to integrate these facets into our sense of self as a human being in a social and physical environment. I introduce Boal's rules: that no one in the group shall oppress anyone else and that none of us is in competition with each other. Warm-up exercises are so crafted that they prepare the group or the individual for the development of the session and future sessions. Since we are dealing with emotionally charged issues, the warm-up exercises introduce these issues, but in a playful way. Supposing the purpose of the session were to delve deeply into parental relationships, then I might introduce role-play with a game like '101 Uses of an Object', where a simple object is 'changed' by members into all kinds of different things, followed by the 'Transformation Game', where members improvise and change themselves from role to role. In this way, the client is allowed to play, thus releasing pent-up energy; meanwhile, she is introduced to the emotional meat of the session, but in a gentle way.

Counselling and role play

When an actor approaches a character or a role, she brings to it projected aspects of herself as well as her observations of others and her close reading and interpretation of the text. Similarly, the client, when she enacts a role, involves herself and her own emotions in the characterization. The group of actors rehearse their parts and the clients play their characters within the group drama. In what Phil Jones (1991) calls 'dramatic projection', the clients project aspects of themselves or their experience into theatrical or dramatic materials or into enactment and thereby externalize inner conflicts. Through this dramatic projection, the client reintegrates material which may lead to a change in awareness. The counsellor helps the client work with the character, by moving her body as the character would walk and move, thus writing it into a form of kinaesthetic memory. The client is helped to develop skills of improvisation to facilitate role-play; this role-play is not impersonation but enactment. But throughout, the counsellor will help the client make a distinction between the dramatic reality of the role and the external reality of her own life.

Counselling and emotion

The empathic director helps the actor understand the text and his role in the play and she facilitates the actor to find access to his emotional life and to bring these insights to his character or role. In the same way, the counsellor helps the client discriminate between her feelings so that she can distinguish between them and prevent them from getting in the way of her understanding. The counsellor helps the client when her feelings appear not to be under her control. Murgatroyd (1985: 84) argues that 'The aim of the helper is to encourage the person in need to attend to their feelings whilst at the same time connecting these feelings to their understanding of themselves as persons in a social world.' So the director encourages the actor and the counsellor the client, to explore their emotions and connect them with the emotional characteristics of their characters within the structure of the drama.

The director/counsellor listens to the person, to her text and her subtexts. She gives feedback in a supportive, reflective manner and she gives the person what Peter Brook calls the 'empty space' to express herself. In this empty space all that is superfluous is eliminated (Brook 1992). The empty space for Brook the director is thus a psychological space, just as it can be for the counsellor. In the empty space, Brook says, there is no clock or 'linear' time. In internal life there are memories and dreams, fears from the past and apprehensions about the future and they can be embodied and realized in the empty space. Brook talks of giving the actor an empty space to help him become what he calls 'a real person':

What do I mean by a 'real person'? A real person is someone who is open to all parts of himself, a person who has developed himself to the point where he can open himself completely – with his body; with his intelligence, with his feelings, so that none of these channels is blocked . . . This is the ideal image of the real person.

(Brook 1987: 232)

For the client to become a real person, the counsellor helps her work with her body, recognize her emotions and bring to cognitive awareness the reality of the here-and-now. In drama (as in real life!), we do not necessarily have to talk to express our feelings and emotions: we can and do use our bodies to embody what is in our minds. As I wrote above, those who are articulate and who speak in a literate language have power – power over those who cannot express themselves, either literally and physically or physically and psychologically. Drama – and arts therapies in general – are particularly suitable for people without language. The big contrast between arts therapies and talking therapies is just that – the talking. In drama, the client finds ways of 'saying' what she means without the use of words.

However, by definition, counselling has become a 'talking' enterprise and it is hard to think of counselling someone without the use of language. Murgatroyd (1985) writes of techniques akin to drama, such as the empty chair technique used in Gestalt psychotherapy and role reversal, a technique central to psychodrama, which demonstrates that counselling is not simply talking treatment, but may allow the person literally in her body to 'take the role of the other'. Drama can give counsellors greater awareness of non-verbal ways of helping the client become aware of herself.

Counselling and the observer

The counselling group operates like Boal's Theatre of the Oppressed, where clients are 'spectators' – both spectators and actors: they watch and they take part. And as the client/spectactor watches the drama of other members of the group, she sees in their stories multiple mirrors of herself. Through performance or sharing, the actor and client express the integration of the work they have done and experienced during the sessions. When we give people the opportunity to express themselves in an atmosphere and environment of trust and unconditional positive regard, when we allow and encourage them to use their physical and mental capacities, then we are enabling them to show the complexities of their emotional and cognitive natures.

Central to the relationship between counsellor and client is the dual role that the director/counsellor plays. On the one hand, the director is audience for the actor as well as companion on his journey; on the other, the counsellor is observer and participator. Yalom (1991: 113) talks of this dual role of the therapist: 'As observer [the therapist] must be sufficiently objective to provide necessary rudimentary guidance to the patient. As participant, one enters into the life of the patient and is affected and sometimes changed by the encounter.' Because the counsellor is exposed to the same existential issues as her client, both must be prepared to examine them within the same rules of enquiry. Therefore, Yalom urges us not to use with our clients phrases such as 'You and your problems', but rather we should speak of 'Us and our problems'.

Drama is not mysterious. Drama uses metaphor and aesthetic distance in the empty space (which are in themselves metaphors) but not in any mystical way. It is the human mind that is complex.

Case study: Shade's story

Shade heard that I am a dramatherapist through friends who worked with me in a theatre group and she approached me for help. She said that she was 'going through difficulties' and wanted some help to sort them out. I agreed to meet her to see if we both thought it possible for me to counsel her.

The assessment

Shade is a very pretty and alluring African woman, small and graceful with a flare for unusual clothes, which she wears with style. I observed in her a chameleon-like quality of responding to the expectations of others and of a kittenish, flirtatious response to men and a wariness and often critical approach to women.

At the assessment meeting I was consciously observing Shade's body language and appearance, particularly direction of gaze and posture, and tone of voice. My experience in drama makes me very aware of non-verbal cues that people supply to the observer, often unconsciously, depicting their state of mind. Posture and stance are very important to the actor in role; very young children will strut and pose, if they are wearing a crown and cloak and are pretending to be a King or Queen. Shade was carefully dressed and made up; she was not, in my opinion, in an emotionally distressed state, but she was tense, with the anxiety showing in her voice. She said that she recognized she needed help to try and 'sort things out'. She and her partner, Martin, were planning to get married in a few months' time, but 'things' were getting in the way and she felt she was 'destroying' their relationship. We made a contract for ten sessions.

As she spoke, I surmised that she seemed to have a deep underlying unhappiness, which seemed to stem from her lack of self-esteem, which was verging on self-hatred. She talked of her irrational jealousy of Martin; she knew she could trust him, but she could not help herself accusing him of outrageous affairs with the most unlikely people and she knew that this aspect alone was in danger of breaking up her relationship. She is an actor, and I surmised that such scenes must have a satisfying (on one level) dramatic flavour. She spoke of not being able to remember 'things', and this made her feel foolish, as though, indeed, she were finding it difficult to recall the script of her life. She spoke of her difficulty in relating to other women and her need to live more on a cognitive than an emotional level. As she put it, 'I go through life just feeling and I want to think.' It was as though she had constructed a role for herself and she was unhappy in it, but it had become so habitual that she was finding it very hard to change into a less destructive role. I made it as clear as I could that I felt we could not expect miracles in a short period of counselling, but that we could at least address some of the issues.

Aims of the sessions

I planned the structure of the sessions round a drama model of warm-up, development into drama and closure. We had already been through the 'audition' period with the assessment meeting; now we were approaching what Peter Brook calls the 'preparation' or rehearsal stage.

My aim was first of all to find out more about Shade and what she thought about herself. If, as I predicted, she had a very low self-image, I wanted to discover her coping style and what mechanisms she used and to help her develop different social strategies. As a warm-up, I planned to begin each session with relaxation, leading to a guided image at first and then to encourage her to produce her own image, which she would then explore. We would next move into breathing and voice exercises to help her find her inner voice, reflected in the image, which she could then speak about. I planned to use various projective techniques and masks. I decided to close each session by asking her to colour a mask template expressing her emotional reaction to each session which would be incorporated in a mask diary, which we should reflect upon at the end of the sessions.

The sessions

At our first meeting, I asked Shade to draw the map of her life, showing the various milestones along the way. She drew a winding road, beginning with her birth and ending, or rather 'stopping', with two arrows pointing in different directions signifying that her life could now go in one of two directions. Along the road she drew neat pictures of little people and a house and a building and a heart – it was a task she enjoyed. She then told me a strange story about her early life. She was born either in Nigeria or Ghana of a Lebanese man, who abandoned his Yoruba wife at the child's birth. The baby was called Tina and she went to live with her grandmother because her mother didn't want her. Eventually, the mother met a British soldier and accompanied him when he was posted to Germany. She then decided to bring back Tina, but it didn't work and the couple abused the child who was taken away and handed over to foster parents. But this family also rejected her and she was sent to a children's home in Britain where she was very happy, because everyone was in the same position and she did not stand out. When she was about seven (Shade was very uncertain about the passage of time), her stepfather came down to open a fete at the home, saw her singing in the choir and decided to adopt her because, she said, 'It was the time when people were adopting "coloured" babies, so I suppose it was fashionable.' She went to live with the family of mum, dad and brother of the same age as herself and she was very happy until she was sixteen when her father and mother divorced and her father went to live with another woman and she left home:

> Then I met Martin and he asked me my name and I said 'Tina, but I want to be called Shade Farmer'. My dad was very upset. He didn't want me to change my name. My name was Tina Parnell but the new name was mine. One that I chose for myself. It's me. It's mine and then I got depressed.

The map of her life, a projective technique, had led straight into what she really wanted to talk about – her deep misery because she had been so rejected all her life, first by her real parents, then by her mother and her soldier husband, then by the foster parents, then by the children's home, then by her mum and dad when they were divorced. I was struck by her passivity, but most of all I was interested in the two people: Tina and Shade. Shade told the story in a dreamy, almost expressionless voice; her body was still; her eyes fixed in the distance; she paused as though watching the drama of her life on a stage. I found it significant that in the early part of the story she used the third person. She said she could not recall anything about this period and that she knew nothing about herself then. I was also struck by the reason why she thought she had been adopted – 'because it was the fashion' – as though she were a thing and as though there were nothing in herself as a person which had contributed to her being wanted by her new parents. There was also something extreme about the father's reaction to her change of name. When she had finished telling the story, I asked her to move into a mime enactment of the drama. Slowly she enacted her life in her body, first as the rejected child, then as the hopeful child smiling at the nice man who was going to adopt her and then the adult holding out her hands to the new man in her life, yet with her head bowed looking down. This mime was as affecting to me as the audience as the story. At the end of the session, when she drew her mask for the diary, she said, 'How empty my head is feeling'. She gave the mask template no distinguishing features and left the eyes blank.

In the second session, we returned to her life map. At the children's home, she came to love the Matron, Mrs Murdoch, who is now dead and who looked after her and cared for her. She placed all her love and affection on this woman who, of course, arranged the adoption and handed over the little girl, Tina, to the new family. When she spoke of her love for this woman, I felt that it seemed too good to be true. I felt that Shade might be playing a role that she felt she *ought* to play; there was something of the soap opera actor in her words. I thought we might find out by using the 'empty chair technique'. I placed a piano stool in front of Shade and asked her to pretend that Mrs Murdoch was sitting on the chair and asked her to say what she wanted to say. We found that her feelings of extreme despair at what she construed as rejection and her anger against Mrs Murdoch were intense. This technique is frequently used in dramatherapy, and I use it in drama as a way of directly encountering the emotional content of past interactions and present, often deeply felt and previously suppressed feelings. She was amazed at the anger and bitterness she was able to express and it frightened her. When I tried to encourage her, I made the mistake of calling her a very courageous 'girl'. I corrected myself and said 'woman': 'I don't want to be a woman. I want to be a child. That's the trouble'. So, in this second session, there in front of me, sobbed the despairing and rejected child. The carefully constructed roles and masks had fallen away. I felt that she had been ready for the sharing of these massive emotional reactions and I was glad I was there to help her channel them. Her mask diary showed a blank face, except for tears.

My aim in the next session was to bring in a projective technique to help Shade find a way of coping with the real unhappinesses that had been brought up in the previous two sessions by using the 'Six Picture Story Making' technique of Mooli Lahad (1992). The structure is to ask the client to make a story containing six elements and pictures: picture (1) shows the main character in the story; picture (2) shows what the main character wants or desires; picture (3) shows the main character's helper; picture (4) shows the obstacles in the main character's way; picture (5) shows how the main character deals with the obstacle; and picture (6) shows the ending or resolution. The story constitutes the drama of the session; people inevitably express something – usually a great deal – of themselves in their stories. Shade told the story of a totally isolated little creature who lived at the bottom of a well and was rescued by a Bubble and taken over a wide river to a land filled with Smiley creatures of all sorts of different colours, so that the creature did not feel different. I felt her story had real relevance to the way she was feeling at the time: she does not know her parents; she had a feeling of deep isolation; she felt that she was different; and she wanted to belong. After making this story, she gave her mask eyes and eyebrows, cheekbones and nose and a hairline and half a smile, which I felt was a significant advance into personhood, despite the negativity of her story.

In the following session, I wished to help Shade look at herself and her self-image, not directly but once again through the drama of story. I deliberately chose a tale from a children's story book, called 'The Brave Little Kitten'. This kitten went out on her own and was brave and faced all sorts of dangerous animals in the forest but eventually found a surrogate mother in a tigress. At the end of the story, I asked Shade to take on the role of the kitten and to write a letter to her real mother. She wrote that she was happy and that if she never saw her mother again, she wished her well. While I felt Shade was projecting some of herself in this letter, I sensed that she was also holding things back. When I look back on all the sessions, I realize that this is a strong coping mechanism for Shade; she does not wish to address the rejection of her real mother; it is not the case that she has forgotten. Once again, her mask diary became more defined, which was an indication of change.

I planned at the next session to open the stories out into a drama improvisation or a role-play using her own story and proposed that she and I would take different roles and play around with them; but when I arrived for the next session, it was apparent that Shade was ill. I also realized that she was feeling very anxious about playing in role after her experience with the empty chair. While recognizing this resistance and because she was unwell, we agreed to explore memories through photographs instead. From a large bag she brought out the early photographs which were in a separate container: 'This was when I was Tina', she said. 'Look at me', she said, 'I was dressing like that to please other people. When I was Tina I was always trying to please other people. You can see that.' When she went to change her name about three years ago, she said she felt at first like a criminal, filling in all the forms and denying her former name, but it was the best thing she had ever done, she had taken her *real* name. In this session, I was aware that she was playing the role of herself as a small child, curled up on cushions and picking up pictures and casting them away, while I sat and observed. After this session, her mask was looking straight out at her from the page, its features clearly defined.

At the beginning of the next session, because I knew Shade is a musician, I suggested that the warm-up take the form of a song. She took her guitar and sang a song called 'The Wise Woman's Song': 'You will like it', she said, 'because it can be seen on two different levels, but the important point is that this song was written by Tina and now Tina is singing her song to Shade'. Once again, I found that the warm-up led directly into the drama of the session, which was about the two different characters within her, Shade and Tina. Through the song we seemed to have discovered the key which would integrate Tina and Shade into one person. It was a quiet but exhilarating moment as we looked at each other in recognition! As Shade, she wrote a letter to Tina in which she expressed her happiness at finding a new person who had learnt to forgive. I felt – we both felt – that through the drama of the song and the letter we had made a significant therapeutic breakthrough. Her mask template was full of colour and joy, expressing her feelings of integration.

As the final drama, I suggested that Shade make an actual mask with paints and paper and coloured fabric of her feelings now of herself in her new role and new emotional state – an integrated mask, which would take up the remaining sessions. Using a white neutral mask, she performed a ritual, trying it on and moving and dancing with it on her face before starting to decorate it. The first thing she did was divide the mask in half. As she worked, she spoke of 'finding the key to herself' and that it was a significant step in her life. Half the mask, the yellow, pretty, conventionally made up face was Tina, and the other half, colourful, starry, full of colour and life and very different was Shade. She said:

> The most important fact is that I realize things have to come from within and then it can spread out. So now I am happy. I was confused. This new person [represented by the mask] was ready to take over. The sessions have given me a chance to find out what was happening to me. Tina was so hurt that Shade was reacting like a small child. I realized Tina was not to blame because other people hurt her. I can now laugh and joke about my dad without feeling guilty. I don't blame my real mother because she was always out of the story. She never wanted me. She always wanted to get rid of me so there was no point in thinking about her. I was hurt in the beginning but I soon put her out of my mind. My mum is my mother and my dad is my dad – that's why he can hurt me. I am so much more open about it now.

'It seems too good to be true', she commented; she was now able to approach the plans for her wedding with so much more equanimity. She had been afraid to plan before; afraid that her partner did not really love her, afraid that she was so fragmented that she couldn't really love him, afraid that she was so horrible that he couldn't possibly love her – who could love her? Afraid that if she thought about it too much and did any of the planning it was bound to go wrong. Now she was happily planning her dress and the invitations had gone out and so life was really good.

We closed the session by taking photographs of the mask and acknowledging the mask as the fused individuals of Tina and Shade.

Conclusion

In this contract of ten sessions, Shade and I came a long way together. She was caught in destructive social roles where she played the flirtatious kitten with men and the judgemental critic with women. She felt that she was ruining the most important relationship in her life through her irrational jealousy born of her fear of being deserted, unloved and unlovable. She kept silent in company because she felt that she hadn't anything interesting to say and yet felt resentful because she wanted to be able to talk. And she was deeply unhappy.

Through the drama of counselling, she found the intermediary circle between her core self and her social self and was able to link positive emotions with her everyday roles of fiancée, step-daughter, employee, colleague and friend. Through the mask diary, she was able physically to portray her emotions and, in the final mask, she actually integrated the two parts of herself. Shade was able to see multiple images of herself in the stories we used and those she made up. Through exploration of the emotions of the characters in the stories, she was able to explore her own emotions and understand them better. We used the empty space of the sessions in an actual and psychological way in our joint endeavour to find her 'real' person in the here-and-now.

As counsellor, I changed my original aims because of Shade's needs, while keeping to the theatrical framework of warm-up, rehearsal, performance and closure using techniques from drama, dramatherapy and counselling theory. The integration Shade achieved was much more than she and I had dared to predict. But my feeling is that because she was so motivated and ready to change, she allowed herself to experience the painful emotions counselling brought up in a healing and positive way and to move on by reframing them cognitively through understanding and integration. The submerged emotions were no longer dangerous, because she could accept them and understand them and she realized that they no longer had the power to destroy her.

As I found when I was a child, there is a great deal of comfort to be found in literally playing the roles and characters of other people. In drama, it is not simply a question of 'pretending' to be someone else in one's mind, but we embody the role; we move as the character, we use the tone of voice we think the character has; we try to think as we imagine the character thinks. How do we do this? Because as children we learn to take the role of the other and we recognize what other people feel, because we have experienced the same emotions ourselves. When we ask clients to try to play different roles and characters, they are allowed to practise what it feels like to 'try on' different aspects of themselves. The discoveries they make can sometimes be life-transforming.

REFERENCES

Berry, C. (1992) That secret voice. In Murray Cox (ed.), *Shakespeare Comes to Broadmoor*. London, Jessica Kingsley.
Boal, A. (1992) *Games for Actors and Non-Actors* (Translated by A. Jackson). London, Routledge.

Brook, P. (1992) Interviewed by Jean Kalman. Any event stems from combustion: Actors, audiences, and theatrical energy. *New Theatre Quarterly*, No. 30, May, pp. 107–12. Cambridge, Cambridge University Press.

Brook, P. (1987) *The Shifting Point.* London, Methuen.

Campbell, B. (1990) Metaphor in dramatherapy. *Dramatherapy*, 13 (1), 1–6.

Dunn, J. (1988) *The Beginnings of Social Understanding.* Oxford, Blackwell.

Johnson, L. and O'Neill, C. (eds) (1984) *Dorothy Heathcote: Collected Writings on Education and Drama.* London, Hutchinson.

Jones, P. (1991) Dramatherapy: Five core processes. *Dramatherapy*, 14 (1), 8–15.

Lahad, M. (1992) Story-making: An assessment method for coping with stress. In S. Jennings (ed.), *Dramatherapy Theory and Practice 2.* London, Routledge.

Murgatroyd, S. (1985) *Counselling and Helping.* London, British Psychological Society and Methuen.

Neelands, J. (1990) Introduction. In T. Goode (ed.), *Structuring Drama Work.* Cambridge, Cambridge University Press.

O'Neill C. and Lambert, A. (1982) *Drama Structures.* London, Hutchinson.

Taplin, O. (1978) *Greek Tragedy in Action.* London, Methuen.

Wilshire, B. (1982) *Role Playing and Identity: The Limits of Theatre as Metaphor.* Bloomington, Indiana University Press.

Yalom, I. (1991) *Love's Executioner.* Harmondsworth, Penguin.

7

PSYCHOLOGY AND COUNSELLING

Michael Carroll and Eileen Pickard

About twenty years ago, one of us was becoming a psychologist, the other a counsellor. We had separate starting points and little knowledge of the discipline of the other. It was through our work in psychology and counselling that our paths converged. We talked, developed ideas and courses and wrote together and, as a result, we each became influenced by the starting point of the other. In this chapter, we invite you to share in a journey of minds; our own and some of our clients, through the psychology–counselling relationship.

PSYCHOLOGY AND OUR ENGAGEMENT WITH IT

Undergraduates sometimes embark on psychology courses in order to explore people and to extend self-understanding (Morris *et al.* 1992). We did likewise, but our early impressions of our courses were of apparently unrelated theories, statistics and practical experiments as well as the experience of conflicting philosophies of the person argued out by academics who seemed to be into point scoring. One of us was a teacher with experience of real-life human development and learning and found some of the areas encountered on the undergraduate psychology curriculum far removed from those experiences. For the other, the first encounter with psychology as a discipline came after courses in philosophy and counselling. In philosophy, a good deal of time had been given to thinking about people, their nature and inner aspects. And in counselling, of course, exploration of the person was very central. In many ways, our experience of working and training in education and counselling created within us a contempt for the scientific and non-applied approach to psychology which we encountered. It appeared to deny issues of spirit, mind, subjectivity and affectivity. The psychology we had encountered had, of course, been very selective. We were introduced to Carl Rogers, who was so person-centred and concerned with meaningful education and to Freud, hardly an orthodox psychologist, with his emphasis on inner dimensions of people, the mind, and its unconscious aspects and his much criticized methods of studying people which included dreams and hypnosis. As we studied psychology, we began to build up a sense of the discipline.

Psychology is a science

'Psychology is a science', we were told. Tutors emphasized scientific method and talked of the need for objectivity. We carried out experiments both on people and animals and learnt the importance of valid and accurate measures. We also learnt that well-conducted experiments should be repeatable, that is, it should be possible to gain the same results on subsequent occasions, given that the experimental conditions were identical. We could see that this might work well in the physical sciences, from where the procedures had been borrowed, but we were not so sure that people could be controlled in this way. However, at the time we were too inexperienced to realize that there were other world views and that ideas about the nature of science were themselves under discussion.

Psychology is a science of people

Psychology is a science of people, we learnt. We also read that Watson (1925) had insisted that 'we should make what we can observe the real field of psychology' and that he had rejected claims that the person had abstract dimensions such as mind or soul. We could see that this approach to the person would go hand in hand with a neat and tidy experimental approach. It is not easy to subject the mind or soul to controlled experimentation, but this did not seem a good enough reason for ignoring questions about them. We were reminded of Freud who struggled with this very issue and wrote: 'the doctor cannot understand hysteria . . . He regards [hysterics] as people who are transgressing the laws of his Science' (Freud and Breuer 1956). If psychology was to be a science of people, then it seemed essential to us to develop methods of investigation and experimentation that could be systematic and rigorous but respectful of the complex nature of the person.

Quantitative or qualitative methods?

We were final-year students before we really began to understand that psychology is open to interpretation, that there are different views in the psychology community about the nature of persons and different ways of investigating them. Those who hold views rooted in the positivist tradition emphasize external measurable features of the person and use a methodology which enables them to quantify their findings. Those struggling with less tangible, human issues, such as insight, creativity, self-perception and extra-sensory perception, know that methodologies capable of respecting and encapsulating qualitative dimensions of the person are needed. In other words, our concepts of science and person will determine the methods we use. Suddenly, we realized that psychologists are interpreters of people and that, as students of psychology, like psychologists themselves, we were becoming interpreters, making sense of the insights, ideas, theories and research findings passed down the years in the attempt to understand the complexity of the person.

The range of psychology and its applications

We graduated with a range of knowledge about people culled from developmental, social, cognitive and other fields of psychology. Through the courses we followed and our own reading we became aware of the range of our discipline. We also realized that the range was being extended as psychologists faced new questions. Some concentrate on human life-span issues, others on interpersonal matters. The research and publication on culture, cognitive science, parapsychology and many other fields makes clear its range and relevance. In our final years, we began to understand that this science of people was a developing one with a range of approaches to people and to ways of studying them. We were also becoming aware of the many applications of psychology including occupational, educational, clinical and counselling situations as well as para-medical, sporting, welfare and business contexts.

Understanding and using psychology

Though we graduated with some understanding of the nature of psychology and its applications, it was not until postgraduate level that this knowledge was *used* by us and it was the use that began to turn us into interpreters of psychology as opposed to fact gatherers. At this stage, our experiences, of psychology began to take us down different paths. One of us researched the development of creativity. It had to be done scientifically because the hoped for award was a PhD from a Faculty of Science, but researching creativity involved a confrontation with issues which confront counsellors. How can one investigate insight? How does one get inside a person's mind or interpret their insights and actions in relation to creativity? Suddenly, much of the scientific methodology, the backbone of our university studies, appeared inadequate for the task. New paradigms, capable of dealing with qualitative aspects of the person, were needed. At the same time, there was a need to retain appropriate scientific rigour.

   While one of us struggled with the methodological challenges of researching creativity, the other became a practitioner keen to understand and research the efficacy of counselling processes and the conditions which appear to influence them. Though engaged in different areas of postgraduate research, both of us were finding a need for new research methodologies capable of dealing with the qualitative issues which confronted us. By the 1980s, we were working together. Debates about the nature of science and its relationship with psychology were well established (Fransella 1975) and the scientist–practitioner debate had commenced (Howard 1986). We were preparing lectures on the nature of psychology and encouraging students to reflect upon it. The *Oxford Dictionary*'s definition, 'the science of the nature, functions and phenomena of the human soul and mind', makes it clear that psychology isn't just about external behaviour, but includes soul and mind and is a science. However, how does one explore these abstract phenomena in a reliable and scientific way? That was the stage at which we became jointly involved in exploring research methodologies that could be sensitive to human subjectivity, and trying to enable students to appreciate that ideas about the nature of science were themselves under revision (Reason and Rowan 1981).

Though our routes through psychology and counselling have been different, our paths have converged and we have come to a number of common conclusions. Psychology is a science, but its theories and methods are open to imaginative and sensitive application. People-appropriate methodologies are developing and contemporary psychologists are struggling with difficult qualitative tasks, such as the investigation of the unconscious, human relationships, creative insights and psychological aspects of healing. We have come to the view that counselling can only benefit from a partnership with psychology. Indeed, we would go further and say that counselling has deep roots in psychology. Many of the theories which colour counselling practice were developed by psychologists, as were some of the skills and training schedules. More, if counselling is going to develop reflexive practice, it needs a body of research to inform that practice and here it can benefit from the experience of psychologists. But it is also true to say that psychology has been influenced by counselling. The discipline has changed a great deal since 1879 when Wilhelm Wundt set up the first psychology laboratory in Leipzig and William James established his in Harvard, USA. Then, psychology was a very new discipline and sought respectability and entry into academia by adopting ideas and methods devised for the physical sciences. People, however, are not so easily controlled and cannot, for all aspects of their behaviour, be fitted into this particular kind of scientific precision. The humanistic psychologists, like Carl Rogers and Maslow, really challenged this kind of psychology and the challenge has led to methodological developments. Today, psychologists are working to create people-appropriate methodologies (Barkham 1990) and are raising questions about human dimensions which are deeper than external observables.

Summary

Psychology is a science in that it is trying to be systematic in its study of human issues. From its beginnings, different concepts of person have influenced both the theories and methods of psychology and today, in the community of psychologists, there is a range of views, theories and methods. We are interpreters in that, like psychologists and counsellors before us, we have to develop the insights and methodologies of yesterday to make sense of today's issues.

PSYCHOLOGY AND OUR UNDERSTANDING OF PERSONS

Understanding the person through theory and practice

It is the interaction of theory and practice which has formed our ideas of person. But they are ideas which have taken many years to develop and because we try to extend our own knowledge and because psychology itself is developing, they are always under revision. As practitioners, we are both essentially person-centred in our approach but we are sufficiently eclectic to want to learn from other approaches and, where appropriate, integrate concepts and practices from different theoretical orientations. It was practice that encouraged this integration and it was practice that brought theory to life for us. There was the student, with whom one of us worked, profoundly distressed about his work habits and aided by an essentially behavioural schedule. And, suddenly, some of the work of Skinner began to have something to offer. There was the client, troubled by early childhood experiences, who brought Freud to life and gave meaning to some of his claims about repression and the unconscious. And there were the children in the classroom, who illustrated better than any lecturer could do, the power and benefits of Carl Rogers' idea of meaningful learning. As undergraduates we had both covered areas of knowledge very relevant to practice. We still remember lines from Skinner urging us to 'turn from the inferred to the observed, from the miraculous to the natural, from the inaccessible to the manipulable' (Skinner 1973: 196). We did laboratory exercises and laboratory reports on learning and anxiety. We read Sigmund Freud, Carl Rogers and Abraham Maslow. But somehow it all remained on the page, eventually finding some form of expression on an examination script. It is our practice which has informed our early academic notions of people and which has made us return to the great theories and the research to deepen our knowledge and, as a result, enable us to be more effective practitioners.

Understanding human development

For both of us, the study of the development of the human person has been central to our counselling practice, enabling us to make sense of human issues in relation to life tasks, transitions and stages. Developmental psychology has itself developed, extending its knowledge of the person. At the beginning of this century, developmental psychology, then referred to as child development, drew to a close with adolescence. Major theories stopped there. Adolescence was an arrival point for cognitive, psychosexual and other areas of development (Pickard 1990). Since then, there has been an extension of developmental psychology into what is now lifespan psychology. If we were to draw a line across a page and label one end uterine life and infancy and the other ageing and death, we would have a quick statement about the start and end of human life. Between those two points is a range of human developments all brought together in the human person and expressed over a time-span. Developmental psychologists now research the tasks and experiences of adulthood, which include the formation of stable relationships, marriage, parenting, career development, divorce, bereavement and death. Part of the ongoing task of being a psychologist engaged in counselling is to remain in touch with new insights into human development.

Exploring the boundaries of human potential

Pursuing the development of psychology itself is a massive task because there are so many issues of significance to our understanding of the human person. Psychologists explore areas ranging from racial prejudice, the influence of television and drug use to neurological and genetic issues. Some of the most exciting work is that which breaks new ground leading us to new conceptualizations of the potential of the person. In the USA, Stephanie Simonton has, with her husband Carl, developed a technique of guided imagery which appears to indicate that the individual can have some control over their immune system and over illnesses, such as cancer, related to this system. Biofeedback studies make similar claims in relation to an individual's control of his or her autonomic nervous system, suggesting that he or she can control blood pressure for instance. Studies of this kind are often seriously exploring the boundaries of human potential. They are a long way from Watson's idea that 'we should make what we can observe the real field of psychology'. From a methodological point of view, they are difficult areas to tackle, but it is often through work of this kind that we enhance and extend our understanding of human persons whose complexity and fascination grows as psychologists and related researchers reveal more and more about them.

Understanding the person through research

Just as practice has led us back to a consideration of major theories and related research, each one enhancing the other, so we have been obliged to give serious thought to the development of research methodologies. For both of us, memories of research methods courses were about statistics, formulae, lectures on interview techniques and engagement in practical experiments of a sometimes trivial kind. It was the real-life questions presented, usually unwittingly, by clients, children and students, which drove us back to seek for developments in research methods and made us realize that lecturers were right when they insisted that becoming a researcher was pivotal to sound knowledge and practice because our understanding of people is as sound as the research upon which we base our conclusions. The development of research is dependent upon knowledge of the area in question, upon imaginative interventions and processes and sometimes upon technology. Carl Jung, for example, tried to assess reactions to emotive stimuli but he lacked the technology, available today, which enables more reliable measures. Audiologists working with psychologists have shown us that babies in the womb can recognize and remember certain sounds. Researchers like Tom Bower (1982) have, through creative research methodology, found ways of putting very complex questions to infants. It is through creative research that we are able to pose and answer questions about the human person that once seemed to be beyond practical investigation. For the psychologist and counsellor, there is an important partnership in unravelling human questions. Why is it, for example, that bereavement influences individuals so very differently? How is it that some practitioners appear to be able to help cancer patients by using guided-imagery, a technique in which the mind appears to control the body? Does the personality of the therapist influence counselling outcomes? Does life really proceed via stages of development? In what sense can we remember in the womb? Devising methodologies to respond to questions of this kind is central to an ongoing understanding of people and human potential.

Summary

As undergraduates, we were somewhat black and white in our thinking, failing to appreciate that all academics and practitioners are engaged in the task of better understanding the person and that though they may be fired by different philosophies and approach the person from different perspectives, there can be meeting points (Chapman and Jones 1980). With experience we have come to understand the growing dialogue between psychologists and practitioners. We have also come to understand that psychological theory and research must be made sense of in its historical context. Modern day behaviourists do not reject the inner dimensions of persons in the way in which Watson did, but they have the benefit of years of thinking and of technological advances. Today, we no longer believe that babies are born blind and that the deaf are unintelligent. Research and technology have dispensed with those myths. In other words, in the light of our own experience of psychology and counselling and drawing upon the knowledge and research of the psychological community, we are better placed to come to less fragmented views of the person.

The human person, with his or her many different dimensions, is at the centre of the psychologist's theorizing and research. Over the years, psychologists, influenced by philosophers, have held and worked with different views of the person. Some have focused upon external, measurable behaviours; others have attempted to explore less tangible aspects of the human person. These different views of the person have contributed to different methods of practical investigation, some of which have been aided by technological developments. Whatever the methodology, psychologists aim to work in valid and systematic ways so that the knowledge we build up about the human person is reliable and helpful. Like the academic psychologist, the practitioner has a range of questions about the human person. To begin with, how are practitioners influenced by psychology? Are they? How much psychological knowledge should the counsellor have? Is the counsellor who is ignorant of psychological advances likely to be a less good counsellor? In the next section, we intend to explore some of these questions.

PSYCHOLOGY AND OUR UNDERSTANDING OF THE COUNSELLING PROCESS

Psychology will influence, or more precisely, be allowed to influence, the counselling process depending on the counselling orientation espoused by the practitioner and the resulting emphasis on either insight by the client, cognitive restructuring, catharsis, the therapeutic relationship or alliance, and/or learning new skills.

The five elements of the counselling process

Our understanding of the counselling process revolves around the client–counsellor and the counsellor–supervisor relationships and our perceptions of the three key figures involved: the client, the counsellor and the supervisor. Figure 7.1 connects the persons and the relationships and provides an overview to help us show how psychology influences our practice of counselling.

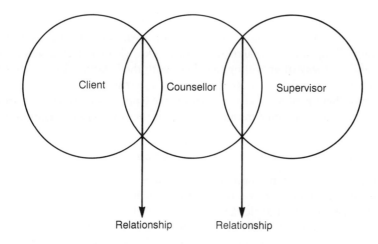

Figure 7.1 The counselling process (Carroll 1992).

The client

The client is central to the counselling process. Each individual client is rich and varied, coming from a range of backgrounds which include family, friendships and various communities. The clients arrive for counselling accompanied by a whole range of people, who still live within them, who have influenced their lives in one way or another. Some counsellors argue (e.g. Egan and Cowan 1979) that clients come into counselling because they are searching for the skills and knowledge to deal with the various systems of their lives. These clients are also at a developmental stage of life (Erikson 1950), process information in a certain way, have values and a certain level of moral development (Kohlberg 1964) and have built up defences and ways of interacting with the world.

The counsellor

The second element in the diagram is the counsellor. The counsellor will have background issues in his or her life from similar general systems (family, community, world), will also be in a developmental stage of life, will have certain personality characteristics and an interpersonal relating style. And, presumably and hopefully, will have undergone training in counselling.

The counselling relationship

The third factor in the diagram is the relationship between client and counsellor. The counselling relationship has many aspects and differs when viewed from within a variety of counselling orientations – the working alliance, the real relationship, the transference, the reparative and the transpersonal relationships, for example (Clarkson 1990). Our own approach to psychology and counselling views the real relationship as a key element in counselling outcome and as a way of providing the client with the basis needed for change. This means we function as counsellors in a particular way with clients, relating to them professionally but with more emphasis on the real relationship and working alliance than on the use of the transference relationship.

The supervisor and the supervisory relationship

A fourth and fifth dimension have been added to the diagram, viz. the person of the supervisor and the relationship between the supervisor and the supervisee as essential elements in the counselling process. Supervision is the forum where counsellors bring their client work to 'ensure that clients receive a certain minimum quality of care while trainees work with them to gain their skills' (Bernard and Goodyear 1992). The supervisor, like both the client and the counsellor, has personality characteristics unique to self, is at a developmental stage and is living within certain key systems of life. All these are brought to the supervisory situation. We agree with Doehrman (1976) that the supervisory relationship has a significant influence on the relationship between client and counsellor.

Together, these five elements go to make up the counselling process, that is, the factors involved in the change process. Our view, as psychologists, is that psychology has a lot of potential influence in all these areas and we have isolated three main ways in which psychology can influence counselling theory and practice, and does so in our work.

Psychological theory and counselling practice

First, psychology provides theories that directly influence counselling interventions (e.g. personality theory and life span developmental theory). Our own backgrounds in humanistic psychology have enabled us to draw on the work of Maslow to understand motivation and what helps an individual change. Using the writings of Rogers, Berne and Perls, as well as Jung (who is also seen within the humanistic field), enables us to create counselling interventions that trust the inner drive of the individual towards self-actualization. For this reason, we are more experiential in our work with clients than, for example, a psychodynamic counsellor, drawing on experiential learning, homework, experimenting with different roles, keeping journals, using techniques from various theories as ways of engendering insight and rebuilding new methods of interacting with life. Our belief is that, given the right atmosphere, which often means the right sort of relationship, the person will blossom and become the individual he or she was meant to be.

We are keen to build a supportive and challenging relationship that will allow the client to experiment with new ways of thinking, feeling and acting within the counselling relationship as a prelude to translating these to real life.

Developmental psychology and counselling

As we indicated earlier, we use insights and knowledge from developmental psychology to help our work with clients. One of us worked with a 73-year-old woman in a hospital setting who was dealing with what Erikson called 'despair', that is, almost at the end of her life and not able to accept how she had lived. Knowing something about 'integrity' – that is, being able to see one's life realistically and accept it, despite its limitations – resulted in using particular counselling interventions. These revolved around helping her recall incidents in life, tell her story, and stories, in an acceptable atmosphere, 'mine out' the good experiences of life, re-interpret what had happened in the past, and slowly come to see that, close to death, she had lived meaningfully. This insight helped her write some letters to significant people in her life.

A knowledge of stage theories influences intervention with this person. However, a rigid interpretation of stage theories is to be avoided. Stages are not hurdles through which the individual must proceed, but helpful landmarks to facilitate intervention; for example, being aware that clients who are grieving sometimes need to express anger and helping them deal with that when it is appropriate.

Contexts and counselling

Psychology can influence counselling by reminding it about the contexts from which clients emerge and the impact those contexts have on individuals and groups. Cultural aspects of counselling, in the past an interesting option, have now become ethical issues. Gender issues in counselling are coming to the fore with serious questions around cross-gender counselling. Research into language used by men and women (Coates 1986) shows that in men/women conversations there is serious damage done to women's right to speak. This research has been used by some to indicate the need for same-sex groups for women and the need for same-sex counselling at certain stages of development (Wray 1992). In our counselling work, we have found it invaluable to be able to offer potential clients a choice of working with either a man or a woman and to have the opportunity of talking to a counsellor who comes from a similar racial background.

It may be here that counselling can provide questions for the psychologist to research, questions about the importance of contexts, the culture of the individual, and itself struggle with what counselling interventions are most helpful when an understanding of context is seen as important.

Psychological research and counselling

A second major connecting link between psychology and counselling is in the area of research. Psychological research has given assistance to counselling in three areas: psychological assessment, psychological research methods and by providing information from psychological research.

Counselling and psychological assessment

Psychological tests are methods for helping the practitioner assess some aspect of the personality of the client; for example, the Myers-Briggs Type Indicator believes people to be different and that individuals have preferred ways of interacting with the world and with other people. This test will summarize these preferences and help clients to understand which type of job will be more suitable, or indeed which kinds of relationships will be easier or more difficult for them to work within. Bayne (1991) connects the Myers-Briggs test and counselling: 'Type has implications for counselling itself, for counsellor training, and in time, perhaps, for "matching" of clients, counsellors and strategies.'

There are tests for decision making, for personality type, for leadership qualities, for depression, for anxiety. Testing can be used in diverse contexts, such as redundancy counselling (matching the right person to the right job), suitability for counselling and what counselling is best suited for this person, team development and how the personalities in a particular staff team interact with one another.

Psychological tests can be used in a number of ways by counsellors. Some use them to assess what is happening to the client or what particular outlook a client may have. Using the Heimler Scale of Social Functioning or the Myers-Briggs test may provide helpful insights into how best to intervene with a client. Knowing a client is highly introverted will undoubtedly change the counsellor's way of interacting with him or her. An extroverted client will take more easily to the counselling relationship and use it for growth; the introverted client, who is more at home in the internal world, will respond less vigorously to the relationship (Bayne 1991).

Secondly, such tests, we have found, can be used as ways of monitoring progress. If a client is attempting to be more outgoing, more socially and interpersonally involved, then scoring the Myers-Briggs test before counselling and after three months of counselling will help designate changes (or the lack of change) that have taken place. Change here can be monitored from various perspectives: from within the person (e.g. depression, locus of control) or from outside (e.g skills development or interpersonal relationships). One large counselling agency uses the Beck Depression Inventory ('for the detection of depression, anxiety, hopelessness and suicidal intent') as a way of monitoring client progress or lack of it.

We have both used tests as ways of initiating dialogue with clients; for example, asking a young person to complete a sentence test with half completed sentences such as, 'One thing I like about myself is . . .', 'I get sad when . . .', 'A recent problem I've handled very well is . . .'. With some young people, especially those who are not very articulate, filling in sentences such as those above can be an easier way of getting in touch with information about themselves. Counsellors can then ask them to choose a sentence and use it as a basis for talking.

Psychological methods

A further way in which psychological tests are used is to help research projects within the area of counselling. One recent dissertation, written through our psychology department, used the FIRO-B Test (Schultz) to monitor interpersonal changes in groups of nurses undergoing introductory counselling skills training. The nurses were tested before a ten-week skills training programme in interpersonal skills on their levels of relating. After the course they were again tested. The conclusions were fairly clear: training in interpersonal skills were viewed as more helpful for nurses in their work with their patients and in their relationships with one another than no training.

Information drawn from psychological research

All of us are researchers in some form or another. We draw conclusions from our counselling work about what works best with which clients. Some of these conclusions are common sense, others are opinions, others possibly inherited without any grounds for validity. Research is an organized way of drawing some conclusions from the work we do.

Psychological theories provide research methodologies and research findings that can be used to research the counselling process (Heppner *et al.* 1992) and provide information useful to the counsellor. Some findings are simple statistical facts whose knowledge is helpful to the counsellor. For example, in 1911 the average marriage lasted twenty-eight years, whereas in 1970 it lasted forty-two years; most women have finished child-bearing by the age of twenty-six or twenty-seven; fifty per cent of all divorces occur in the first nine years of marriage. These three pieces of statistical information can be of great help to the couples counsellor or the family therapist. There is a fund of 'working knowledge' useful to counsellors that allows them to understand what is happening to clients and why it might be happening.

Psychology has traditionally been based on quantitative or experimental methods or research. Criticisms have been made about adopting this method or research especially in studying counselling (Pilgrim 1990; Van Deurzen-Smith 1990). Other research methods are being considered as more applicable to studying the counselling process (Reason and Rowan 1981; Reason 1988). Some of these involve methods such as analysing the conversations that take place between a counsellor and a client, coding the issues in transcripts of counselling sessions, having clients keep diaries summarizing their thoughts after each counselling session. One of us is at present researching clinical supervision by interviewing supervisors and coding tapes of live supervision sessions.

The debate continues within psychology about the relative merits of differing research methods. Alternative methods such as those listed above are only slowly being accepted as part of psychology and the lack of skills in using these research methods by psychologists is again being slowly addressed in psychology training. Counselling psychologists are now part of the conversation themselves, offering suggestions about how best to research the complex relationships involved in counselling. As practitioners and researchers in the counselling field, we want to try and answer some key questions about the value of counselling, what counselling models work best with which clients and what are the longer term effects of counselling.

Psychological information and counselling

Psychology also contributes to counselling in providing information about human behaviour from a variety of psychological backgrounds.

Developmental knowledge and counselling

A friend who is a 'primal therapist' has talked about his interest in the psychological work being done on individuals before birth. We know the developing foetus responds to external stimuli and probably has some memory. What else is it capable of? What can it know? It is an interesting historical fact that the parents of Oedipus intended killing him when he was born. Did he know this in some unconscious, preverbal way in the womb? It would be interesting to speculate on how far that knowledge influenced later developments between himself and his parents. There is a certain amount of clinical evidence that the 'birth experience' affects later life and that clients in some counselling orientations can regress and relive the experience. Medical and psychological insight into these areas will provide further information that will, undoubtedly, influence counselling interventions, not just with primal therapists, but with all those who recognize the relationship between past, including the prenatal period, and present.

Kohlberg's work on the stages of moral development indicates that it does not help to challenge someone more than one stage above their developmental level. He outlined six stages of moral development that individuals go through in a systematic way as they struggle with life's moral issues. Many individuals stop and remain at particular stages, seeing moral issues in restricted ways, e.g. I do to others what is done to me. Understanding these stages has been of great help to us in reviewing values with a client and challenging them to look at racist attitudes. It would have been unhelpful to initiate the dialogue by suggesting that they view all people as valuable individuals (fifth and sixth stage) when they were still at the bargaining stage of development.

Marcia's work on identity in adolescence (Mauss 1975) explains characteristics of teenagers at different stages of identity (identity foreclosed, confused, achieved or moratorium) and influenced one of us who ran a Youth Counselling Agency for a number of years. To a counsellor working in a young person's Drop-In Centre, knowing that a 16-year-old has already foreclosed identity (and therefore has problems making personal choices) will be helpful. The counsellor will concentrate on helping the young person learn how to make choices and the subsequent commitments. Knowledge of the various forms of resolving identity will influence working with the 40-year-old woman who foreclosed her identity with marriage at eighteen and is now desperately trying to make sense of her world. Allowing her to tell her story and revisit that earlier commitment will help her know if she wishes to choose again or change that decision.

Psychological knowledge, while never absolute, continues to challenge counsellors to rethink the cognitive base of their theory and practice.

Conclusion

There are three connected ways in which psychology can influence the counselling process. The first is in providing the counsellor with the array of theories that influence counselling interventions. A second is in psychological research which results in information, assessment procedures and methodologies to help the counsellor practise and research that practice. And a third way is to provide psychological information as a basis for conceptualizing what is happening to a client and how best to intervene.

This psychological influence can be handed on directly to the client and we have found it useful to share psychology in counselling practice. We base this on research by Frank (1973), who found that a common element in all the helping professions was the ability to offer clients clear frameworks that explained mental illness and mental health. Psychology can do that for the client. We sometimes suggest appropriate reading. Parents, finding great difficulty in understanding their teenage children, can be helped with reading from developmental psychology – for example, Martin Herbert's *Working with Children and their Families* (1988) or Egan and Cowan's *Moving into Adulthood* (1980). Very moving accounts have been written by adults who were sexually abused as children (*My Father's House*, by Sylvia Fraser, 1989) and there is academic literature on adult life crises (*Passages*, by Gail Sheehy, 1976).

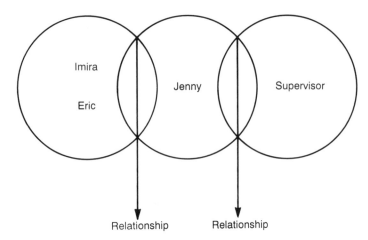

Figure 7.2   The counselling process as seen by the counsellor.

A second way is to share with clients what we consider to be the issues with which they are dealing. It comes as a great relief to know that a mid-life crisis does not mean that the client is going crazy. Explaining some of the stages of grief (if a grieving person is experiencing the lost one as still around physically) can allow the client to view as quite 'normal' what they were interpreting as 'abnormal'. Our belief is that 'giving psychology away' to clients, either through suggested reading or through direct explanation, is both helpful and effective.

Case studies

In reviewing some case examples where psychology is seen as influencing counselling, we will use the eyes and thoughts of Jenny, a counselling psychologist, and utilize two contexts in which Jenny works. Figure 7.2 personalizes the counselling process. Jenny has two clients, Imira and Eric, one of whom she sees in a youth counselling agency, the other in a GP practice.

Jenny works in a youth counselling service in which young people refer themselves or are referred for counselling. Even before seeing clients, Jenny has helpful psychological information that influences her way of working in the agency. She knows from work on the family life-cycle that the most difficult time in a family is when there are teenagers, not simply because teenagers are teenagers, but because the adolescent transition time often coincides, and indeed triggers off, the parents' mid-life issues. From this, Jenny concludes that counselling work with young people should never isolate itself from its context – that is, parents and home, school, peer group. Jenny spends a lot of her time with parents and teachers and her counselling work has an outreach element she considers essential to good practice.

From an informative viewpoint, the work of Marcia (1966) is particularly helpful to Jenny in assessing and working with individual young people. Marcia's studies revolved around identifying the patterns and issues emerging from the adolescent struggle towards identity. For him there were two key areas that go to make up identity: personal choice and personal commitment –choice being the ability to choose from alternatives, commitment the ability to invest energy in choices made. From these twin viewpoints, Marcia unfolded four areas of identity: identity confused, identity foreclosed, moratorium (identity on hold) and identity achieved. From his interviews, he was able to designate the features and characteristics of individuals in each of the stages of identity formation. For some the key issue in their lives was an inability to choose or commit, for some it was pre-commitment, (i.e. commitment without choice), for others it was choosing without commitment and a final group had both chosen and committed themselves.

The value of this research for Jenny allows her to make general statements about the identity issues of the young people she is seeing and will be seeing and to be able to gear her interventions accordingly. An obvious example is a 17-year-old girl, Imira, who wanted to talk through her arranged marriage.

Imira

Imira was in a dilemma. She had been born and lived her life in London; her parents had come from India. She had gone to school and learned British ways and customs while still retaining Indian customs at home. She dearly wanted the freedom to date boys and make her own choice of husband when she felt ready to marry. On the other hand, she needed to be part of her family and follow traditions valuable to them, one of which was an arranged marriage. From Marcia's viewpoint, she was identity foreclosed, that is, she had committed herself to marriage without choosing it and was prepared to go through with this decision.

The second area in which Marcia's work helped Jenny was in choosing interventions. With 'identity foreclosed' clients, it is important to help them reflect on their areas of freedom and what choice they can make and will allow themselves to make. Denying themselves personal choice is a way of overcoming the difficulties of choosing and the responsibilities involved.

A review of this case from a psychological perspective might look like this from Jenny's stance:

Imira	*Jenny*
Seventeen years old	What adolescent tasks is she facing?
Asian girl	What does this mean for her? What effect is this having on her family? What inter-/cross-cultural problems affect her life?

Family	What are her values regarding her family? What is happening there? What kind of family system is involved?
Personality	How is Imira's personality assessed? What kind of person is she?
Choices	What are the implications of the choices open to her? How are these understood in the context of her culture and her family?

Working with Imira allowed Jenny to support her while challenging the choices she made or did not make. With an awareness, in this instance, of the cultural values involved, and how easy it could be to change one set of foreclosed issues with another (i.e. allowing the counsellor to make the decision), Jenny worked with Imira helping her see what choices she had, and how these fitted in best with the values she wanted to remain in her life. She also reviewed possible ways of negotiating with her parents that might release other options. At one stage, she met with Imira and her parents and an Asian social worker who had worked extensively with cultural issues. From her initial no-win situation (either she refused to go through with her arranged marriage and lost her family or she accepted her husband and forgot all the new values she had learned about choosing her relationships), she and the family were able to work towards a 'both . . . and' agreement, in this case where she had some choices over her future husband.

Eric

Jenny's second client is Eric. Eric was referred to the GP Counselling Service by one of the doctors who simply indicated that Eric was depressed and had been depressed for some time. The doctor was getting anxious about Eric becoming dependent on anti-depressants and suggested counselling as a way of dealing with the depression. Eric agreed.

Eric is fifty years old. He has been married but the marriage broke up fifteen years ago. He has a daughter aged twenty-six whom he sees occasionally. He lives alone in a little bedsit run by a housing charity. He has not worked for several years and has given up trying to get a job. He used to undertake labouring and casual work but has no trade and no special skills.

Eric has been hospitalized several times for his depression (he tried to commit suicide twice). He visits the doctor regularly, but it would appear for social rather than medical reasons. He comes from a family where there was little sign of affection and some violence . His father drank a lot, his mother was constantly depressed. He has two brothers and two sisters but he has lost contact with all of them. His parents split up when he was fifteen and he has had to look after himself since.

Several possible interventions come to Jenny's mind when she talks to the doctor about the referral:

1 Can I get (a) an up-to-date psychiatric assessment or (b) a psychological assessment of his depression?
2 Can I find out what medication he has been on and why? What are the effects, and possible side-effects, of his medication?
3 What (tentative) conclusion can I draw from Eric's notes about: (a) the developmental stage of his life and the task he is facing (seems more like the task of wisdom *vs* despair rather than generativity); (b) his sense of identity – seems confused (maybe foreclosed); (c) his interpersonal life (he doesn't seem to have the skills to form and maintain relationships); (d) his suicide attempts?
4 Has any research been done on (a) depression, (b) suicide and (c) counselling depressed people.

Jenny looks up the psychological literature on the above areas and comes up with a number of conclusions:

1 A number of theories of depression: what causes it, how people react to it, and the medical and psychiatric responses to it.
2 Some statistics and reflections on suicide and parasuicide. One theory suggests that suicides involve a lack of certain chemicals within the blood. This, she discovers, is not widely accepted but makes Jenny aware that there are interesting biochemical theories of depression and suicide. Statistics show Eric is very vulnerable.
3 One theory in particular looks interesting in working with depressed people – Beck's model of depression. (Beck and Emery 1985)

Jenny reads up on Beck's work with depressed people.

Jenny meets Eric for their first session. She allows him to speak freely and explain the problems as he sees them. In particular, she talks to him about his depression and his suicide attempts. Eric obviously likes the opportunity of talking to someone interested in what he has to say and wants to continue to see her. She asks him if he will have an assessment and, when he agrees, makes a note to contact the clinical psychologist in the local hospital. From this report Jenny sets up time to meet with Eric and look at his problems with a particular emphasis on cognitive work. She also enlists the help of the social worker to see if there are places Eric can attend locally to meet and talk with people. Her hope is that Eric might join a therapy group after some individual work with her.

The following is an overview of how Jenny might think psychologically with Eric:

Eric	Jenny
Fifty years old	Developmentally, where is Eric and what life tasks is he facing? Does he have the skills to deal with the issues in his life?
Personality	Is his depression a personality disorder? Where will I get a suitable personality assessment?
Social context	What does his lifestyle, social contact, lack of friends tell me? Is Eric lacking in social/interpersonal/assertiveness skills?
Suicide attempts	Any research on suicide? Any information that might help me work with him?
Counselling	What form (s) of counselling seem to have worked well with people like Eric? Should I see him myself or refer? Any research on working with depressed clients?

Jenny is very aware that, although her psychological background is helpful to her client work, it is all too easy to fit the client to the theory and so she works hard to keep the individual differences of her clients in focus. She knows that individual journeys will have elements common to the human journey, but is also aware that each person handles that in a unique way. One area of major importance to her is the cultural background from which clients emerge and how important a facet it is of their lives. She has known for some time that rigid Western views of personality and development have to be carefully monitored before being applied to other ethnic backgrounds.

She has also realized that people learn differently and is beginning to adopt new methods in her work. With some clients she can involve them in skills training; others, she knows, will find that incredibly difficult. Some clients utilize visualization, art work, relaxation; others find it very difficult to do so. Adapting the theory to the person has become more of an approach for her.

She wants to continue researching her work and has devised an evaluation form she gives to her clients who post it back anonymously. With the statistics she is already keeping on clients (age, sex, presenting problem, number of sessions, family and social backgrounds, etc.), she hopes to be able to draw up yearly diagrams of who is presenting with what and how her counselling work is being evaluated by her clients.

She is wondering about the long-term effects of counselling provision and is contacting former clients after six months with a further questionnaire to assess how lasting have been the effects of counselling. As yet she has not introduced psychological testing into her work except in a very informal way (e.g. sentence completion), but the number of depressed clients through the doctor's surgery is making her consider using Beck's Scales for Depression.

In summary, Jenny's work is based fairly solidly in her psychological background. She uses information, intervention, research methods, and tries to keep up to date with psychological findings that will influence her practice.

Conclusion

Psychology and counselling have had a special relationship for some time. Since 1950 counselling psychology has been a well-established branch of psychology in the USA. Recently, the British Psychological Society, in the regulations for its new Diploma in Counselling Psychology, emphasized counselling psychology's grounding in psychology,

> Counselling psychology is a branch of applied psychology concerned with the interplay between psychological principles and the counselling process and is developed by substantial reflection on practice and research . . . In counselling psychology, there is an emphasis on the systematic application of distinctively psychological understandings of the client and the counselling process to the practice of counselling.
> (BPS 1993, Regulations for the Diploma in Counselling Psychology)

In this chapter we have tried to show how psychology, with its interpretation of human behaviour, its application to a number of settings and its use of research, offers information, interventions and findings that influence counselling work.

However, the influences are not simply one way. Psychology itself has also been influenced by counselling practice and research. The practitioner meets human questions and issues in the course of counselling work which defy existing psychological theories and new methods are explored and in time modify existing theory or result in new theories. Both Freud and Rogers developed and modified their theories through insights from practice with clients. And that is the way it should be, practice modifying theory and theory directing and giving meaning to practice.

REFERENCES

Barkham, M. (1990) Research in inductive therapy. In W. Dryden (ed.), *Individual Therapy: A Handbook*. Milton Keynes, Open University Press.

Bayne, R. (1991) Psychological type, the MBTI and counselling. *Employee Counselling Today*, 3 (1): 9–12.

Beck, A. and Emery, G. (1985) *Coping with Depression*. New York, Institute for Rational Living.

Bernard, J. and Goodyear, R. (1992) *Fundamentals of Clinical Supervision*. Boston, MA, Allyn and Bacon.

Bower, T. G. R. (1982) *Development in Infancy.* San Francisco, Freeman.

Carroll, C. (1992) Psychological therapies and the counselling process. Unpublished paper.

Chapman, A. and Jones, D. (1980) *Models of Man.* Leicester, British Psychological Society.

Clarkson, P. (1990) A multiplicity of therapeutic relationships. *British Journal of Psychotherapy,* 7 (2): 148–63.

Coates, J. (1986) *Women, Men and Language.* London, Longman.

Doehrman, M. J. (1976) Parallel process in supervision and psychotherapy. *Bulletin of the Menninger Clinic,* 40, 3–104.

Egan, G. and Cowan, M. (1979) *People in Systems.* Monteray, CA, Brooks/Cole.

Egan, G. and Cowan, M. (1980) *Moving into Adulthood.* Monteray, CA, Brooks/Cole.

Erikson, E. (1950) *Childhood and Society.* New York, Norton.

Frank, J. (1973) *Persuasion and Healing,* 2nd edn. New York, Schocken Books.

Fransella, F. (1975) *Need to Change?* London, Methuen

Fraser, S. (1989) *My Father's House.* London, Virago.

Freud, S. and Breuer, J. (1956) *Studies on Hysteria.* London, Hogarth Press.

Heppner, P. P., Kivlighan, D. M. and Wampold, B. (1992) *Research Design in Counselling.* Pacific Grove, CA, Brooks/Cole.

Herbert, M. (1988) *Working with Children and their Families.* London, Routledge.

Howard, S. (1986) The scientist-practitioner in counselling psychology: Towards a deeper integration of theory, research and practice. *The Counselling Psychologist,* 14 (1): 61–105.

Kohlberg, L. (1964) Development of moral character and moral ideology. *Review of Child Development Research.* New York, Russell Sage Foundation.

Marcia, J. E. (1966) Development and validation of ego identity status. *Journal of Personality and Social Psychology,* 3, 551–8.

Mauss, R. E. (1975) *Theories of Adolescence,* 3rd edn. New York, Random House.

Morris, P., Cheng, D. and Smith, H. (1992) How and why applicants choose to study psychology at university. *The Psychologist,* 5, 247–51.

Pickard, E. M. (1990) Creative potential in adolescence. *International Journal of Adolescence and Youth,* 2 (3): 157–64.

Pilgrim, D. (1990) British psychotherapy in context. In W. Dryden (ed.), *Individual Therapy: A Handbook.* Milton Keynes, Open University Press.

Reason, P. (1988) *Human Inquiry in Action.* Chichester, John Wiley.

Reason, P. and Rowan, J. (1981) *Human Inquiry: A Source Book of New Paradigm Research.* Chichester, John Wiley.

Sheehy, G. (1976) *Passages.* New York, Bantham Books.

Skinner, B. F. (1973) *Beyond Freedom and Dignity.* Harmondsworth, Penguin.

Van Deurzen-Smith, E. (1990) Philosophical underpinnings of counselling psychology. *Counselling Psychology Review,* 5 (2): 8–12.

Watson, J. B. (1925) *Behaviourism.* New York, Harper.

Wray, G. (1992) Same sex counselling? A discussion on neutrality, social conditioning and issues of gender. Thesis for Extra Mural Certificate in Counselling and Groupwork, University of Cambridge.

8

EDUCATION AND COUNSELLING

Mhairi MacMillan

EDUCATION AND MY ENGAGEMENT WITH IT

When I think back on all the crap I learned in High School
It's a wonder I can think at all;
And that my life of education hasn't hurt me none
I can read the writing on the wall . . .
                    (Paul Simon, 'Kodachrome')

Paul Simon's song may well reflect the views of many as they look back on their own 'lives of education'. Many people feel that the best they can say of the time they spent in school is that they managed to survive it. This is small consolation for years of compulsory schooling characterized by, at best, boredom and empty busyness and, at worst, by humiliation and failure. There are few people who do not react emotionally to their schooldays: second only to the family, schooling has a profound and lasting effect on people's lives.

Yet it is not the case that everyone has a bad time in school. My own experience of school was largely positive, probably because I was a 'good' – that is, a conforming and academically able – pupil. This may explain why I have spent so much time there.

I first went to school when I was four and a half years old; I finally left school forty years later. I attended primary school then secondary school for a total of thirteen years; one university as an undergraduate followed by teacher training college. I then taught in secondary schools in Scotland and England, teaching general science and physics and, briefly, in a primary school. I held two guidance posts in Scottish secondary schools. Twenty years after my first graduation, I returned to university (number two) for a postgraduate qualification in counselling; then took a Master's degree in Education at a third. At the same time, I taught in an experimental, progressive project in Scottish secondary education. As that was ending,

I finally left schools altogether to work in the counselling service of a
(fourth) university.

All the above, however, refers to *formal* education which takes place
in institutions within an educational system. *Informal* education goes on
continually as a result of human interaction and human experience. It has
been said that 'education is learning in the context of the search for truth'
(Stenhouse 1984). Few people would argue that truth is to be found only
within the walls of a school or university. With that reservation in mind,
I shall nevertheless outline some concepts which have shaped formal education, such as the acquisition of knowledge, the curriculum, pedagogy and
learning, and indicate two contrasting views of its purpose and function in
society.

Educational concepts

The nature of *knowledge* is complex. There is 'knowing' as remembering,
understanding and reproducing facts and information. There is 'knowing
how to', i.e. the acquisition of cognitive skills as well as manipulative
and social skills. Knowledge and skills, in this sense, are capable of being
organized and transmitted in some way from those who possess them
(teachers) to those who do not (learners). This view of knowledge is useful,
but limited. Some knowledge does not fit into any of these categories.
More and more, this kind of 'personal knowledge' is being recognized as
independent of facts and skills that have to be taught. It emerges only during
a process of personal discovery known as the 'heuristic' process.

The *curriculum* is the way in which a body of knowledge is organized
for transmission. It sets out criteria for selecting, structuring and pacing
the knowledge that is to be transmitted. The curriculum is structured into
different subjects and a syllabus is drawn up detailing what is to be taught,
in what order and in what space of time. In determining curricular content,
value judgements have to be made. How to decide who are qualified to
make these judgements remains a contentious issue.

Pedagogy, the art or science of teaching, is the practical expression of
underlying beliefs and theories about the nature of knowledge, the nature
of the learning process and the capacities of the participants in it, teachers
and pupils. It is developed as the means whereby knowledge is transmitted
and the objectives of the curriculum attained. For example, if learning is
seen as primarily a group activity, teaching will be directed towards pupils
as a group; when learning is seen as an individual activity, teaching is
directed towards individual pupils.

One important aspect of teaching is *instruction*; yet teaching also comprises
a range of skills and attitudes which facilitate learning. Language is not only
the medium of education, but the manner of its use in the classroom teaches
something about the way in which the teacher views the world and those in it.

On the face of it, *learning* is the principal activity promoted in school. Yet, despite successive learning theories, many aspects of learning remain mysterious. Even experts in the field of learning psychology change their ideas about how learning takes place. A leading advocate of discovery learning or 'learning by invention', essentially an individual activity undertaken by a single child, has written more recently:

I have come to recognize that learning in most settings is a communal activity, a sharing of the culture. It is not just that the child must make his knowledge his own but that he must make it his own in a community of those who share his sense of belonging to a culture.

(Bruner 1986)

Education as social control

Formal education can be seen as a system of social control. The transmission of the culture of our society is viewed as one of its major functions. Control is exerted by the way in which the culture is interpreted and by the extent to which varying interpretations are allowed to be transmitted. By means of streaming and selecting within schools, by maintaining a privately funded (and differently valued) school system alongside the state-funded system and by controlling assessment for entry into higher and professional education, the system can be seen as maintaining existing disparities between career and economic groups.

Control within schools is maintained by socio-legal, institutional and classroom rules. School attendance is compulsory; schools have rules concerning uniform, punctuality and acceptable conduct with sanctions against rule-breakers. At the classroom level, pupils soon learn what they can 'get away with' from particular teachers. There is often covert negotiation as pupils and teachers find ways to co-exist in a situation neither are free to leave. At the end of the day, the hierarchical authority structure ensures a power gradient with the pupils in the lowest position.

Education as a forum for negotiating meaning

We now live in a rapidly changing, post-industrial society, where there is a tendency to impose even greater control on formal education. An alternative would be to allow and support students and teachers to negotiate openly within school and higher education. When a Scottish newspaper consulted school students about educational reform, a typical respondent wrote, with unassailable logic:

Every young person is constantly told to be more responsible by parents, teachers and governments. If they want us to be more responsible for ourselves, they should let us have the opportunity.

(*The Scotsman*, 15 January 1992, letter from a pupil)

Such opportunity would be an integral part of a system based on the concept of education as a forum for negotiating knowledge and values, that is,
for the re-creation of meaning. 'The language of education is the language
of culture creating, not of knowledge consuming or knowledge acquisition
alone' (Bruner 1986). This does not entail those who know renouncing their
knowledge, but does require renunciation of the belief that they know
everything and, in its place, the adoption of an attitude of openness to learning, even from the learners.

EDUCATION AND MY UNDERSTANDING OF PERSONS

Experiencing myself as teacher and learner

Soon after I started school, I decided that I would be a teacher when I grew
up. Six months after my class intake, the Infant Teacher put me in charge
of looking after a new class which had just started. I did this very proudly.
At five years old, it was satisfying to me to tell other people how to do
things and to teach them about the world.

After graduating from university and teacher training college, I taught
science in a secondary school. I was dismayed to find that the pupils did not
always want to learn what I had to teach them and I felt a failure if I could
not keep a class under constant control.

Some years later, I worked as a guidance teacher with responsibility for
the personal, curricular and vocational guidance of pupils. To learn how to
do this job better, I took an in-service course, 'Helping interviews and
groupwork skills', and was introduced to the ideas of Carl Rogers on the
facilitation of learning. I began to understand school students as potentially
autonomous learners, not as people who always needed to be taught, and
to question the view that they were incapable of evaluating their own
experience and learning from it.

I then returned to learning in a way different to any that I had previously
experienced. In the intensive group workshops of the Facilitator Development Institute (see Thorne 1988), I learned about myself and my ways of
interacting with others. Before this, I had learned in the standard academic
mode with much use of books and with a teacher to instruct and explain.
In experiential group learning there was no explaining or teaching. Instead,
the basis of my learning was an inner conviction that my own experiencing
was valid and meaningful for me.

People are learners

People have the capacity to learn from birth until death. This learning
capacity is an essential part of being human. Human beings (persons) also

have the capacity to reflect on, and to learn about, their own learning. This predisposition to learn is basically constructive and creative; people do the best they can in the situation in which they find themselves. Learning, nevertheless, may be disadvantaged because of factors in the outer environment or distorted by previously learned beliefs and attitudes.

Even the most superficial look at the evolution of humanity reveals a rich history of learning. From the earliest times, cumulative learning, bodies of knowledge, have been passed down from generation to generation, starting from 'the oral traditions in which history and ways of seeing the world were passed on by elders' (Oatley 1980).

Equally, from the beginning, the human species has, by questioning and enquiring, discovered facts and laws governing ourselves and our world and has invented technologies which can expand and enhance human life. In the present time, it is not necessary, in formal education, to oblige human children to 're-invent the wheel', although they may enjoy discovering its properties and what can be done with it for themselves. Thus, one definition of 'action learning' brings together two important aspects of learning in an equation, $L = P + Q$. That is, learning consists of the acquisition of existing programmed knowledge (P) along with questioning insight (Q) (Zuber-Skerritt 1991).

An understanding of persons as learners, however, must also include some understanding of *how* persons learn and how their learning may be helped or hindered.

How people learn: The perceptual field

The earliest learning is experiential; all that a newborn person has to go on, in this world, is experiencing. Throughout life, there is no 'objective reality' that is common to all individuals. Each of us has our own perception of our inner and outer worlds and it is to this individual 'perceptual field' that we respond and react. Therefore, in order to participate in a learning process that is personally meaningful to the learner, we need to take into account the inner perceptual world of that learner.

From the very earliest stage of life, the perceptual field is individual and complex. Studies of the arousal effect produced by different stimuli on newborn infants show that this depends not only on the nature of the stimulus but also on the baby's internal state, as inferred from its behaviour. For example, infants either in deep sleep or fully awake and crying did not respond to sound or touch, whereas those sleeping irregularly or quietly awake did. The internal state also influenced the nature of the response; a researcher found that infants when quiet were startled and activated by the whirr of a camera, but when they were already active, the sound had a quieting effect. 'All this shows how important "state reading" is when dealing with an infant . . . we see the dangers of arbitrarily imposed stimulation; a baby's response is not only determined by the adult but also by the baby himself' (Schaffer 1977: 51).

Self-concept

Part of this complex, highly organized 'perceptual field' forms the self-concept (Rogers 1951). It seems, therefore, that the self-concept consists of a part that is learned and a part that is innate. Each of these parts varies in its accessibility into the awareness of the person. The learned part, when available to awareness, can be re-learned and is therefore, potentially, open to change. It is the innate part that Rogers called the 'organismic self'. This appears to be a similar, although not identical, notion to those found in other, typically more spiritual, traditions such as the 'higher self' of the Sufis. When people can remain or become aware of the experiencing of the organismic self, sometimes called 'the felt sense' (Mearns and Thorne 1988), they can use it to further self-understanding and to inform their dealing with both inner and outer worlds.

People do not develop in isolation, however, and their learned image of themselves incorporates much that has come from other, often more powerful, people around them. When powerful others impose their perceptions, including their perception of the child itself, on to the child's own perceptual field, the child's inner world is invaded, and the child may be forced to deny or distort the meaning of its personal experiencing. This is deeply damaging to its self-image. The child learns to expect nothing, either of its self or of the outer world. When the self-concept can no longer be based on trust in the person's own organismic experiencing, trust in the outer world and the people inhabiting it is also lost.

By the time children go to school, they already have a highly developed self-concept, which influences their ability to learn and their manner of learning. Their behaviour, including learning behaviour, is influenced by the whole of their perceiving and the personal meaning this holds for them. Teachers and others who relate to young people must take into account their individual inner worlds if they are to encourage not only their intellectual but also their emotional and social development.

Learning is an emotional as well as cognitive experience

In studying newborn children and mothers, researchers noticed that 'mothering' consisted not only of an emotional process but also of cognitive learning aspects. The effect of the mothers soothing and holding their babies was to free them sufficiently from the demands of their internal stimuli (their inner state) so as to allow them to explore and form perceptions of their external environment. One study concluded: 'When caretakers do not have the time or sensitivity to help a baby to reach a state in which he can maximally profit from encounter with his world, even the richest environment will fail to "get through" to him' (Schaffer 1977: 53).

In later life, when a person is experiencing (or repressing) strong emotions (anxiety, fear, anger, resentment – even euphoria, being in love!), their capacity for learning is likely to be impaired until the emotion subsides or is given attention. Formal education is loaded with emotional content. The relationships of learners with teachers and of learners with fellow learners are emotional experiences. Evaluation and assessment procedures, however 'objective' their design, are bound to produce emotional reactions in the pupils and in their parents. Not only in them, for the emotional tension of staff on the occasion of a school inspection is palpable!

Enhancing and hindering learning

Evaluation is inevitable in formal education. Continuing assessment of learning can help to detect blocks to progress for the learner and some sort of evaluation at the end of a course is necessary for various purposes. However, additional, unhelpful judgements are often made not only of pupils' learning but also of their characters. Here are some comments on pupils about to enter a special group project: 'A. and M. inseparable puddings, interesting to see if you can spark any enthusiasm; D. hopeless in a large group, incessant demands for attention; L. frequently knocks off, completely apathetic' (White and Brockington 1978).

Such judgements serve to reinforce the negative aspects of the pupils' own self-concepts. They do not help young people to learn, nor do they enhance their experience of formal education. Neither is it helpful, in the long run, for young people to be over-rewarded and praised for achievement in school. Being valued for one's achievements is not the same as being truly accepted for oneself. It becomes harder and harder for high-achieving children to allow themselves to make mistakes or to fall short of the expectations of others. Such young people come to feel acceptable only as performers, not for themselves. It is a sad experience to meet a university student, much praised for achievement in academic work, sport, music, drama, etc., who finds no satisfaction, far less pleasure, in any of it because she has no feeling of being valued for who she is rather than what she does.

The best facilitators of learning are those who can work with, rather than against, the young person's intrinsic motivations, such as curiosity and a need to know. They take into account their pupils' ways of seeing themselves in relation to the rest of the world and treat them with respect and liking. If teachers can respond to their students honestly, and if they themselves are trustworthy, the students are more likely to fulfil their potential as learners (Aspy and Roebuck 1977).

For some years, I worked in a project known as the 'Alternative School' within a local community high school. The major aim of the project was 'to allow students to make decisions about themselves in relation to curriculum and conduct'. The students found themselves in a situation that they had not previously experienced in school. One commented to the project evaluator: 'It was quite difficult at first when a teacher actually said, "What do you want to do this period?", and you hadn't really thought you could think for yourself' (Mearns 1986: 24). Despite (or because of) the struggle, for teachers as well as for students, to come to terms with a new way of relating to school and to each other, one of the most significant findings from the project evaluation was that 'over the period of one academic year compared with a control group of mainstream students of similar age, the Alternative School students show a significant gain in self-esteem as well as an increased appraisal of their relations with others' (Mearns 1986: 61).

Valuing the whole person as a learner

Carl Rogers said, 'People are wiser than their intellect'. Unfortunately, most formal educational methods fail to take this into account. Not only does education, especially after primary level, tend to concentrate on 'thinking' skills, but much of what actually passes for thinking in the classroom is actually 'remembering'. People, especially the young, have valuable creative abilities of imagination and fantasy. In school, these capacities are often regarded as distractions or signs of instability and severely discouraged. Neville (1989) points out how, in a technologically biased education system, the dismissal of imagery skills leads to 'metaphor blindness' and, possibly, to actual harm to the human organism. By restoring imagination and fantasy to a valued position in formal education, the currently over-valued mode of linear, rational thinking can assume its proper place again. We can then invite (rather than try to compel) the dreamers among us to use logical thinking to ground their fantasies and realize their visions.

One of the most essentially human capacities of all is that of creativity, especially the ability to create meaning. The creative process is usefully conceptualized as containing four stages – preparation, incubation, illumination and verification. In this process, 'learning as accumulation of information' and 'learning as acquiring insight' come together (Neville 1989). Neither is sufficient without the other. Without preparatory collection of information, there can be no insight; insight then requires to be verified through testing in the world.

If education – formal and informal – is to do more than merely 'hurt us none', it must be shaped to foster creativity.

EDUCATION AND MY UNDERSTANDING OF THE COUNSELLING PROCESS

General reflections

From teaching to counselling

It was becoming increasingly clear to me, working in the formal educational system, that opportunities for encouraging creativity on the part of pupils or myself were very limited. As my views of the educational process and of the formal education system changed, I came to feel alienated from the role of a physics teacher. Only with pupils in the early years of secondary school, or with those pupils who were considered 'non-academic', could teaching move away from the passing on of a body of knowledge to a more open, creative negotiation of what science meant to the pupils concerned. In teaching older and 'more able' pupils, the examination syllabus rapidly took over.

Through participating in experiential group workshops, where I was able to gain a measure of self-knowledge and self-acceptance and to try out new ways of interacting with others, my style of communicating with colleagues and pupils changed. I became less able to identify myself with the group of teachers and, through meeting people involved in the world of counselling and personal relations, I was led to consider whether I had some of the qualities and personal attitudes to fit into that world. It seemed to me to be a world with more scope for a creative approach to learning.

For a time, nevertheless, I continued to believe that I could be of use to more people in education since that affects everyone, whereas few people are affected by counselling. Eventually, I decided to leave schools, for ever I believed, and enrolled in the postgraduate diploma course in counselling in educational settings at the University of Aston. Thus began a new stage in my personal education in which I gained experience, developed skills and reflected on the meaning of counselling.

A learning process

Counselling can be understood as part of the whole educational process that goes on throughout a person's life. It is not part of, nor does it have much similarity to, formal education. Nevertheless, there is a formal aspect to counselling which distinguishes it from other informal learning. As the British Association for Counselling definition makes clear, to be called 'counselling', the activity is marked by one person (client) formally coming to another (counsellor) for help.

Counselling is a learning process; that is, one of exploring, clarifying and re-creating personal meaning. In this process, client and counsellor both learn from the interaction between them but the learning is led by the client's need and motivation and is at the client's service. It is useful to consider how learning through counselling fits into the contrasting modes of 'experiential learning' and 'learning from the elders' (passing on a body of knowledge) referred to earlier. I would argue that all counselling approaches include both modes, albeit in widely varying proportions and differing styles of expression.

For example, some approaches to counselling follow a fairly strong didactic line in which, at least early on, the counsellor sets out to teach the client the framework or language that structures the therapeutic work. Such approaches include Transactional Analysis, Rational Emotive Therapy, Gestalt and cognitive-behavioural counselling. There is a sense of 'the elder' instructing the client in a specific method of viewing the world, thus enabling the client to adopt a different and more constructive set of perceptions. Counsellors may also teach clients interpersonal and communication skills, such as assertiveness techniques, social skills, study skills, methods of stress management and so on. The pedagogical methods adopted by the counsellors will reflect their beliefs and theories about the nature of learning and knowledge acquisition.

My own practice reflects the beliefs and theories underlying the person-centred approach; thus I view the learning process in counselling as primarily experiential. In this approach, the theoretical framework is implicit rather than explicit, although it can be explained if the client wishes.

Feedback assists learning

In order to learn effectively and meaningfully, a person needs to be fully involved in the process, emotionally as well as intellectually. Thus, learning can be seen as having two facets: '(1) confronting some new experience and (2) discovering what it means to the self' (Combs 1989). Carl Rogers gives a simple but clear example of how driving over a favourite shrub caused him to learn (painfully), 'Don't turn your wheel until you're out in the street' (Rogers 1974a).

People are least likely to learn when they are bored and unengaged and most likely to learn when they are interested and challenged. Yet challenging situations are threatening for many and support is needed to render the challenge bearable. A sense of 'supportive challenging' (Mearns 1986) can be conveyed in the feedback given to the learner. Giving feedback is a skill that can be learned by teachers and has to be re-learned when moving from teaching to counselling. In the classroom, the feedback has to take into account the 'body of knowledge' and the students' understanding of it, whereas in counselling the feedback is directly personal, immediate and continuous and arises from within the mutual relationship between counsellor and client.

How can this skill be learned? There cannot be a formula for giving feed-back since each situation requires the personal involvement and judgement of the counsellor. Similarly, in the classroom, teaching is a living process, not the technical reproduction of a set of instructions. 'Good teaching is created by good teachers . . . Good teachers are necessarily autonomous in professional judgement. They do not need to be told what to do', wrote Stenhouse (1984). This does not mean, he went on to say, that they arrogantly reject advice, consultancy or support. Stenhouse views teaching as an *art*, by which he means 'an exercise of skill expressive of meaning' which leads to the creation of new meaning for both teacher and learner. The learning process is created by teacher and learners together.

Counselling is also a living process. Good counselling, in effect, is created by good counsellors who reflect on and develop their work, assisted by supervision, consultative support, reading and research. Furthermore, the counselling process is not created by the counsellor alone but by client and counsellor together, and it is led by the client.

Good teachers know that 'reaching toward the truth through education is a matter of situational professional judgement' (Stenhouse 1984). In counselling, seen as an unfolding of personal learning ('in the context of the search for truth'), my responsibility is to use my 'professional judgement' intuitively, yet as consciously as possible in each situation. When I am with a client, the situation is unique; all my prior learning and reflecting may inform but cannot determine what I should do.

A relationship between counselling and education

Carl Rogers and a number of his associates working in education have shown that the characteristics of the kind of relationship within which therapeutic change occurs are similar to those marking the kind of relation-ship that facilitates learning (Aspy 1969; Tausch and Tausch 1980; Rogers 1983). That is, students learn more effectively when they experience a relationship to the teacher that is open, honest and trusting. This kind of relationship is likely to be built up when the teacher can show enduring warmth and respect (unconditional positive regard) for the students, acts genuinely and authentically as a person (is congruent) in the relationship and listens to the students to understand their perception of the situation (shows empathic understanding). (For definitions of the facilitative condi-tions, see Mearns and Thorne, 1988.)

Over three years, Aspy and Roebuck conducted a major longitudinal study and many smaller supporting studies across the USA, all of which pointed to the conclusion that 'a teacher who provides high levels of facili-tative conditions (empathy, congruence, positive regard) tends to enhance students' positive growth, but a teacher who provides low levels of these conditions *may retard students' learning*' (Aspy and Roebuck 1974; emphasis added). Thus, the study also supported the contention that young persons are intrinsically inclined to learn, but this capacity can be damaged when teachers do not respect or value their students, make no attempt to listen empathically to them and act dishonestly or hide behind an authoritarian façade.

What did these 'facilitative conditions' mean to me as a teacher? Positive regard, especially when free of conditions, stands in stark contrast to the judgementalism experienced by many in the school setting. Praise, approval, scorn, denigration, the awarding of good and bad marks are the antithesis of valuing the person and, as Aspy and Roebuck's work shows, militate against learning. It is not possible to function effectively as a teacher, a facilitator of learning, just as it would not be possible to continue to function as a counsellor, without the belief that human beings are basically a decent part of creation.

The validity of empathy is shown in the powerful effect of actually listening to students. When teachers listen to their students and try to understand their existing ideas and perceptions, the students are helped to clarify their own thinking. At those times when the students' learning is blocked or inhibited by affective constraints such as worry, anxiety or sadness, the teacher's understanding and acceptance of these feelings often clears the way for learning to proceed. Students feel valued for themselves as well as for their learning abilities.

Many teachers find it very difficult to be genuine and congruent in relating to students. Such an attitude is opposed by much teacher training which emphasizes the role or persona of the teacher. Role 'refers to prescriptions about the behaviour of a person occupying a given position' (Hargreaves 1972) and, as Aspy and Roebuck have shown, when teachers behave according to these prescriptions rather than according to their own experience in relation to the learners, then their students' learning is disadvantaged.

The concept and practice of congruence marks out the significance of power differentials in human relationships. Where one person is in a position of greater power than another, it may be very dangerous to be open about personal feelings. As O'Hara (1989) points out, 'There are situations in which silence may be the only power oppressed people have'. This is seen very clearly in the school situation; pupils being questioned often know that they will be trapped whatever they say. Clients, who may have experienced such situations in the past, are often very sensitive to feeling that they are giving away their sole power by confiding their true selves to a counsellor. The teacher's, and the counsellor's, consistent authenticity and congruent responding is perhaps the only way that she can be perceived as vulnerable also, and thus, perhaps, trustworthy.

Differences between counselling and formal education

The person-centred approach has had some influence on educational practice and research in Britain and abroad (Rogers 1983; Mearns and McLeod
1984; Merry 1988), but it has significantly failed to bring about a revolution. This is not only due to a misunderstanding of the nature of student-
centred education and the intransigent attitude of established educational
institutions, although this undoubtedly exists (Woods 1983: 32), but also
because the context and settings in which counselling and formal education
take place are different.

Parallels have been drawn between the ideas of Paolo Friere, the Brazilian
educator, and those of Carl Rogers: 'Both men share a conviction that
what characterises the fully human life is *consciousness* and that the exclu-
sive human activity is the *search for knowledge*' (O'Hara 1989; original
emphasis). To liberate educational systems, the focus must be on the
inequality between dominated and dominant groups, whereas to liberate
the person through counselling, the focus is on the disparity between
individual organismic functioning and group (family, cultural) conditioned
functioning.

Even in the most liberal and progressive approach to education, there
is some kind of learning agenda or syllabus that exists outside the learner.
There is a body of knowledge which, although it may not be transmitted
as such from teachers to students, is at least subject to negotiation between
them. The experiments to give 'responsible freedom in the classroom'
reported by Rogers (1983) all involved negotiation on the basis of at least
a minimal external requirement: 'to learn French' or 'to pursue the study
of ecosystem management' with resource materials provided in the study
environment. The Alternative School (see p. 135) was based on the principles of student-centred education but failed to the extent that the resources
of the students themselves were not sufficiently backed up by material or
structural resources in the surroundings.

Experiential learning, as in counselling, follows no external syllabus and
the learning is paced at the rate set by the client as learner. The end-point
and the route towards it are determined by the learner. It has been stated
as the 'fundamental hypothesis' of the person-centred approach that whatever resources are needed for self-understanding and for bringing about
constructive change can be found within the person (Rogers 1980). It
requires a great deal of trust on the part of the counsellor to believe that
the client knows, somehow, where she is heading, even if she herself is
unaware of the destination. In other words, 'the client is the master; when
the client knows what the master knows, the client is healed' (Sims 1989).

It is both a great relief and a challenge for an ex-teacher turned counsellor
not to feel responsible for the client's learning. The relief is obvious after
years of being judged as a teacher by 'results' such as students' examination

passes. The challenge is to drop years of habit, to discard the old feeling that if I do not do something to direct the learning process, nothing will be achieved.

Heuristic process – counselling as personal research

I find it useful to look on counselling as a process of personal research, in which both the chief researcher and the subject of the research is the client. I sometimes use this metaphor to describe my concept of counselling to clients, especially since I work in a university where the idea of research is familiar. I see myself, as counsellor, in the position of research assistant to the client. This notion has been developed by O'Hara (1986), who states 'the dialogical process of client-centered therapy is viewed as a joint study of the nature and meaning of human experience as seen from the client's point of view'. This indicates the open-endedness of the process and that the direction resides with the client. As research assistant, a counsellor's main role is as co-investigator with a special responsibility for tending the working relationship.

The type of research to be undertaken contrasts with much of the research done in universities. Hutterer (1990) describes the concept and nature of an 'authentic science' in which 'science becomes a search for personal and meaningful insights'. Investigators acknowledge their subjective involvement in the research, which is still 'objective, in the sense of making contact with a hidden reality' (Polanyi, cited in Hutterer 1990). An essential condition is that the enquirers are open to receive the results from the investigation; they cannot be attached to an already formed view of truth. It follows that the process of enquiry is valued for its own sake, although it may be difficult and painful at times:

> The confidence of the client-centered therapist is in the process by which truth is discovered, achieved and approximated. It is not a confidence in truth already known or formulated.
>
> (Rogers 1974b)

This confidence need not belong to client-centred counsellors alone. As Hutterer points out, a commitment to authentic research does not prescribe a particular research methodology. This choice is based on personal values, as should be the choice of therapeutic methodology for both of the co-researchers – client and counsellor. Hutterer puts forward four requirements for authentic research which can equally be applied to the therapeutic undertaking. These are intrinsic motivation, personal involvement, attention to personal and subjective experiences and commitment to the person's individuality. I suggest that these criteria hold good for the client researcher as well as the research assistant counsellor.

The field of research might start out by being quite clearly defined, as when a student wants to find a more constructive way of approaching academic work. At other times, the enquiry is wide open, as in the case of a client who feels something lacking in his life but cannot pinpoint what it might be. The element of unexpected discovery is liable to emerge in any counselling process, however cut and dried it may appear at the outset. Over and again, I am surprised by the direction in which the client's enquiry leads. Just when I think I can foresee the next step, the client, without prior indication, starts to follow another track or, without warning, gets lost.

Creative process

Unexpected turns are typical of the creative process. The amount of work that clients can do between sessions is familiar to most counsellors. Not infrequently, a client uses a casual remark or an apparently minor incident as the basis for a breakthrough in self-understanding. This may be understood as evidence of the client's creation or re-creation of personal meaning.

I have already described the creative process as having four phases: preparation, incubation, illumination and verification. In counselling, much of what goes on in the sessions – exploring the client's experience, identifying feelings and clarifying understanding – constitutes the preparation stage. This can go on for some time. Between sessions is the incubation time, after which a fresh perception or a new meaning may illuminate the client's awareness. Verification of the insight received comes through the counsellor's feedback in subsequent sessions and through observable changes in the client's attitude and behaviour.

Teaching as part of the counselling process

Although I understand counselling as a client-centred and client-led process in which the relationship between counsellor and client facilitates the client's experiential learning, I recognize that I do, from time to time, take the part of an 'elder' in passing on acquired knowledge. Much of this 'teaching' arises from the expression in the relationship of my underlying beliefs and values. From my understanding of counselling as a process of exploration of personal meaning, I respond most consistently to those aspects of the client's communication that deal with inner experiencing and its associated meaning. This may have the effect of teaching clients to turn inward and to become aware of their organismic felt sense. The way I respond to clients may also influence their style of thinking. My belief is that the most constructive counselling relationship is a cooperative effort between client and counsellor. Thus, I am inclined to promote an open system of thinking, focusing on such matters as personal responsibility, internal motivation and egalitarian philosophy (Combs 1989). Those clients whose thinking is similar, or who can learn to adopt such a thinking style, are most likely to benefit from my style of counselling.

Conversely, those whose thinking style is different might well be helped by a different therapeutic orientation. For example, the aims of a rational-emotive approach in counselling have been stated to include 'to train clients to identify and change their distorted inferences and irrational beliefs' and 'to teach clients that such change is best effected by the persistent application of cognitive, imagery, emotive and behavioural methods' (Dryden 1984). Here the educational objectives are explicitly outlined in terms of the 'training' and 'teaching' of clients by the counsellor.

In my own practice, direct teaching or training of clients is rare and always in response to clients' own perceived needs. I use language – frequently employing modal auxiliary markers, such as 'might', 'could' and so on, to indicate uncertainty and probability – as an invitation to clients to consider if what I am saying fits their experience, not to give a diagnosis or interpretation. Nevertheless, I may, by this means, teach clients to be less rigid in their own thinking and, by paying close attention to clients' language structures and choice of words, encourage them to explore the personal meaning of their language for themselves.

Jerome Bruner, the developmental psychologist, writes: 'I do not for a minute believe that one can teach even mathematics or physics without transmitting a sense of stance toward nature and toward the use of mind' (Bruner 1986: 128). Similarly, I do not believe that I can engage in another's learning process as facilitator, research assistant or consultant without language and the way I use it transmitting a sense of my underlying belief system and values.

Further learning for myself

Having gained my Diploma in Counselling, I did not immediately start to work as a counsellor. An innovative project in student-centred education had recently started in a new Scottish secondary school and I joined the teaching team.

It was a challenge to attempt to facilitate learning rather than to teach a subject discipline. Using what are regarded as counselling skills in communicating with the students and drawing on my capacity for empathic understanding of the students' worlds and my respect for them as learners and persons, the project provided an intermediate stage in my transition from teaching to counselling. In striving to be genuine and honest with our students, sharing our not-knowing and allowing negotiation on curriculum and learning methods, yet acknowledging that disparities in power and responsibility between us and the students still remained, I often felt vulnerable and tested. Compensating for this were the sense of increased freedom for all in the classroom and the willingness of the students to trust us and to become engaged with the process to their own and others' benefit.

Shortly after joining the Alternative School, I enrolled for a Master's degree in Education. This gave an opportunity not only to develop my ideas on education but also to observe myself as a student. I discovered that I did better in examinations than in written course work, enjoying the stimulation and challenge of the former while finding the discipline and attention to detail of the latter irksome. Experiences such as meeting essay deadlines, sitting in the hall waiting for the examination to begin, the frustration of not being able to find the right section in the library but being too proud to ask have all added to that fund of life experience that underlies the ability to communicate and empathize with others.

For my degree dissertation I undertook a research study, investigating perceptions of the Alternative School held by other (mainstream) teachers in the same school. This was an interview study, conducted along the lines of 'new paradigm' research in the social sciences (see Mearns and McLeod 1984). The interviewer uses similar approaches to those in counselling (e.g. empathic listening, acceptance, having no fixed agenda). Thus, in this case, when the teachers were enabled to explore their own perceptions and the associated personal meanings of the Alternative School, it was not unusual to find that these perceptions shifted or were less rigidly held between the beginning and the end of the interview. In this, the process of educational enquiry overlaps with that of counselling.

The Alternative School project ended, I completed my dissertation and left school at last, to take up my present work in the counselling service of a university.

Counselling in an educational institution

Counselling in an educational institution brings together the two aspects of education, as an experience of life-long, personal learning involving the whole person and as formal, externally structured and evaluated learning in a setting which places great emphasis on intellectual achievement. It is to be expected, therefore, that when students come to the Counselling Service, there is often some tension between themselves and the formal system of higher education. In some cases, the emphasis remains on dealing with the demands of higher education (approaches to studying, organizing work, preparing for examinations and so on). In others, the emphasis moves to the person's self and relationship with others and the world (for example, exploring self-concept, searching for direction in life, coming to terms with past trauma).

Case studies

Two illustrations

Peter was referred to the Counselling Service by a tutor after doing badly in a term exam. This was contrary to expectation on the basis of classwork marks and had shocked Peter quite considerably. He saw himself as a 'serious', conscientious student and wanted to be recognized as such by his academic department. It seemed that Peter had worked hard to acquire a body of knowledge about social anthropology, by reading, memorizing and reproducing facts and opinions in required essays, yet he had not created personal meaning from the material in a way that made the knowledge his own.

Emotionally, he felt confused and distressed by his situation. He felt bitter that other students, whom he did not regard as 'serious', since they appeared not to do much work, were scoring higher marks in exams than he was. His feelings had to be heard, accepted and understood in order for Peter to be able to give attention to the cognitive aspects of the problem. It was important also for myself and Peter both to acknowledge that he was, indeed, a serious student, but that in itself was not sufficient to achieve an integrated learning.

Exploration of the personal meaning to Peter of his difficult situation was followed by considering the different ways that he might become involved in his own learning. This meant that Peter was learning something about how he learns. He accepted my suggestion that as well as understanding and memorizing the material, he could also allow his mind to roam around the subject matter, 'play' with it and create a sense of engagement with it. In the exam situation, he needed to learn some strategies to cope with his anxiety before being able to accept the challenge to respond to the questions on the basis of a personal and creative knowing. That is, to learn that he could engage with the test questions, make decisions on which ones to attempt, allow his mind to access information and to be aware of his stance on the issue, rather than to force the answers. In fact, in a sense, Peter could learn to become a less *serious* student without becoming a less effective one.

Kate's learning process was even more personal and complex. When she first came to the Counselling Service, she was worried about her ability to cope with her final examinations (at that time over a year and a half in the future) and wanted to find out if counselling could be a source of support for her. I discussed with her the kind of support that I could give: help to structure course work and examination preparation in a way that felt right for her, exploring her anxiety and what it might mean for her, working together to understand and find ways of coping with the intellec-tual and emotional demands of preparing for and undergoing a major evaluation process. Throughout this brief meeting, Kate was very tense and kept a fixed smile on her face. She almost seemed to be going through the motions of consulting a counsellor. I found it hard to form a sense of her as a person but suspected that Kate's sense of self-worth depended very much on her academic achievement.

I did not see Kate again until the start of the next term, three months later. This time she was in a very tense and edgy state, still smiling fixedly and giving the impression of being so brittle that she might break up into little pieces. She recounted that during the vacation she had taken part in a business training exercise which had involved working in groups. She had felt so bad in the group, completely alienated from the other participants and from her own feelings, that she had thought she might go mad. Her anguish had brought her back to counselling. This illustrates how the stark awareness of the desperation of one's situation can be a great spur to seeking help in learning how to change it.

Kate had learned to view herself as someone quite worthless, except in outward achievement and service to others, neither of which, however, gave her any sense of lasting fulfilment. Since coming to university, she had felt increasingly separate from fellow students and detached from her own experience and now described herself as completely incapable of having a real relationship with any other person. She described herself as 'everybody's servant', feeling compelled to be 'nice' to everyone all the time. Despite her outward appearance as a successful student, she expected her whole life to come crashing down at any time. In her own words:

> My life on the surface seemed great. Sometimes I wonder how on earth I could have done well academically, done so many uni activities, had a good social life, put on a great cover-up and battled through with my own self-hatred for so long.

Kate's perception was that the source of her difficulties lay in her traumatic childhood and schooldays, yet nobody took her seriously when she mentioned this. After all she had been to a highly regarded private school, her parents (whom she loved) were anxious to do all they could for the family and were liked and respected in the community. In other words, Kate's perceptual field was discounted by others and so remained closed to the possibility of exploration and change. Kate could hardly believe it when I listened closely and accepted what she was saying. She felt an enormous relief to have found a person who did not try to talk her out of her own experience of her childhood. My acceptance, as counsellor, of her perception relieved her emotional intensity enough to facilitate Kate's new learning process.

She embarked on a project of researching her childhood, my role being largely that of research assistant. At an early stage, I mentioned the work of Alice Miller. Kate found Miller's books in the town library and read them eagerly. They gave her a basis for beginning to understand why her growing up had been so difficult for her. She used the 'received' knowledge, passed on from the writings of an experienced therapist, to augment her own understanding, which, along with the growth of a trusting relationship in counselling, provided something for Kate to hold on to as she experienced great waves of emotion. Personal learning is in no way an 'objective' process but is accompanied by strong emotional changes. She described how she experienced this time:

> Those moods are so painful, you basically feel all the pain you've been denying yourself all through your life. Now, they aren't quite as heavy and dominating as they used to be and my outrage is beginning to be replaced by a deep, deep sorrow and sadness.

In her research, Kate used her own diaries from the period to help her reconstruct the past. Her re-creation of the meaning of that time and her re-evaluation of it continued in her stream-of-consciousness writing, which became an integral part of the counselling process. However, when a person is experiencing strong emotional demands, formal educational activities and learning are likely to be inhibited. Kate had thrown herself so completely into the counselling process that she could not attend to her academic work as well. She began to consider asking her department to allow her a year out before she took her finals. I had some doubts about this at first, but by this time I trusted Kate to know what was best for herself, and we discussed how she would approach the department.

Kate's trust in her own experiencing felt very new and fragile but it had to be tested out in the setting of her family and the outer world. It was difficult; her parents found what Kate was saying hard to hear, but they did not follow Kate's 'worst scenario' fantasy and throw her out.

Kate obtained permission from the university to take a year out and organized working and learning opportunities to fill that time, both abroad and in Britain. She has not abandoned her formal education and returns to the university to take her final examinations and complete her degree. Here she sums up her personal research and comments on her own learning style:

> I feel a lot more broadminded, able to cope on my own and confident about everyday life. My attitudes to life have changed now that they reflect who I really am – this indicates a lot about how detached and separate the external me that other people were exposed to was from the inner me. I hate being told what to do, rather than learn it for myself. Counselling provided the basis for me, taught me about myself, I learnt who I was. Also, I think it's important for me, almost a *gift*, to be able to get an insight into my past and the *truth* that it wasn't my fault! When I gradually found myself getting to know myself, the world really seemed to start to fall off my shoulders. Although life was being really shaken up and I felt so lost in all the pain and confusion it was still exciting because it was the start of me discovering myself and life – myself first, life later.

Conclusions

Educational research and developmental studies have shown that persons are autonomous learners, able to set their own agenda for learning and to follow their own curiosity and desire for knowledge. Even within formal education, knowledge cannot be said to be truly acquired until the person has made it his or her own. Within counselling, learning is an on-going process of discovering personal meaning. Motivation arises from the person's needs and desires, but the progress of the learning is greatly influenced by the kind of relationship between the persons of client and counsellor.

When I am in the position of counsellor, my responsibility is to look after this relationship, or working alliance; clients are responsible for their own learning and for the use they make of it. Persons do not need to be pushed into learning or to have their learning directed from outside. When they feel free from external threat or evaluation, their learning will proceed at their own pace in their preferred direction.

Education has the potential to change people. Personal learning may well bring about irreversible changes in the person's perceptual field. As Polanyi has said, 'Having made a discovery, I shall never see the world again as before . . . I have made myself into a person seeing and thinking differently' (cited in Hutterer, 1990). The discoveries made through counselling, when persons feel safe enough to accept and absorb them, make them into persons who experience themselves differently.

In counselling, I am committed to the process by which truth may be discovered and to the relationship of trust that enables that process to take place. There are many people who have been hurt through their 'life of education', both in the formal education system and in the education dealt out by life experiences. Such hurts can force people to deny their own feelings and beliefs. By understanding people as capable of learning throughout life and of having within themselves the resources and direction for exploring personal meaning, counselling as the most personal educational experience can help people retrieve and confirm their particular truth. Then, indeed, we can allow ourselves to 'read the writing on the wall', however much it has been overlaid by layers of scribbles.

For myself, I am grateful, now, to believe that my education, formal and personal, has hurt me less than it has helped me in my own search for truth and that it has fostered my capacity to think and to reflect on my counselling practice. For without reflection, based on the foundation of a coherent system of belief and values, there cannot come about that transformation of personal experience which leads to the creation of meaning.

REFERENCES

Aspy, D. N. (1969) The effect of teacher-offered conditions of empathy, positive regard and congruence upon student achievement. *Florida Journal of Educational Research*, 11, 39–48.

Aspy, D. N. and Roebuck, F. N. (1974) From humane ideas to humane technology and back again many times. *Education*, 95 (2): 163–71.

Aspy, D. N. and Roebuck, F. N. (1977) *Kids Don't Learn from People They Don't Like*. Amherst, MA, Human Resources Development Press.

Bruner, J. (1986) *Actual Minds, Possible Worlds*. Cambridge, MA, Harvard University Press.

Combs, A. W. (1989) *A Theory of Therapy*. London, Sage Publications.

Dryden, W. (1984) Rational-emotive therapy. In W. Dryden (ed.), *Individual Therapy in Britain*. London, Harper and Row.

Hargreaves, D. H. (1972) *Interpersonal Relations and Education*. London, Routledge and Kegan Paul.

Hutterer, R. (1990) Authentic science: Some implications of Carl Rogers's reflections on science. *Person-Centered Review*, 5 (1): 57–76.

Mearns, D. (1986) *Inveralmond Alternative School*. Glasgow, Jordanhill College.

Mearns, D. and McLeod, J. (1984) A person-centered approach to research. In R. Levant and J. Shlien (eds), *Client-Centered Therapy and the Person-Centered Approach*. New York, Praeger.

Mearns, D. and Thorne, B. (1988) *Person-Centred Counselling in Action*. London, Sage Publications.

Merry, T. (1988) *A Guide to the Person-centred Approach*. London, Association for Humanistic Psychology.

Neville, B. (1989) *Educating Psyche*. Melbourne, Collins Dove.

Oatley, K. (1980) Theories of personal learning in groups. In P. Smith (ed.), *Small Groups and Personal Change*. London, Methuen.

O'Hara, M. M. (1986) Heuristic inquiry as psychotherapy: The client-centered approach. *Person-Centered Review*, 1 (2): 172–85.

O'Hara, M. M. (1989) Person-centered approach as conscientizacao: The work of Carl Rogers and Paolo Friere. *Journal of Humanistic Psychology*, 29 (1): 11–36.

Rogers, C. R. (1951) *Client-Centered Therapy*. Boston, Houghton Mifflin.

Rogers, C. R. (1974a) Can learning encompass both ideas and feelings? *Education*, 95 (2): 103–14.

Rogers, C. R. (1974b) Remarks on the future of client-centered therapy. In D. A. Wexler and L. N. Rice (eds), *Innovations in Client-centered Therapy*. New York, John Wiley.

Rogers, C. R. (1980) *A Way Of Being*. London, Constable.

Rogers, C. R. (1983) *Freedom To Learn*. Columbus, OH, Charles E. Merrill.

Schaffer, R. (1977) *Mothering*. Glasgow, Collins Fontana.

Simon, P. (1973) 'Kodachrome'. Burbank, CA, Warner Bros Records Inc.

Sims, J. M. (1989) Client-centered therapy: The art of knowing. *Person-Centered Review*, 4 (1): 27–41.

Stenhouse, L. (1984) Artistry in teaching: The teacher as focus of research and development. In D. Hopkins and M. Wideen (eds), *Alternative Perspectives on School Improvement*. London, Falmer Press.

Tausch, R. and Tausch, A. M. (1980) Verifying the facilitative dimensions in German schools, families and with German clients. Unpublished manuscript, Psychologisches Institut III, University of Hamburg.
Thorne, B. (1988) The person-centred approach to large groups. In M. Aveline and W. Dryden (eds), *Group Therapy in Britain*. Milton Keynes, Open University Press.
White, R. and Brockington, D. (1978) *In and Out of School*. London, Routledge and Kegan Paul.
Woods, P. (1983) *Sociology and the School*. London, Routledge and Kegan Paul.
Zuber-Skerritt, O. (1991) *Action Research in Higher Education*. Sheffield, USTD.

9

PHILOSOPHY AND COUNSELLING

Campbell Purton

Working in philosophy – like work in architecture in many respects –
is really more a working on oneself. On one's own interpretation. On
one's way of seeing things.

(Ludwig Wittgenstein 1980: 16)

PHILOSOPHY AND MY ENGAGEMENT WITH IT

Bertrand Russell once said that the aim of the philosopher is 'to see the world
steadily and to see it whole'. I think I felt the need to do something of this
sort from quite early childhood, but my engagement with academic philosophy dates, I suppose, from the time when I studied physics as an
undergraduate. I was always more interested in the philosophical than the
technical aspects of the subject, and after obtaining my degree I undertook
a Master's degree in the history and philosophy of science. By then my main
interest had moved from physics to psychology, and I completed a thesis on
the philosophical problems involved in giving satisfactory explanations of
animal behaviour. I then studied the philosophy of psychology for my doctorate, and for a number of years lectured in philosophy at universities in
Canada and Scotland. During my time in the academic world, I always felt
that philosophy could be relevant to people's lives, rather than being an 'ivory
tower' subject, but there seemed little opportunity to put such thoughts into
practice. This dissatisfaction, together with other circumstances, took me
out of the academic world and led me in the direction of counselling. I completed the FDI (now PCT) course in person-centred counselling and psychotherapy, and since then have worked both in private practice and in a
university counselling setting. Following a period in which I gained much
from the work of Jung (who referred to himself sometimes as 'a philosopher
manqué'), I am finding it increasingly important to relate my counselling
practice to the philosophical interests which were undoubtedly my first love.

It may be best to say at the start that there are several different schools or traditions of philosophy, just as there are different schools or styles of therapy, and that the differences between them can go very deep. Partly for reasons of limited space, and partly because of my own involvement with it, I shall draw here on a style of philosophy which in this century is associated especially with the name of Ludwig Wittgenstein, but which I think has recognizable connections with the thought of earlier Western philosophers such as Kierkegaard and Socrates, and in the East with the approach of Nāgārjuna and Buddhist Mādhyamika philosophy. (For the remarkable parallels between Wittgenstein and the Mādhyamika philosophy, see Gudmunsen (1977). I should say that I have become increasingly impressed by the relevance of Buddhist philosophy to counselling theory, and will make some reference to it in what follows.)

For me, the deep division in philosophy is between those approaches which set out to establish a body of knowledge about the world, and the approaches which probe, question and draw out our confusions. 'Philosophy', Wittgenstein wrote, 'unties the knots in our thinking; hence its result must be simple, but philosophising has to be as complicated as the knots it unties' (1967: Section 452). According to this latter view, there are no philosophical truths to be discovered; rather there is the unravelling of the tangles of thought which constitute philosophical problems. It is impossible in the space available to illustrate this procedure adequately, but the reader who is interested in the difference between 'discovering the truth' and 'untying a knot in our thinking' may wish to reflect on the following illustration, adapted from Wittgenstein (1953: Section 350): When it is five o'clock in London it is half past ten in Delhi. Now what time is it *on the sun* when it is five o'clock in London? Must it not be *some* time on the sun? Perhaps it is for the scientists to discover the truth about this? But on further reflection we can come to see that really there is no answer to this question, and when we see why there can be no answer we no longer see it as a genuine question at all. The problem has not been *solved*, i.e. no answer has been found. Rather the question, on a deeper understanding, *dis*solves and no longer troubles us.

Wittgenstein's view of philosophy is that it is a procedure akin to therapy. He writes 'The philosopher's treatment of a question is like the treatment of an illness' (1953: Section 255). 'There is not *a* philosophical method, though there are indeed methods, like different therapies' (1953: Section 133). 'A philosopher is a man who has to cure many intellectual diseases in himself before he can arrive at the notions of common sense' (1980: 44). Philosophical problems, for Wittgenstein, are disturbances in our thinking. Something has become diseased or tangled, and just as the restoration of health or the untying of a knot does not create anything new, so philosophy 'leaves everything as it is' (1953: Section 124). The pattern in the relief of philosophical puzzlement was beautifully expressed by the eighth-century Buddhist Ch'ing Yuan:

Before I studied Zen for thirty years, I saw mountains as mountains and rivers as rivers. When I arrived at a more intimate knowledge, I come to the point where I saw that mountains are not mountains and rivers are not rivers. But now that I have got its very substance I am at rest. For it's just that I see mountains once again as mountains and rivers as rivers.

Not all, not even a majority, of contemporary philosophers accept this view of what the philosopher is doing. There are philosophical traditions in which the goal of philosophy is to discover the Truth about the ultimate nature of Reality, even if in modern times this quest proceeds under the guise of an 'analysis of our concepts'. The idea of coming to know what the Ultimate Nature of Things is has a great appeal, a great 'charm' as Wittgenstein put it. Like most philosophers I have felt, and can still feel, the pull of this approach, but I have come increasingly to think that it is to be resisted. What has drawn me in the Wittgensteinian direction is not any general argument, but rather the experience of seeing how at least some philosophical problems really do dissolve under a sustained Wittgensteinian approach.

Perhaps more than anything it was my experience of the application of the Wittgensteinian approach to what philosophers call the 'other minds' problem which convinced me of the value of the approach. I shall say a little more about the other minds problem later, as it has a bearing on issues surrounding the theme of 'human nature', but very briefly it amounts to the following. It can seem that only *I* can know what I now experience. I can hypothesize, guess, even be quite certain that you now experience pain, say, yet I could always be wrong, since I have direct access only to my own experiences. In your case, I have to deduce what you feel from observing your *behaviour*, and it could always turn out that I have made a mistake. In the same way, it seems that I can never really know whether another person's visual experiences are the same as mine. When I look at the sky on a clear day, how do I know that the colour sensation which I have is the same as that which you have? How do I know that they are even remotely similar? We all *call* the colour of the sky 'blue', but isn't it possible that our experiences are systematically different, so that for instance your experience of the sky is what I would call 'red', and vice versa? Might we not, for all we know, inhabit quite separate experiential realities?

In my experience of teaching introductory philosophy classes, I find that some students quickly appreciate the force of this line of thinking, and may well have discovered it for themselves. Others find it more difficult to see the point, but once they have understood, the effect is unsettling, and occasionally even frightening. For the direction in which the line of thought leads is towards a sense of isolation. You can't ever know what I am feeling, and I can't know what you are feeling. Nor, it seems, is there any way in which I can reasonably assess how likely it is that your experiences are similar to mine. I can't get inside your mind to *check* that by and large when you behave in such-and-such a way you have the experiences which I have when I behave in that way. When taken seriously enough, this thought can be quite deeply disturbing. It can become not just an intellectual exercise but an existential experience of loneliness and disconnection from people, so that in speaking of the work of the philosopher as a form of therapy Wittgenstein is not presenting a mere analogy.

The background to the 'problem of other minds' is complex, and involves issues which go back to the picture of the world which we inherit from the seventeenth century and the impact of modern science on Western thought. Descartes crystallized the most important themes in his division of a human being into a 'mind' and a 'body', and I will say something about this picture of the person in the next section. I will be reflecting for the most part within the framework of Western thought, but here and there I will draw attention to aspects of Buddhist philosophy which I have found illuminating.

PHILOSOPHY AND MY UNDERSTANDING OF PERSONS

In this section, I hope to provide some further illustrations of what is involved in philosophical reflection, and at the same time begin to focus attention on two themes which I believe are especially relevant for an understanding of the nature of counselling. One theme is that of 'the nature of persons', and the other, closely linked, is that of our *perception* of people. These are both very large topics, and I can only hint at the complexity of the philosophical issues involved. However, I hope to be able to say enough to give some indication of what it is in philosophy which provides me with a framework for my counselling practice.

Persons

I will focus first on a view of human beings which has dominated much of Western thought since the seventeenth century, and which found its classical expression in the work of Descartes. Crudely, but I hope not too misleadingly summarized, it goes like this. A human being is a composite entity made up of a physical body and a non-material mind. Clouds, stones and so on have the physical bit, but not the mental bit. Angels, if there are such, have the mental bit but not the physical bit.

Human life involves both action and perception. In Descartes' view, when a person acts something like the following occurs: a mental event takes place such as the formulation of the intention to raise one's arm. This mental event causes (we don't know how) certain changes to occur in the brain which themselves cause changes in the nerves, which stimulate the arm muscles in such a way that the arm rises. Similarly, when a person perceives a tree, a chain of events takes place in the opposite direction. Light is reflected from the tree into the eye, causing chemical changes on the retina which produce a pattern of impulses in the optic nerve. These produce certain changes in the brain which cause (we don't know how) an image of the tree to appear in the person's mind.

Something like this picture of human beings has filtered through into our 'common sense' ideas, but philosophical reflection on the picture since the time of Descartes has revealed more of what the implications of the picture are. What Descartes is depicting is the human person as a mind which is directly aware only of its own states. Knowledge of the externally existing table is an inference from my mental image of a table; I am not directly aware of the table, but of the image which has arisen at the end of a long causal chain of events. So far as my knowledge of other people is concerned, it can at best be an unverifiable hypothesis that associated with the external objects I believe cause my images of their bodies, there are states of consciousness, i.e. minds, other than my own. But I cannot know that there are such other minds; *other* minds are outside my experience. Thus Descartes detaches us from the *world*, and condemns us to living within a bubble constituted by our subjective experiences. Here we have again the 'other minds' problem to which I drew attention above.

It is important to see that what I have described is not just the concern of philosophers. Descartes' picture of human beings lies behind much twentieth-century psychology. Behaviourism, for example, arises from the view that we can't observe other people's subjective experiences, so that if there is to be a science of psychology it must either limit itself to the study of physical behaviour, or define mental concepts in terms of behaviour patterns. (More recent moves in this game involve trying to define the mind in terms of states of the nervous system, or in computer terms as the 'software' to which the brain stands as 'hardware'.)

One of the most important developments in twentieth-century philosophy, I believe, has been Wittgenstein's unravelling of the tangled Cartesian knot. Here I can only give a glimpse of what I take to be involved in this process. The simplest approach is perhaps to look at how we can conceive of a young child's early experience. The traditional view, based on Descartes' picture, is that the child begins life with a bare awareness of sensations, the experience, as William James put it, of a 'blooming, buzzing confusion'. As time goes on, the child (like a little scientist) notices regularities in his patterns of sensation, and gradually builds up concepts of enduring physical objects. Then he notices that his own body is rather similar to other bodies which he frequently encounters. Since these other bodies behave in ways rather similar to the way in which he behaves, he infers that they are like him *also* in the respect of having thoughts and feelings. Thus the child arrives at the idea that there are other people in the world.[1]

What the Wittgensteinian approach shows, in effect, is that this story – this picture – really makes no sense (it is a muddle, like 'the time now on the sun'). The baby can't acquire the concept of red, for example, by noticing that this flower and that mug and that pen are *all the same colour*. It doesn't yet know what *counts* as being of the same colour. One could (and different cultures do) classify coloured things in a variety of ways. Where, in contrast to orange and purple, do the limits of 'red' come? Is it all right to lump together crimson and scarlet in the 'red' category? These are matters which are settled by the *community* into which the child is born. In its early months and years, the child is drawn into ways of doing things, ways of classifying things, ways of seeing things that are normal for that community. It makes no sense to suppose that a child could acquire a view of the world all by itself. This is because acquiring a view of things is a matter of acquiring standards of judgement. The child has learned what red things are when it can *correctly* put all the red counters in the box, select all the red books from the shelf, and so on. Learning a concept (here the concept of red) is a matter of coming to be able to *get it right*. This often goes along with learning the correct word, though not always – deaf and dumb children can pick up the concepts involved in, say, setting up the signals for an electric train set without learning any words. What is essential is not verbal language, but the picking up of interpersonal ways of doing things, ways that are open to the correction of others. Very soon, of course, the child is able to assume the role of corrector: 'Not David naughty, *mummy* naughty'.

In short, we must reject the view that human life begins with a baby's subjective awareness, out of which it constructs an external world of material objects and other people. It is, rather, the other way round: the baby starts as a nexus in a network of personal relationships. There is, as it were, a place for the baby in the interpersonal network even before it is born. Without the presence and care of others, the baby will not survive physically, and even if its physical needs were somehow supplied by machines, it could not, without personal interaction, develop as a person. To develop as a person *is* to be drawn into a shared life with others, into ways of taking things which are characteristic of the community. Once this shared life is established, the child can begin to raise doubts and objections. Having learned 'That's red' it can now begin to learn 'That looks red to me, though perhaps it isn't red really' and progress to the philosopher's 'I am having a subjective sensation of redness'. But one can't do it the other way round. One can't begin with objections, or with how things *seem* to be, or with subjective experience. The interpersonal comes first, and only within it can develop those aspects of human life that we call 'subjective' and 'individual'.

The view of human nature which emerges from these considerations is that people exist as people only in relation to others. (This is one way of expressing the Buddhist doctrine of *anatman*, i.e. the view that there can be no self-existent soul.) Thus solipsism, the doctrine that only I exist, is necessarily false; there logically could not have been a world in which there was only one person, a world without personal relationships. Of course, everyone else might die, so that only one person was left. But that would not be a world without personal relationships. This hypothetical, solitary last person views the world with the eyes of those who have died, thinks in terms of concepts common to that community within which he grew up. He sees that the bird above the crag is an eagle, not a kestrel; but the difference between eagle and kestrel is not *his* distinction, and that the lake below is turquoise rather than blue is not a purely private matter. *Nothing*, we might say, is a purely private matter.

The view of human nature which I have sketched has important implications for our view of what is involved in *seeing* things and people. I shall focus the rest of my discussion very much around the notion of 'seeing', because I think this notion is of especial importance in understanding the nature of counselling. [The reader who is interested in other aspects of the relationship between philosophy and counselling may find it helpful to start with such philosophers as Ilham Dilman (1983, 1984, 1988) on Freud, Alasdair MacIntyre (1958) on the notion of the unconscious mind, and Richard Lindley (Holmes and Lindley 1989) on the ethics of psychotherapy. For a different approach to the thesis that people exist only in relation to others, see Macmurray (1959, 1961).]

Seeing persons

> We find certain things about seeing puzzling, because we do not find the whole business of seeing puzzling enough.
> (Ludwig Wittgenstein 1953: Section 212)

'Seeing' seems at first sight a very simple notion. In the case of physical objects, we just open our eyes and the objects enter our awareness. Yet on reflection this is absurd: *a physical object* like a corkscrew can't literally *come into my mind*. Isn't it rather that the corkscrew produces physical effects that result in an *image* of it coming into my mind? A mental image is just the sort of thing that can enter a mind, but here we are back with Descartes' picture of perception, and its disastrous consequences.

We have to get away from this picture of 'seeing' being a matter of opening our eyes and letting the images of things come in. On reflection we know it is not like that. Someone who hasn't learned to read doesn't see words in a newspaper when the newspaper is before his eyes. Congenitally blind people who through an operation have been given their sight for the first time don't see apples when apples are before their eyes. We have to *learn* to see, we have to be taught, we have to be put in the way of taking things, visually, as those around us take them. Coming to see something for what it is a complex interpersonal affair. Even with aspects of our experience as seemingly straightforward as colours we may need to negotiate with others what the truth of what we see is. For instance, we are choosing some new curtains. They are to be blue. We see some excellent specimens in the shop, and I suggest that we take them. You reply that they are not blue. They look blue to me. Now I know very well that seeing something blue isn't just a matter of having it in front of my eyes and experiencing a sensation. It may depend on the light. So we take the curtains over to the window and inspect them again. This time we may agree that they are blue (or, say, turquoise). On the other hand, we may still not agree, and now a more complex round of negotiation is called for. Perhaps we go through colour charts together, and negotiate where the boundary between blue and turquoise comes. Then back to the store. 'But you agreed that this sample is turquoise!' 'Yes, but colours on small shiny bits of paper look different from when they are the colours of big pieces of material', and so on.

Seeing what colour a thing is doesn't *normally* raise such issues, but it is important to see that it *can* do so, since this helps us to appreciate that the concept of seeing is not a simple one. And if this is so as far as seeing colours is concerned, it is much more clearly so in seeing *people*. I see Fred as being a rude, uncouth person. Then I get to know him better, I hear other people speak of him in quite other terms, I am persuaded that it could be worthwhile to think of him more as a 'rough diamond' than 'uncouth'. Next time he does something untoward I try to see it in this light. I think – yes, you *could* see him that way. I talk over with someone why, in spite of this possibility, I still can't help seeing him as rude. We talk, and things come up about how rudeness has been a painful issue in my life. It's something that is hard for me to see straight. This conversation shifts my feelings a bit. I do begin to see Fred differently. He just says what he thinks. He is straight with people, although he can upset them. I gradually cease to see him as rude. [For a more extended discussion of a similar example, see Iris Murdoch's essay 'The idea of perfection' (1970, pp. 17ff.). It was this essay which first made me realize the significance of 'seeing' for an understanding of the counselling process.]

Seeing, one might say, is an achievement rather than a passive state or the mere having of sensations. Seeing isn't a matter of 'having certain experiences', nor is it a matter of *doing* anything (compare other 'achievement verbs' such as 'winning'), but through doing certain sorts of things one can help to bring it about that one sees. The things which facilitate seeing are very various and depend on what it is we are trying to see. It is often largely a matter of overcoming sources of distortion, or removing of obstacles to clear sight. We need, for example, to take the curtains to the window, because artificial light distorts the appearance of colours.

In the case of seeing people the sources of distortion often lie in wanting to fit a person quickly into a familiar pattern (stereotyping), in our wanting people to be other than they are, in our perceptions being distorted by irrelevant past experiences, or present fears or hopes and so on. For instance, in the early chapters of *Middlemarch*, Dorothea does not really *see* Mr Casaubon. Her need for intellectual and spiritual companionship makes it almost impossible for her to see him as he is. (Still less is Casaubon able to see Dorothea.) In the course of the novel, it is life and experience which bring Dorothea to a clearer view of her husband. There is then disillusionment, which distorts her view in a different way, but shortly before his death we sense that Dorothea is beginning to see him more truly.

PHILOSOPHY AND MY UNDERSTANDING OF THE COUNSELLING PROCESS

General reflections

Two main points which I would like to draw out of the previous section are, first, that people only exist as people within a network of personal relationships and, secondly, that interpersonal perception is inherently liable to distortion. These points are connected, in that seeing things clearly, or at all, involves the perceiver in an interpersonal network which sets the standards of what counts as genuine seeing. All *real* seeing, we might say, is seeing *together*. Consequently, any disturbance in one's interpersonal relationships will have the potential to affect clear perception and, conversely, the lack of clear perception will tend to disturb one's interpersonal relationships.

People come for counselling for many reasons: for advice, for support, for sympathy, and so on. But while a counsellor, like a teacher, may usefully be able to give clients something of what they need in these respects, I do not see such things as being central to what counselling is. Freud says somewhere that his aim is the modest one of replacing neurotic pain with ordinary pain, and I find this a helpful way of locating within the spectrum of human pain those varieties of emotional suffering which are the special concern of the counsellor. Roughly speaking, the counsellor is primarily concerned with *confused* emotional pain, with the sort of pain that arises from a distorted view of things. In Western thought, there is no concept which quite catches that with which counselling deals. In Buddhist philosophy, the Sanskrit term '*duhkha*' catches it very well indeed. '*Duhkha*' is variously translated as 'pain', 'suffering', 'ill', 'unsatisfactoriness', but with the connotation that the pain arises from delusive perception for which one bears some responsibility.

Something needs to be said now about how the emotions link with interpersonal perception and its distortions. As in the case of 'seeing', philosophical reflection on the concept of an emotion reveals how confused our understanding of the concept can be.[2] Emotions can easily be assimilated to *feelings*, and feelings can be regarded as a kind of sensation. So just as 'seeing something blue' gets represented as 'having a blue sensation', so 'being jealous', for example, gets misinterpreted as 'having a jealous feeling'. Thus jealousy, like blueness, comes to be thought of as a 'subjective mental state'. It is tempting to say 'But surely jealousy *is* a feeling – it is a tight wound-up sort of feeling, with at the same time a bit of a sinking feeling in the stomach'. Someone who is jealous might indeed notice that these are exactly the feelings he now has. Yet on reflection it is clear that physical sensations like these are neither necessary nor sufficient for jealousy. Not necessary, since we usually recognize whether people are jealous without having any information about their bodily sensations; not sufficient, because a person could have just such sensations in connection with a quite different emotion, such as fear.

But if jealousy is not a set of feelings or sensations, then what is it? Perhaps the best answer is to say that it is a recognizable pattern in interpersonal relations. Roughly speaking, we say that A is jealous of B if A is upset by the fact that some third person, C, in some way prefers B to himself. Jealousy has an interpersonal structure which cannot exist without there being at least three people in relation to one another. It is not a 'private subjective state', but a perception of a relationship pattern. It may involve a *false* perception, of course. It may be that C doesn't in fact prefer B to A, but once A comes to see this it will necessarily make a difference to his emotional state. If A no longer sees C as preferring B to himself, then whatever he now feels in this connection it isn't jealousy.

In the same way, the emotion of guilt isn't for example, a gnawing feeling in the pit of the stomach (though such feelings may be present). To feel guilty involves seeing oneself as having done something wrong. One may not *believe* that what one did was wrong, but that is how one *sees* it. The difference here is like that between believing that the rope-bridge is safe (people are walking across it, the ropes are thick, and firmly attached, etc.) and *seeing it as safe*. In spite of all the evidence, which I accept as conclusive, the bridge doesn't *look* safe to me. And in spite of all the evidence I may still feel guilty. Another helpful illustration can be found in visual illusions, such as the Müller-Lyer (see Figure 9.1). Careful measurement can lead one to believe that the two long lines are of equal length, but no amount of rational argument can make them *look* equal. To make them look equal, you have to make some quite different move, such as erasing the other lines from the diagram, or adding compensating lines.

Our emotional lives cannot be disentangled from our perceptions of our relationship with the world, and especially our relationships with other people. If a client's emotional life is disturbed, we can then expect that there will be disturbances in her perceptions of how she relates to the world and to others. It follows that if the counsellor can help the client towards a less distorted view, then the client's emotional disturbance will be correspondingly alleviated. The general idea here is far from new. It is found in the Stoic philosophy of Epictetus (see White 1983: Section 5), and in the thought of

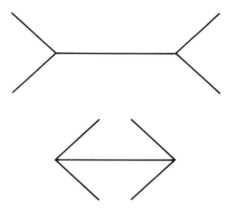

Figure 9.1 Seeing and believing.

the cognitive-behavioural therapists (e.g. Trower *et al.* 1988). I find much in this approach congenial, but I think the cognitive therapists do not always fully appreciate the difference between unfounded beliefs and distorted perceptions. Unfounded beliefs can be approached through rational argument, but the transformation of perception may require quite different moves, a few of which I mention shortly.

The counselling process

In the light of the above discussion, the counselling process can be seen as beginning with the client's presentation of a state of emotional disturbance. In the simplest possible terms, something feels wrong in the client's life. This 'feeling of something wrong', or sense of *duhkha*, needs to be explored, and the counsellor needs to provide an environment in which such exploration can effectively be carried out. The client needs to be able to see more clearly, and the counselling situation therefore should be one in which factors which tend to distort perception are eliminated as far as possible.

The possible distorting factors are very various, but can perhaps be classified under three main headings which I draw from the classical Buddhist analysis of *duhkha*. They are emotional repulsion (e.g. fear, hate, guilt), emotional attachment (e.g. dependence, possessive love) and emotional inertia (e.g. repeating old patterns, stereotyping). The counsellor needs to provide an environment in which these three are discouraged, and their opposites encouraged. Thus the ideal counselling setting will be one in which (1) the client can feel safe, appreciated and accepted, (2) the client will not become dependent on or emotionally 'involved' with the counsellor and (3) the client will be stimulated, challenged and encouraged to look at alternative possibilities.

Within this counselling setting, the client has the opportunity to see more clearly what his or her emotional disturbance consists in. Given what has been said above about the interpersonal nature of human life, the exploration of the disturbance, with the help of the counsellor, is likely to focus on the client's relationships with other people, including as a special case of this, the relationship with the counsellor. Other foci of attention are likely to be the possible distorting factors which have led to the disturbance, so that the counsellor may find it helpful to encourage attention to areas of the client's life where such things as guilt, dependency or force of habit may have played a role in distorting the client's perceptions.

If the client is to see his or her life in a truer way, there needs to be an openness to alternatives. The counsellor may need to challenge gently the client's general emotional inertia, the tendency we have simply to go on seeing things as we always have done. Or to look at it from another angle, the counsellor may need to help clients to be less *attached* to their habitual way of seeing things. The restructuring of perception is bound to involve periods of confusion and feelings of being adrift: the pieces of the puzzle have to be thrown in the air before they can come down in a new pattern. Appeals to logic and rationality are likely to be of limited value in this process, since logic works with categories and rules of inference which have already been laid down. In the restructuring of perception, new categories and rules are gestating, so that at this stage there is nothing for logic to get to grips with. [A very interesting comparison would be with Thomas Kuhn's (1962) view of what happens in the historical development of scientific theories. In Kuhnian terms, counsellors tend to see clients during revolutionary rather than normal phases of the clients' lives.]

The ways in which a counsellor can help with the client's emotional restructuring are naturally various. I find that attention to dreams can be very helpful. Dreams provide emotional pictures which often are at variance with, or are completely disconnected from, the client's own perceptions. They provide at least a novel point of view, yet it is a point of view which is nevertheless in some sense the client's; it is the client's dream, though it may need to be fed back to the client by the counsellor if it is to be effective.

The use of dreams in counselling can be seen as just one aspect of the importance of the use of the imagination in emotional restructuring. To get from an old way of seeing things to a new way, one needs at least to imagine the possibility of things being different. Questions like 'What would you do if all the current restrictions on your life were removed?' can be very revealing. So, I think, can questions such as 'How else could you have responded to that situation when you were a child?' or 'How do you imagine it all felt to the other people involved?' Such questions can help to free the client from old, fixed patterns of perception.

The counsellor may need to slow the client down, if enough attention is to be paid to the relevant details which may be significant in the restructured view. It is well known that most of what we call 'perception' is based not on what is before us, but on our expectations. We see things as the way they need to be if they are to fit into our familiar conceptual structures. Now this is as it should be; we couldn't, as I have argued earlier, see *at all* if we were not seeing within a broadly agreed conceptual framework. Yet where certain details of the framework have become distorted, the pattern which normally facilitates our shared life with others becomes a source of separation from them, and we cannot see what is wrong because we are so used to viewing the data of our lives in a particular way. It is as it is with proof-reading: if you read the proofs quickly you just don't see even glaring errors. To proof-read effectively, you have to slow down, and perhaps even read the lines backwards to break up the familiar flow of words. One interesting technique I have encountered recently in a programme of Buddhist-inspired therapy (Irwin 1990) is to tell the story of one's *life* backwards, so that one doesn't fit the various phases into the over-familiar patterns.

What the client *does* also has its impact on his perceptions. A client who is not able to imagine seeing himself differently may be able to put himself into a situation in which he will inevitably *be* different. Experimenting with doing things differently can reveal just how powerful the forces of fear, attachment and habit have become. Consider for example clients who say 'I couldn't do *that*,' where the act in question, once done, is reperceived as something quite ordinary.

I have mentioned a few ways in which the counsellor may be able to help the client to see more clearly, and while I am sure there are many others, I doubt whether there can be any systematic deployment of techniques in all this. People come to see things differently as a result of all sorts of curious events, and acquiring the art of counselling seems to me to be largely a matter of coming to be able to trust one's hunches about what is likely to help in the individual case.

Case study

The counselling process I will describe is not that of any particular client, but rather a composite and therefore 'fictional' study. I hope nevertheless that it is as true to the relevant 'facts' as is necessary for its illustrative purpose. The whole issue of the use of 'case studies' in writing about counselling practice is something which has not yet received the study it deserves. It is obvious that any description of a counselling series involves a great deal of selection, emphasis and interpretation, and to make a client 'come alive' the counsellor really needs to have the gifts of a novelist. Literary critics know better than counsellors the devices that are required to portray characters and human situations effectively, and the writer of a really good case study is going to need to employ such devices. Some may want 'case studies' to be 'fully objective', but the fact that this is impossible does not mean that stories like the one I tell here are just 'subjective inventions'. The 'truth' of a counselling session may be closer to the truth of a work of art than that of a scientific theory;

there are, I suspect, quite deep philosophical issues lurking here, issues not to be explored on this occasion. My purpose, in any case, is not to try to convey the reality of the sessions, but simply to give some indication of the ways in which my philosophical background influences what I do.

Jeremy, a journalist who had taken early retirement, contacted me initially because he felt blocked in his creative writing. He was at first emphatic that he did not need therapy as such, but help in freeing himself to work. Early in our sessions, however, he acknowledged that there was something wrong not just in his writing but in his life. He suffered from a pervasive mixture of anxiety and depression, though just what this was all about was obscure.

This to me is a typical situation at the start of counselling. The client has a problem which at first sight seems fairly specific, but which on closer examination turns out to be a tangled '*duhkha*-ish' knot, where there is pain but no clarity about what the pain involves. Here I feel very much as I feel in the presence of a *philosophical* problem, the sort of problem which, as Wittgenstein (1953: Section 123) put it, 'has the form: "I don't know my way about".'

Jeremy was anxious, and my concern as a counsellor to understand *his* anxiety was to some extent informed by my concern as a philosopher to understand the nature of *anxiety*. (Compare Plato's dialogue *Laches,* where Socrates investigates the related concept of *courage*.) In thinking about anxiety, I find helpful the reflections of the philosopher-theologian Paul Tillich (1962), who divides anxiety into three broad categories, each of which Jeremy experienced to some extent. The three categories are (a) the anxiety of fate (and ultimately of death), (b) the anxiety of doubt (and meaninglessness) and (c) the anxiety of guilt (and condemnation). In Jeremy's case, he was very concerned (a) that people should not know that he was receiving counselling. This was an anxiety about his fate if he entered counselling, and he needed to be reassured very explicitly about confidentiality. He was also very concerned (b) that I might not understand him, so that accurate empathy was important from the start. In addition (c) he had vague guilty anxieties connected with being found out to be a different person from the one he pretended to be, and I have little doubt that he would have abandoned counselling if he had not felt fully accepted by me. Reflecting on these aspects of Jeremy's initial anxiety in connection with coming to counselling helped me to survey something of his more general emotional landscape.

The reduction of anxiety is important if the client is to see things more clearly. Yet, as I suggested earlier, emotional repulsion (of which anxiety is one variety) is itself only one of three main distorting factors to be considered when first exploring a client's state of *duhkha*. The second factor I referred to is that of 'emotional attachment'. Jeremy had toyed with the idea of seeking help from a hypnotist, and would have liked me to conduct some deep relaxation sessions with him in order that I might 'draw out deeply buried feelings' from him. I felt we had to look a little at whether this request should be taken at face value. (That things are often not what they seem is a truism, but one which is central to philosophical thought. Both in Wittgensteinian and more traditional metaphysical philosophy, the effort to distinguish reality from appearance is a fundamental philosophical aim.) After some discussion, Jeremy agreed that part of the appeal of hypnosis was that it would allow him to hand over the responsibility for his progress to someone else, and that such abdication of control over his life was a tendency which he could recognize in himself in other contexts. Here is the opposite problem from that of being anxious about engaging in therapy; it is the problem of being in a sense not wary enough, the problem of clients who, once a minimum of trust has been established, will attempt to throw their lives into the counsellor's hands. Fear, anxiety and hate will distance the client too much from the counsellor; dependency, need for 'love' and collusion will not allow a proper working distance.

Thinking within the general philosophical framework which I outlined above, there is finally a third source of distortion to consider, the one which I called 'emotional inertia'. After the first three sessions, it seemed to me that Jeremy was going round in circles in much of what he said. His main complaint was that, in spite of now being retired, and devoting only a few hours a week to his adult education work, he never had time to write. He believed that he had a real talent for the short story, and had in fact had a number of stories published in the past. However, his week was filled with mundane gardening tasks on his rented allotment. Each week he resolved that he would write, and each counselling session became centred around what he had done instead of writing. I said that it seemed to me that just as the rest of his days went round in a frustrating circle, so it seemed to be the same in our sessions. I saw it as important to identify the emotional inertia here and to do something to help him to break the circles of habit into which he easily fell (and into which I found myself falling in our sessions). We reached an agreement that the following week he would devote Friday morning to writing, *whatever* happened, and this agreement he kept to.

In the early sessions, I try to be especially aware of the three dangers just mentioned. They *are* all dangers because each of them is likely to disrupt a clear view of what is happening in the client's life. One can't *see* clearly when one is afraid, when one is emotionally attached or when one is steeped in habit. The reduction of emotional repulsion, attachment and inertia remains a desideratum throughout the counselling process, but given that this desideratum is at least moderately fulfilled, the way is open for the client and counsellor together to try to see more clearly the nature of the client's *duhkha*.

Jeremy was depressed. He was a writer who was not writing. He didn't write because his allotment needed constant maintenance. Yes, he had chosen to cultivate the allotment, but there followed a long string of reasons why he could not relinquish it. I felt confused; I couldn't see how Jeremy saw the situation. Did he really *want* to write? In response to this direct question he rather irritably said that of course he wanted to; it was just that external circumstances prevented it. We had to agree that we were seeing the situation differently, and after we had talked about it at some length, he agreed that logically he could devote more time to writing, by cutting down on his other chores, but in practice 'it didn't work out like that'. Here again I felt the Wittgensteinian 'form of a philosophical problem': *I don't know my way about.* Given my general view of what is involved in *duhkha*, it seemed likely that something was distorting Jeremy's perception here. However, since neither of us had any idea what the distorting factors were, we agreed it might be best if we spent some time simply looking about in the rest of his life and background to see what might emerge.

Jeremy came from a working-class family and had, from as early as he could remember, felt alienated from his parents. His father, in particular, he saw as an uncouth person, and while neither parent was exactly unkind, neither seemed very interested in him. His parents were often away from the house, and from an early age they expected him to look after his younger sister while they were out. Jeremy had wanted to go to college, but his parents had no sympathy for education, and at fifteen they arranged for him to take up a job in a market garden. There he was fortunate enough to meet an older man who befriended him, and who later encouraged him to obtain a place on the local newspaper.

Most of his story Jeremy told without much feeling. However, there were moments when speaking of his father that tears came to his eyes. Just once or twice during his childhood his father had talked with him, and in these moments his perception of his father as an uncouth labourer living a pointless life seemed to shift. More often, however, his feelings in connection with his father were distant and despising. He began to speak of how in his teenage years his aim above all had been *not to be like his father.*

From all this emerged, through his talking and my reflecting back to him, a realization that he had never wanted to be grown up, because being grown-up would mean being a man (like father). Although other people often saw him as something of a leader, he felt himself to be a boy. Other emotional pressures helped to sustain this picture: as a child he had been forced into a parental role in relation to his sister, and he had seldom experienced any parental care himself. (As one expects from an interpersonal view of human nature, the distorting factors arise from distorted *relationships*.) In our sessions, the question now arose of whether he would *like* to see himself as an adult. He felt confused about this. There were feelings of 'It's too late. I was was never really allowed to be a child. Later I could not be a real adult because I still needed to be a child. Now I may have only a few years left . . . I don't know who or what I am.'

Jeremy's habitual view of himself had been thrown into confusion, but there was no logical foundation on which to build a new view. Here it seemed to me that we were in territory very similar to that described by Kuhn (1962) in connection with what happens in science when one paradigmatic view has broken down, but no new theory has yet emerged. This by its very nature is trackless country, and one has to find inspiration where one can. One form of 'inspiration' is the dream, and Jeremy now told a dream in which he had embraced his grandfather. He told this dream briefly, then quickly went on to talk about problems he had been having with his neighbours on the allotment. I drew his attention back to the dream (an instance of slowing the client down, to allow time for new perceptions to emerge), and asked him about his grandfather. It emerged that grandfather was the one adult male in his childhood whom he didn't despise. Following this dream, he began to reflect along the lines of 'I could be a bit like my grandfather', and this new picture of himself was naturally facilitated by the fact that he was indeed of an age to be a grandfather. This struck me as a good example of the sort of situation in which intellectual discussion is of no help (Jeremy knew intellectually that he was not a child). He nevertheless saw himself as a child, and to counter the power of that picture another picture was needed, which the dream helped to supply.

Following this we worked for some time on the difficulties he had in relationships to men whom he saw as 'authorities'. This seemed to be linked with his difficulty in experiencing himself as an adult with some authority. When he took his car in for repair, for example, he saw the garage man as having the right to decide whether certain non-essential, cosmetic repairs should be done. This man was the 'expert' and Jeremy typically came away resentful at having spent money on work he had not really wanted done. We looked at where this picture of the garage man as an authority was coming from. What exactly did he say and do? Could he be seen differently? Jeremy felt that however irrational it was, he just did see the man in that way, and compared it with the fact that with ambiguous drawings one can know that there is another aspect, yet can't *see* it. (This was a – rather rare – example of a client explicitly referring to an issue in the philosophy of perception.) We discussed the analogy, and together realized that there were in fact things one could do to see the other aspect. You have to say to yourself such things as: this is the *front* corner, we are looking *down* on it, try to see that as the *top*, etc. There is an element of imaginative play in this, and no guarantee that the new aspect will dawn. Yet often it does, and with people as well as drawings. (Philosophers from Kant to Iris Murdoch have emphasized the important role which the imagination plays in perception, and I find it helpful to keep this in mind in counselling practice.) Jeremy practised imagining what the garage man himself might be thinking, he tried to recall what he actually knew about this man, and the more he focused his attention on these details the more it became possible to see the man's behaviour not as that of an authoritarian tyrant, but rather that of a hard-pressed small businessman. Then, being able to see him differently, Jeremy found himself acting differently next time they met. There are clearly many ways in which a person may be seen, but it is important to my conception of counselling that these different views are not regarded as equally valid subjective visions. Jeremy's two views of the garage man were, I believe, not equally valid. For his first view was clearly distorted by his general tendency to project authority into other men, while the second view he had developed through giving some genuine attention to the garage man himself.

Jeremy had a chance to go to a short-story congress abroad and wondered what to put on the application form under 'occupation'. He had intended to put 'retired', but when I questioned whether this was really how he saw himself, he paused, and then suddenly said 'No, I'm a writer!' I encouraged him to put 'writer' as a way of helping him to fix this view of himself. (As I suggested earlier, 'seeing' is logically an achievement verb. To see himself as a writer was a significant achievement for Jeremy, but achievements often need to be consolidated.) He began to find at least some time to write, and generally came to take more charge of his own life. There were also times when he was able for the first time to relax and be playful, to be *happy* with being a child. It seemed important to encourage this as much as his attempts to be 'more adult'. To return to Wittgenstein's image of the knot, it often seems in counselling that one has to help the client pull a thread of the tangled skein first in one direction and then, maybe, in quite the opposite direction. Untying a knot is not a linear process; one may have to loosen one bit here, another bit there, before the main tangle begins to unravel, and the process will indeed 'be as complicated as the knots it unties' (Wittgenstein 1967: Section 452).

In conclusion, I find that philosophy, and especially the philosophy of perception provides me with a sophisticated framework within which I can deploy a variety of counselling approaches. It is important to me that counselling should have such a framework, since otherwise there is the danger of allurement by the latest ephemeral fashions in 'therapy'. Human beings have always been faced with the issues which the counsellor addresses, and philosophy has always contained as part of its aim that of alleviating the tangled distress of life through the attempt to see things in an undistorted way. It seems to me that the modern counselling movement is rather out of touch with its own philosophical background, and that much remains to be done by way of relating counselling theory to very much older and broader philosophical traditions.

NOTES

1 For a detailed working out of this picture see, for example, Stace (1932). For a
   sustained attempt to develop a Wittgensteinian view of early learning, see Hamlyn
   (1978); see also his 'Human learning' (1971).
2 For philosophical studies of emotion, see Sartre (1962) and Bedford (1957).

REFERENCES

Bedford, E. (1957) Emotions. *Proceedings of the Aristotelian Society, 57.* Reprinted
   in D. F. Gustafson (ed.) (1967) *Essays in Philosophical Pyschology.* London,
   Macmillan.
Dilman, I. (1983) *Freud and Human Nature.* Oxford, Blackwell.
Dilman, I. (1984) *Freud and the Mind.* Oxford, Blackwell.
Dilman, I. (1988) *Freud, Insight and Change.* Oxford, Blackwell.
Gudmunsen, C. (1977) *Wittgenstein and Buddhism.* London, Macmillan.
Hamlyn, D. W. (1971) Human learning. In S. C. Brown (ed.), *The Philosophy of
   Psychology.* London, Royal Institute of Philosophy.
Hamlyn, D. W. (1978) *Experience and the Growth of Understanding.* London,
   Routledge and Kegan Paul.
Holmes, J. and Lindley, R. (1989) *The Values of Psychotherapy.* Oxford, Oxford
   University Press.
Irwin, E. (1990) *Back to Beginnings.* Edinburgh, Tara Trust.
Kuhn, T. S. (1962) *The Structure of Scientific Revolutions.* Chicago, IL, Chicago
   University Press.
MacIntyre, A. C. (1958) *The Unconscious.* London, Routledge.
Macmurray, J. (1959) *The Self as Agent.* London, Faber.
Macmurray, J. (1961) *Persons in Relation.* London, Faber.
Murdoch, I. (1970) *The Sovereignty of Good.* London, Routledge.
Sartre, J.-P. (1962) *Sketch for a Theory of the Emotions.* London, Methuen.
Stace W. T. (1932) *The Theory of Knowledge and Existence.* Oxford, Oxford
   University Press.
Tillich, P. (1962) *The Courage to Be.* London, Collins.
Trower, P., Casey, A. and Dryden, W. (1988) *Cognitive-Behavioural Counselling in
   Action.* London, Sage Publications.
White, N. (trans.) (1983) *The Handbook of Epictetus.* Indianapolis, Hackett
   Publishing Co.
Wittgenstein, L. (1953) *Philosophical Investigations.* Oxford, Blackwell.
Wittgenstein, L. (1967) *Zettel.* Oxford, Blackwell.
Wittgenstein, L. (1980) *Culture and Value.* Oxford, Blackwell.

10

POSTSCRIPT

Brian Thorne and Windy Dryden

The writers of the preceding chapters were asked, on completion of their task, to reflect on the experience of engaging with their original disciplines in this way. Without exception they recorded a process which had involved considerable struggle and for some of them formidable difficulties. One writer confessed to a period when he seriously doubted his capacity to complete the work at all (for him a totally new experience of potential failure). Another spoke of being kept going by the shame he had experienced at the inadequacy of his first draft. A third admitted that if we, as editors, had required further changes to her third draft she would have told us, in no uncertain terms, where to go. In short, all our writers, who had at the outset enthusiastically accepted our invitation to contribute to this volume, discovered that they had let themselves in for far more than they had bargained.

The difficulties encountered in composition were more than outweighed, however, by the deep satisfaction at the final results. In many ways, it would seem that each writer was forced into a process of self-exploration which had about it the flavour of a particularly demanding encounter with aspects of the self which had not previously been fully integrated. The resulting integration was personally and professionally rewarding and several contributors professed to find a new confidence in their therapeutic work as a result and a heightened awareness of their own unique approach to clients. At the same time, there was a decreased concern about their allegiance to any prevailing orthodoxy. Perhaps surprising was their realization on the one hand of the significance of their original disciplines for their personal and intellectual development and, on the other, their comparative failure, prior to the writing of these chapters, to conceptualize in any systematic way, the continuing and considerable influence of these disciplines on their work as counsellors. In one case, a contributor acknowledged that he had not previously been aware that his original discipline was a significant factor at all in his therapeutic practice (whereas it turned out to be of major importance), and in another case the writer admitted to keeping his original discipline in a watertight compartment (or so he thought!), well insulated from his counselling activity. For another the task had put her back in touch with a cognitive and clear-sighted part of herself which she had deliberately suppressed during her counsellor training in the interests of the development of her feeling and intuitive self. For this contributor, the task has opened up a path to a new integration of personality which is having particularly important repercussions in her therapeutic work. As she herself expresses it: 'I no longer regard being clear-sighted and analytical as cold-hearted.'

The experience of our contributors in many ways confirms our initial suspicion that training courses do not encourage trainees to capitalize on their previous academic disciplines either in the task of self-understanding or in the exploration of therapeutic processes. The exception to this was the case of the two psychologist authors who clearly discovered in their counsellor training an arena in which much of their previous psychological knowledge could be revitalized and put to creative use. Indeed, for them counselling breathed new life into what had often previously been dead bones. It would seem likely, however, that the psychologists were aided by the fact that psychology is commonly seen as a natural and logical discipline for counsellors in training to engage with whereas ecology, English Literature, social anthropology, theology, drama, education and philosophy do not so readily appear as 'core curriculum' subjects for the counselling student. Our contributors reveal, however, that their original disciplines have had a profound influence upon their development as persons and no training which professes to encourage the unique resourcefulness of each trainee can afford to reject this powerful dimension of a person's life history. There is perhaps something in us which is resistant to the notion that the pursuit of an academic discipline, even if it is as vocationally relevant as drama or education, can have a determining effect on the persons we become. And yet there is repeated evidence in these pages of a quality of involvement with so-called academic disciplines which reveals an engagement of the personality at a level which is profound and moving. The ecologist concludes that the meaning of the living world to him is, quite simply, that it saved his life. The theologian recognizes that his discipline provides ideas and visions which enable him to cope with the pain of weakness and failure. The social anthropologist sees in his subject the way to a creative compromise between rationality and madness in the face of his father's repeated mental breakdowns. The philosopher finds in Wittgenstein's approach the healing of the loneliness and disconnection which come from the problem of the apparent impenetrability of 'other minds'. The educationalist discovers behind her discipline the unremitting challenge of the search for truth and the negotiation of meaning. The student of drama acknowledges that metaphors and roles and costumes enabled her to bear the traumata of the war years and continue to unlock doors in the edifices she and others construct to avoid the pain of living. The English Literature specialist finds in her discipline not only the peculiar sensitivity to language which renders tolerable the ever-changing nature of meaning, but also the poignant relevance of the social context to the understanding of the suffering individual. In no sense are these academic disciplines characterized by dry-as-dust lecture notes or the threat of final examination papers: they are rather the very stuff of life and as such they have exerted their fascination and their power on the lives of our writers and on their ability to relate with compassion to those who seek their help.

The 'diversity' of approach which such backgrounds bring to the counselling room is strikingly evident in the case studies which our writers present. What is more, we are encouraged that the resourcefulness of each of our counsellor contributors will have been extended and enhanced by the task of writing and by the rigorous self-reflection to which each has submitted. Such a process, we are convinced, should be an integral part of every counsellor training programme as, too, should be the requirement on counsellor trainers to select trainees from as wide as possible a range of original academic disciplines. In this way, every counsellor in training will have the opportunity not only to rediscover the meaning and the passion of his or her original discipline, but also to be enriched by sharing in the academic pilgrimages of fellow trainees. The mysteriousness of human beings and the complex challenges of human relating require that the widest possible range of human knowledge is brought to the theory and practice of counselling and that those who undertake such work neither sell their own experience short nor fail to benefit from the discoveries of their colleagues. We trust that the readers of this book can now at least glimpse the richness of which we speak and discern the outline of the treasure-house which is yet to be built.

INDEX

psychology, 107–27
  applications of, 109
  range of, 108, 109
  research, *see* research
  as science, 108
  sharing, in counselling practice,
    121–2
  theory, and counselling practice,
    116–17
psychosis, 49, 60

race issues, 62–3
Rackham, O., 17
Radcliffe-Brown, A. R., 51
Rapoport, R., 45, 55
rational-emotive therapy, 138, 144
rationality, 163
'real person' (Brook), 97–8, 105
Reason, P., 110, 120
redundancy counselling, 42
Reed, B., 80
Reformation, 70
regression, 62–3, 80
rehearsal stage, 100
religion, 68, 79, 81
  as social change agent, 51
  mythology and, 50–2, 57–8
  see also theology
renewable resources, 10–11
repentance, 85
research, 7, 118–20
  authentic, 142
  methodologies, 110, 112
  'new paradigm', 145
  personal, counselling as, 142
  see also psychological information
research assistant, counsellor as, 147
responsibility, 74, 75, 85, 131
rest home, group supervision in, 65
Richmond Fellowship College, 72
rites of passage, 54, 58, 62
Robertson, J., 50
Roebuck, F.N., 135, 139, 140
Rogers, C., 31, 32, 33, 34, 37,
    107, 110, 111, 116, 127,
    132, 134, 136, 138, 139,
    141, 142

role, 140
role models, 60
Romantic poets, 25–30
  person-centred approach and, 31–5
Rowan, J., 110, 120
Russell, B., 152

safe place, 18, 162–3
salvation, 74, 75–6
salvation history, 69
Samuels, A., 58, 60
Schaffer, R., 134, 135
schizmogenesis (Bateson), 48–9
schizoid personality, 60
science, 7
  development of, 163, 168
  nature of, 110
  subjectivity of, 34
scientist-practitioner debate, 110
scripture, tradition and, 70, 71
sea, archetypal symbol, 14–15
Searles, Harold, 49
seeing, *see* perception
Segal, L., 49
self
  core, 94.
  privacy of, 57
self-acceptance, 41
self-actualization, 31, 116
self-concept, 134
self-expression, 39–40
sex-role stereotyping, 49
sexual abuse, *see* child sexual abuse
sexuality, 36, 59–60
Shakespeare, W., 23
shame, 57
Sheehy, G., 121
Shelley, P. B., 27, 29, 34
shelter, 17–18
Simon, P., 129
Simonton, C., 112
Simonton, S., 112
Sims, J. M., 141
sin, 74–5, 85
  original, 75
Six Picture Story Making technique
  (Lahad), 102

White, R., 135
Williams, R. R., 75
Wilshire, B., 90
Winicott, D. W., 80
Wisdom, Book of, 75
Wittgenstein, L., 152, 153, 154, 155,
  156, 158, 165, 169
women's movement, 8, 49
woodmanship, 17
Woods, P., 141

Wordsworth, W., 27, 29, 31, 32, 34
work, 58–9
working alliance, 149
wounded healer, 46, 84
Wray, G., 117
Wundt, W., 110

Yalom, I., 98–9

Zuber-Skerritt, O., 133